MOTIVATING GIRLS TO START

SPORTS HER WAY

AND STAY WITH SPORTS

Susan Wilson

A FIRESIDE BOOK
PUBLISHED BY SIMON & SCHUSTER
NEW YORK · LONDON · TORONTO · SYDNEY · SINGAPORE

FIRESIDE
Rockefeller Center
1230 Avenue of the Americas
New York, NY 10020

FIRESIDE and colophon are registered trademarks
of Simon & Schuster, Inc.

Designed by Elina Nudelman

Manufactured in the United States of America

10 9 8 7 6 5 4 3 2 1

Library of Congress Cataloging-in-Publication Data

Wilson, Susan M.
    Sports her way: motivating girls to start and stay with sports/Susan Wilson.
        p.   cm.
    "A Fireside book."
    Includes index.
    1. Sports for women.   2. Coaching (Athletics).   I. Title.
    GV709.W53   2000
    796'.082—dc21
                                                                00-037317

ISBN 0-684-86512-2

Acknowledgments

Beginning a book is one thing, completing it is another. I was extremely fortunate to have a team of editors who absolutely believed in me and my project. Dale Fetherling was responsible for building the foundation of the project. He helped me to explore and focus my beliefs about girls in sports. I gained enormous respect for him during the creative process. He was terrific at generating ideas and asking probing questions. Best of all, he always had one hundred ways to make corrections without making me feel inadequate. He has been a wonderful friend and someone who truly gives meaning to the word mentor.

Laura Golden Bellotti refined the manuscript and asked me even more probing questions. She was terrific at helping me to meet my deadlines.

Sharon Hillidge, who reviewed the technical sport information, was never more than a phone call away. Her experience as an athlete, educator, and writer provided a unique dimension to the review process.

Many thanks to my literary agent, Betsy Amster, who polished my ideas and escorted me through the intricacies of the publishing world.

My heartfelt gratitude to the women at Simon & Schuster: Becky Cabaza, Carrie Thornton, and Sue Fleming. Their belief in my ideas launched this undertaking. By giving me a break, these women gave me an opportunity to help parents and athletes make participation in sports an inviting and rewarding pursuit.

There were so many parents, educators, referees, coaches, and student athletes who willingly told me their stories. Their comments gave me an intimate look at the ups and downs of training girls in athletics.

Special thanks to three psychologists: Dr. Patsi Krakoff, Dr. Darrell Burnett, and Dr. John Peterson.

Thanks also go to Dr. Michael Yessis, for his tremendous input on sports and fitness training for youth. His dedication to understanding the value of conditioning for athletes has not only helped his daughter, but all those he has trained.

For their input into my athletic training as a gymnast, my unending thanks to my high school coach, Dr. Joseph Massimo, and my college coaches, Kitty and Eric Kjeldson. Through their respectful coaching, they helped me to grow the life skills that are the underpinnings of my being today.

From the bottom of my heart, I thank my husband who counseled me, computer-educated me, and, most of all, calmed me. His many years of coaching girls provided vital insight into the dozens of discussions we had about the value of sports.

This book is dedicated to my dad, who laid the foundation for sports to be a fundamental part of my life, and to the teachers and coaches who "gave back" and helped me to fulfill my athletic dreams. May your collective counseling help me guide families through the fulfilling world of sports in a more enjoyable and enduring way.

CONTENTS

INTRODUCTION

One November day in 1983 I found myself seated at a desk on the second floor of a converted airplane hangar in Los Angeles. Anyone who knows me knows that sitting is not what I do, especially in nylons and a skirt, but there I was trying to digest everything. Phones were ringing, people scurried about, and the energy was unmistakable. It was a thrilling scene that happens only once every four years. And I was there. All I could think of was that a dream had come true, a fantasy of being part of the highest level of athletic achievement on the planet. You see, two weeks earlier I was recruited to be the director of gymnastics competition for the 1984 Olympics—the dream and the challenge of a lifetime rolled into one mesmerizing event. I couldn't help thinking what a long way I was from Boston, where I grew up enjoying sports but never dreaming that it would dominate my every waking moment.

How did I get started in sports as a girl? The seeds were planted by my parents, who always encouraged me to be active when I was a child. In our house of five children (two girls and three boys) there was no gender distinction as far as sports were concerned. Whatever sport my dad was trying to teach us, everybody tried—for instance, many Sundays after church we would all go to the playground and play baseball. Happily, my days were filled with motion and a built-in play partner, my twin sister, Judy. We loved to skate wearing the old metal roller skates, the kind where you used a key to tighten them onto your shoes; we walked on stilts my dad built for us; we knew every way to duck in and out of a swinging rope. In the winter we would ice-skate, fling ourselves onto our red sleds, or ride the toboggan run at the playground—it was all very electrifying to the spirit. I spent countless hours riding my bicycle, swimming, and playing tennis. It's true I had my dolls, but playing sports of all kinds was a far more addictive activity. It was just bunches of fun and made me feel good.

How did I stay hooked on sports? I found my passion. In my junior year of high school I recall sitting cross-legged on a cold wooden gym floor in my not so flattering green gym suit. But on that fateful fall day none of that mattered, because in front of me was a trampoline and a set of uneven bars, the names of which I don't even think I knew at the time. They must have been in storage. At least I had never seen them before. With a sense of anticipation and excitement, I wondered what you did on those things. Looking back to the day of my awakening, I can vividly see my gym teachers' faces and recollect their names, Mrs. Reardon and Miss Finks. They wore crisply starched, tailored, cotton blouses and bright, plaid kilts. After a brief introduction they called for volunteers to be demonstrators on the apparatus. My arm shot up in the air with all the energy I could find. Luckily I was picked to be a demonstrator. That day is well recorded in my memory as the day I started gymnastics and began a fusion with sports that changed my life—I had found my calling, something that captured my imagination, my heart, my spirit.

The short year and a half that I spent training during my junior and senior years at high school led to four incredible seasons of competition at the University of Massachusetts. Three out of the four years I was fortunate to represent my college at the AIAW (Association of Intercollegiate Athletics for Women) National Championships.

Though I majored in sociology in school, it soon became apparent that sports would be the focus of my career. After a couple of years of searching for a good teaching opportunity, at the age of twenty-five I settled on becoming, with a partner, a small-business owner of a gymnastics school in New Jersey. What I didn't have in terms of business knowledge, which was quite a lot, I made up for with persistence. After six intense years of growing our program, one location became four, and we were training more than a thousand girls and boys.

While running a business, I began to realize that the growing number of gymnastics competitors called for an increased number of gymnastics officials. Using whatever spare time I had on the weekends, I studied, became a certified state official, and judged competitions throughout the state. After a few years I learned that a higher ranking—becoming certified at the regional, then national levels—meant judging more prestigious, higher-level gymnastics. You guessed it, I caught the vision and moved up in my rating until I became an elite national judge. And yes, going to the more prominent meets was a very heady experience.

As gymnastics grew in my state, so did the need for organization. Further compelled to support growth of the sport, I committed my efforts to being part of the board of directors for the New Jersey Gymnastics Association.

Somewhere between running a business, boardwork, and officiating entered a stroke of luck. My business partner (now my husband) was asked to direct an international invitational competition in Madison Square Garden. *Awesome!* I thought. Except for one thing. Most of the judges and the technical committee were European. The next thing I knew, my husband and I were studying German. Miraculously the event proceeded with only minor glitches, and I felt that in a single weekend I learned as much as I had in four years of college. Our efforts couldn't have been all bad, because the next year we were asked to be the directors again. But the big time came when we were asked to be part of the administrative team for the 1979 World Championships of Gymnastics in Texas. My training at the world championships then led to my being hired by the Los Angeles Olympic Organizing Committee in 1983. The eleven months that I spent planning and organizing in Los Angeles was and is the dream of my lifetime. The thrill of the Olympics made me want to share and excite girls about the magic of sports participation. You see, the girl in the green gym suit had come a long way—and sports had become, and *is*, the focus of my life.

What It's All About

This book is about how to get your daughter off to a great start in sports and how to know what the best programs are to keep her involved for a lifetime of enjoyment and personal benefits. Girls play and learn sports *their* way. For a variety of reasons, little girls play and approach physical activity differently from little boys. They don't always spend as much time running, climbing, tumbling, or playing with balls as boys do. Girls are not usually playfully aggressive or competitive. There has been and continues to be extensive scientific research to get to the heart of the matter of how boys and girls play differently. The implications are always controversial.

Many of my thoughts in this book come from countless hours of coaching and watching the play of thousands of youngsters. A group of boys left alone in a room will soon be wrestling, playing dodgeball with an old shoe, a basketball, or any old thing that is found lying around. Girls may engage in some of those activities, but most likely they will form a circle, create a group dance, or do some other cooperative activity. My husband and I have watched this group dancing thing performed by the girl gymnasts in our training center and have wondered if such a phenomenon could ever happen with a group of boys. It hasn't been observed to date. My conclusion that boys and girls are different may not be scientific—it is empirical. Parents will agree. Boys and girls are different in their approach to play.

Our society encourages boys and girls to play differently. Parents buy dolls for girls and balls for boys. Occasionally a boy plays with dolls. These dolls are soldiers, astronauts, or robot sci-fi secret laser ray killers. Boys are encouraged to be aggressive, combative, and daring with their doll toys. Occasionally girls will pick up a ball and play catch.

Here's a news flash. Little girls are very athletic and receptive to sports instruction at an earlier age than little boys. They can listen, they can convert coaching information to skill, and they can strive with the best of the boys through the elementary school years. But then something happens. They may lose self-esteem, interest, and strength unless they are encouraged to keep on the sports track. While you may have started your daughter in sports, your next job is to keep her in sports.

What I Believe

Sports provided me with the opportunity to meet hundreds of new people, whether I was competing against other schools as an athlete, instructing children in my gymnastics classes, attending workshops as a coach, or traveling internationally to athletic events. I have had a chance to share ideas with, struggle with, and be excited about accomplishments great and small with all kinds of people, at all levels of experience. Sports has truly been a way of expressing my personality. It is a joy for me and has enriched my life in many, many ways.

The reason I wrote this book is that I passionately believe that sports can transform a girl's life if she is encouraged and supported right out of the high chair. Having witnessed so many girls discovering their love for sports, and having seen how sports helped them to develop into happier, more confident individuals, I wrote this book to encourage *you* to help your daughter discover that love for sports.

I believe that parents are the key role models for young girls. When you provide an early start out in the backyard playing catch or taking classes in a preschool gymnastics program, your daughter will be ready to play sports as she grows older.

I believe I must set an example as a coach and accept that I am a role model, too.

I believe that physical activity, sports, and recreation should be part of everyone's lives. The benefits of good health, a sense of well-being, and the act of continually striving contribute mightily to the development of the whole person. Every time your daughter makes a gain through sports, she's giving herself a personal promotion.

I want your daughter to have the impression that she can control her destiny—instead of waiting for someone to take care of her. I believe if she's given thoughtful training, she'll be a capable decision maker and self-reliant. My early years in sports marked the beginning of a journey that gave me direction and strength for the rest of my life. And I'm still on the road.

This Is Your Starter Kit

This is a practical book designed to give you the kinds of information you can use in your backyard or while volunteering in community athletic programs. There are three distinct aims for this book. First, to show you what you can do to engage your daughter in athletic activity, regardless of her age or physical abilities—or your own knowledge of a particular sport. Second, to explore the many ways that sports provides mental, emotional, social, and physical benefits to your daughter. Third, to learn why girls stay with or drop out of sports and how you can keep your daughter involved for the long term. Additionally, I will advise you as to certain things that are helpful and are not helpful when it comes to handling a young athlete's fears, failures, attitudes, and sense of "sportswomanship." If you're considering becoming a coach, there is a chapter on how to prepare yourself, what to expect, and how I believe coaching girls is different from coaching boys.

My Hopes and Dreams for You and Your Girls

When you enroll your daughter in a preschool gymnastics class, play catch with her out in the yard, take her to the park where she can master the monkey bars, or sign her up for soccer, you're paving the way for her to enjoy a lifelong relationship with physical activity. My hope is that you will come to believe that sports should be part of her life. The benefits of good health, social interaction, learning to make decisions, mastering physical skills, and continually striving toward personal goals contribute mightily to the development of the whole person. By setting the stage for your daughter to become involved with sports, you're not only giving her the chance to find her passion, you're enabling her to become the well-rounded, self-reliant person she deserves to be.

I hope you take this book to heart and help your daughter grow in body and spirit through sports. It's a remarkable motivator. Remember that your daughter's body has to see her through a long life. Let's give her a healthy and competent one. Her level of confidence and well-being will be the emotional tools that will guide her. Best of all, you will have peace of mind for a job well done. I warmly welcome you and your daughter to *Sports Her Way*. Now, get together with your daughter, lace up your sneakers, and get ready for some fun.

The Bonanza of Benefits

1

Why do we get involved with recreational activity and play sports? If you ask kids, they'll probably answer that it's just plain fun. You lose yourself in the moment as you find that little place inside you that says, "Go for it." This is true whether you are three or thirty-three. Not too long ago, a Girl Scout troop came to my gymnastics facility to earn a sport badge. One of the mothers holding an infant happened to mention that she was in her early thirties and had never been on a trampoline. I could see the yearning in her face to give it a try before she went home. Knowing that it was now or never, I said, "Let me hold that baby and you get yourself up on that trampoline right now." You'd think I had told her she had won the lottery. She was up bouncing on the trampoline in a New York minute—and loving it. Did she experience sheer pleasure and go home happy because she gave herself a psychological boost? You bet. Could she have received benefits in other parts of her life—her social, physical, and educational side—if she was given the opportunity to experience that simple act, that joy as a youngster? Yes, again.

By encouraging your daughter to engage in sports early, you can lay the foundation for a lifetime of pleasure and personal benefits.

Hopefully she'll stay active in recreational activity because at the most basic level it enhances her in some way. Every time she does something physical, she'll realize something about herself. No matter what direction you'd like to see her grow—having fun, staying healthy, representing her high school team, keeping her weight under control, staying away from drugs and early sex—the bonanza of benefits she'll gain by playing sports will serve her throughout her entire life.

Physical Health Benefits

Young girls deserve more credit than we give them sometimes. When I asked eleven-year-old Jennifer, an elementary school student and daughter of one of my friends, about sports and staying in shape, she said, "I want to stay slim, 'cause life is easier when you keep yourself healthy, and it's good for your heart." Jennifer may have a future in marketing because her message couldn't be more simple or clear.

The following are the key physical health benefits your daughter can expect to enjoy when she participates in sports.

Maintaining a Healthy Weight

Pick up any newspaper or magazine article about children's health and you will read that obesity is the "most prevalent chronic illness in North America." According to *Pediatric Review,* as many as 25 percent of children in the United States may be obese. Most girls and young women actually don't consume too many calories; instead they burn too few. Staying physically active is important not only to burn calories, but to promote loss of body fat and maintain lean muscle. That's the reason females should exercise *and* eat properly. If you want to help your daughter reduce the risk of obesity, keep her involved in recreational sports throughout her childhood and adolescence. In terms of future benefits, it's common sense that women who exercise weigh less than nonexercising women. For the best results, as your daughter gets older encourage her to engage in a combination of strenuous physical activity and aerobics to help her maintain an ideal weight for her body size. Sports participation also helps the muscles become stronger. The stronger the muscles, the more calories your body burns even at rest. What? Burn calories while you rest? Science bears this out.

Looking Better Through Toning the Muscles

There isn't a day that passes by when you don't look in the mirror. You need a little less fat here, a little more muscle there. As girls enter puberty they look in the mirror more and more. This can be a pleasant experience when you're satisfied with your body. But sometime around adolescence that vision may not be so pleasing. For adolescents, appealing to how they look is often more alluring than making the appeal for better health. Therefore one of the biggest points I like to make to girls is that if they want to change their shape, they'll have to change their muscles. Your muscles give you your shape. You can literally reshape the legs, for example, by firming the thighs through sports that work the legs—gymnastics, swimming, volleyball, track and field, basketball, tennis, and soccer to name a few. The muscles in the arms, shoulders, chest, and back can be improved through playing tennis, softball, gymnastics, and especially swimming. Teenagers who take regular advantage of weight training under the supervision of a coach at their high school, or under the guidance of a trainer at a fitness center, will over time see themselves change before their very eyes.

Building Strength

If coaches are doing their job, girls will begin to realize that strength is important if they're going to improve at the sports they play. Coaches who want an effective program will include conditioning at team practice. Over time, girls can develop improved levels of strength that will give them a competitive edge. A note to parents: Making an advanced athlete condition at home in addition to what is scheduled at practice may increase the likelihood that your daughter will feel resentment, dislike conditioning, and ultimately be unhappy with "her" sport. You as parents will need to be sensitive and trust your daughter to motivate herself.

Here is one young athlete's observations about her progress through regularly scheduled sport conditioning.

> *I get the conditioning done because I wouldn't get to learn the diving skills I'm doing now without this new level of strength. The new skills are more advanced and more fun. At first you get sore doing the conditioning, but then you can see*

the results. When you do more conditioning, those exercises themselves and the diving skills get easier for you. When I did the President's Council on Physical Fitness test, I did really well. I condition all year because I'm in sports and I beat everybody except for one boy.

—Jessica, 11, diver

By the time girls enter a high school athletic program, they are definitely aware of the value of having a strong body to do their sport. If they have been active in youth sports, they are also aware that they are stronger than most of their friends. Developing muscle strength has a synergistic effect. The stronger your muscles are, the more you can and want to do. Once teens have developed strength and realize what they are capable of achieving, they want to maintain that level. When strength is lost, they are shocked to discover there are activities they can no longer do.

Three important things happen with an increase in physical strength. First, there is a huge leap in sport performance. Second, having physical strength improves girls' confidence and they feel less intimidated by other people. This is particularly true for girls who are small in size. Finally, strong bones and muscles reduce the risk of injury to joints and ligaments by providing them with extra support.

I know some girls may worry a lot about looking "masculine." While strength training does increase muscle size, having strong, toned muscles won't make most female athletes look and feel masculine. This has to do with hormones—women have high levels of estrogen, men have high levels of testosterone. To build sizable muscles, a body needs major amounts of testosterone; to get that look, women have to have the genetics for muscle mass or take male hormone supplements. Be sure to educate your daughter if she has this fear.

Reducing the Risk of Disease

A number of recent studies have found that developing the habit of exercise as a young girl may help females stay active into adulthood and reduce the risk of serious disease later in life. Such evidence provides powerful motivation to get your daughter involved in sports as early as possible. Here are some recent findings on the positive influence an active lifestyle can have on the prevention of disease:

HEART DISEASE

I know if you hear about cholesterol one more time, you'll scream. But chances are you haven't heard about an important finding by the National Cholesterol Education program. Their research indicates that children who have high levels of cholesterol are "three times more likely than other children to have high cholesterol as adults." Findings also show that women who exercise have lower blood pressure.

DIABETES

Regular exercise is believed to manage or even prevent non-insulin-dependent diabetes. This is important because diabetes is also related to the risk of hypertension and heart disease.

OSTEOPOROSIS

Do you know any elderly women who have a curve in their spine? My grandmother did, and now I know why. She was losing bone mass owing to the aging process. Since there is no cure for this condition, we must learn to take care of ourselves throughout our lifetime. Weight-bearing exercise (using fitness machines or free weights) combined with sound nutrition (appropriate amounts of calcium and vitamin D) will go a long way toward protecting our bones. Purdue University researchers found that minimally active women aged eighteen to thirty-one who had engaged in high school sports had a significantly greater bone density than those who had not.

BREAST CANCER

This disease is a woman's nightmare. The good news is that as little as one to three hours of exercise a week over a woman's reproductive life can reduce the risk of breast cancer by 20 to 30 percent; if a woman exercises more than four hours a week, the risk can be reduced by 60 percent, according to the *Journal of the National Cancer Institute*.

Personal and Social Benefits

Most children are socialized by their parents and close family members, but anyone, especially coaches who have regular and often close contact with a child, can influence how qualities like confidence and self-perception are developed.

Growing Beyond the Surrender Gender

Many girls lack the confidence to say what is on their minds and not always give in to someone else's demands. Being involved in sports—interacting with team members and coaches—gives girls an opportunity to learn assertiveness. One of the girls I coached—who was involved in youth, high school, and college sports—told me that developing the ability to speak up for herself was a long-term process. Here are her thoughts about a couple of situations that made her tap into her strength and not cave in when things got rough.

> *When you say what is on your mind, it is not always welcomed with open arms. For instance, one time I needed to talk to my coach about some tension that was developing in the gym. So I went and asked him about my progress. It was very scary because I didn't know how he would react. While we didn't get anywhere, I was glad I had the nerve to say what was on my mind. I knew if I didn't say anything, nothing would change. Later, after I graduated college, that experience gave me the strength to go and talk to my boss when I had a concern. And that discussion turned out to be a positive one, because my boss said, "Thank you for being honest." I was prepared to be fired if that was the result of my assertiveness, but I felt I had enough confidence in my abilities to ask for what I thought I deserved.*
>
> —Amanda, 21, former gymnast

Rubbing Elbows with Athletic Role Models

It's one thing to be inspired by great athletes on television. It is quite another to be near them, to get their autograph, to hear a word of encouragement, to have a smile beamed your way. You feel as though you are being touched by greatness, and it makes you want to try harder to achieve your own goals.

Many young athletes have the opportunity to meet locally or even nationally famous coaches and athletes by attending sports camps. Distinguished coaches from a particular sport come to discuss and demonstrate how youngsters can improve their skills, their strategies, and the value of goal setting. Hearing such advice from the "big shots" definitely makes an impression.

Volunteering at a professional sporting event is another way to rub elbows with celebrities and take advantage of a worthwhile learning experience—and girls who are involved in sports are more likely to land such positions. Most high-profile sport events need recruits to handle nonpaying jobs, and those in charge tend to give special preference to young people who play the sport themselves. For example, when I was living in New Jersey and was asked to be part of the administrative team for the Dial American Cup in Madison Square Garden, a high-level international gymnastics competition, one of the benefits for my competitive team members was to be present on the competition floor during this spectacular event. The girls carried out all sorts of responsibilities that made them feel they were on top of the world, and they also got to be within inches of their heroes. Being part of that atmosphere makes you work harder, and witnessing an elite performance up close inspires young athletes to strive for greatness themselves. They could see how international competitors handled pressure, how they dealt with mistakes, and how they focused intently on their performance. My students will never forget that experience, and I'll never forget the look in those girls' eyes as they absorbed all that magnificence.

Slowing Down Sexual Relationships

The federal Centers for Disease Control and Prevention conducted a study entitled "The Women's Sport Foundation Report: Sport and Teen Pregnancy" and found that teenage athletes are

- less likely to engage in sexual intercourse as teenage non-athletes (54 percent to 41 percent, respectively).
- more likely to begin sex later and to have fewer partners than non-athletes.

- more likely to use contraceptives.
- far less likely to get pregnant than non-athletes.

One reason why teen athletes delay sex is that being on a team requires a commitment to their sport and their teammates. If a girl is having fun, and accomplishing something that supports her self-esteem, she may be less interested in pursuing sexual relationships. When a girl is committed to sports, she has very little time for anything else aside from school, practice, and homework. Along the way she has usually developed the assertiveness to say "no."

Reducing High-Risk Behavior: Smoking, Drinking, and Drugs

Wouldn't it be a relief to think that you wouldn't have to worry about your daughter drinking and doing drugs in high school or even middle school? It's possible, but you've got to lay the groundwork very early. A 1995 report from *Medicine and Science in Sports and Exercise* noted that

- 92 percent of girls are less likely to be involved with drugs when they spend most of their leisure time involved with recreational activities.
- physical activity appears to decrease the initiation of cigarette smoking in adolescent girls.

Having talked to many high school athletes throughout my teaching career, I know that the report's conclusions are true. And even when a girl has been involved in high-risk behavior, there's still a chance sports can turn her around. Take Teresa, for example. In an interview conducted by *Women's Sports and Fitness* magazine, she was described as just another troubled urban youth until she went on a Sierra Club rafting trip. After several successful outings, the seventeen-year-old found that being able to control her raft inspired her to control her life. Teresa, once confined to an alcohol rehab center, eventually became certified as a river guide. "It gave me a sense of direction and a lot of self-esteem and confidence," she says.

Psychological Benefits

Nothing makes parents feel better than to know that their daughter has a good relationship with herself. From your parental perspective, I'm sure it's easy to understand that this relationship will be tested over and over again as time marches on. Your daughter's participation in sports not only builds her physical strength; it is also one of the best ways to insure that she develops the kind of inner strength that she'll need throughout life.

Fortunately, unique research programs around the country are committing time and money to understand the special concerns of females. One such program is the Melpomene Institute in St. Paul, Minnesota. Their mission is to "help girls and women of all ages link physical activity and health through research, publication, and education." They have dedicated themselves to studying all areas of female health since their beginning in 1982. Of their many findings, one study backed up the belief that physically active girls have a better outlook on life than those girls who were sedentary as kids, that they take pride in their physical and social selves.

Positive Body Image

In general, people won't invest in themselves if they don't think they are worth the effort. Developing a sense of worthiness begins with feeling capable. As girls build physical strength through sports participation, and acquire sport skills, they'll feel capable. The more competent girls feel, no matter what body type they have, the more likely they are to cultivate realistic expectations about themselves and accept themselves for who they are. Listen to the story of one high school athlete who has learned to respect her body for what it is.

Every American girl has a complex from watching beautiful actresses on TV shows. The friends that I go to high school with and I don't really want to be thin like a supermodel girl, but then again we don't want to get into the pudgy look. Gymnastics helped me because I was skinny and twiggy, and I found that exercise was the best thing I could be doing for my body. Then I started putting on some weight. Now that I know muscle weighs more than fat, it gives me comfort. I realize I'm

*not fat. I understand that I weigh more than other people be-
cause I'm toned. Being consistent with working out and balancing my eating has allowed me to be okay with my body.*
                                          —Kellie, 18, gymnast

What's great about Kellie is that as a teenager she has come to her
own conclusion that her self-image isn't all about weight. Because
she has continuously stayed in sports, she has an intimate knowledge of her body, and she can deal with body changes. She likes feeling toned and likes the self-confidence that goes along with being
competent in sports.

Emotional Well-being and Confidence
I don't accept the belief of constantly praising children in order to
build their confidence. Any girl who wants to make her way in the
real world has to *earn* self-confidence, which comes through striving
and years of investment in herself. Confidence isn't something you
can "study" for at the last minute, just before you need it during one
of life's many tests. It has to be developed over the course of a lifetime—and playing sports is one of the best ways to make it grow.

*I really had a shy, introverted ten-year-old. She wouldn't
try something unless she saw that she could succeed. When
she began sports, eventually she learned to trust the coach,
and then she learned to trust herself. The look on her face was
incredible when she learned she could do things. When I look
at my daughter now, she goes for things with confidence, without the fear of failing. That is going to get her far in life. She
doesn't shy away from classes at school that are tough. Socially, she's outgoing and has a diverse circle of friends. She's
very self-assured. She's very even tempered.*
                              —Mary, mother of one daughter

What happens to the child athlete as she grows into the role of
mother and coach? Here is what a female coach has to say:

*When I look back at what sports did for me, I'd say that my
well-being was grounded in the fact that I was confident.
Sports has given me the ability to make mistakes and not look*

at it like the end of life. Maybe it's not okay with somebody else, but it is okay with me. I know I can get back on my feet and start over. Now I look at each day as another opportunity to be successful. The opportunities never stop.

—J.D., mother and coach

Bouncing Back from Setbacks

Learning to adapt to life's ups and downs is an indispensable skill. Emmy E. Warner, a researcher at the University of California, Davis, identified several components of resiliency that should be nurtured while raising children and are equally important in raising athletes. The valuable parenting practices pointed out in Ms. Warner's study that relate to sports are

- providing a caring and supportive environment (where coaches bond with the athletes).
- teaching life skills like persistence and confidence.
- communicating and setting high expectations.
- creating the opportunity to have a meaningful experience.

Coaches and parents who embrace these concepts will go a long way toward helping girls learn how to get back on track after inevitable defeats and disappointments.

A mother explains how sports has helped her daughters face difficulties:

What I liked about what I saw in the development of my girls was that if the various teams that they were on lost a game, they wouldn't go home and fall in a heap. The soccer coach was a big help in that he made the players shake hands with the opposing team after every game. He helped them understand that tomorrow is a new day. Even though one of my daughters initially had a perfectionist personality, by the time she finished college she had become very realistic. She knew what she could and couldn't do, and she didn't drive herself crazy. The amount of time and money we have put into the girls' sports is all worth it.

—Corrine, mother of three girls

Self-Motivation and Ambition

Motivation, according to Dr. Sean McCann, who heads the sports psychology program at the U.S. Olympic Committee, is "generally [established] by the time a child is twelve or thirteen. She is either motivated intrinsically by the desire to do well, or extrinsically, by the desire to please or by concern for what others will think."

I think Shannon's sports experience is an example of how far a girl can go when the drive to succeed comes from within. When Shannon first started in sports, she was an ice-skater, and the line seemed to blur about whether she was skating for herself or to please her mother. When she reached high school and changed sports, something wonderful happened to her. For the first time she began to understand how much she could accomplish with motives that were uniquely hers.

> *When I first signed up for team sports in high school I had two different personalities. I was shy off the court, but not on the court, where I was motivated to succeed. I used to hang around with shy kids, and that kept me from being as ambitious as I thought I could be. But slowly I became more confident and motivated to be different as I interacted with my teammates on and off the court. It seemed like it rubbed off on me, how sure they were of themselves, being able to speak up with no problem. I realized that the very act of having to communicate on the court in order to make certain plays made me talk to my teammates. Now, after four years of team sports, I have the confidence to play hard, to speak up, and I like it.*
> —Shannon, 16, basketball player

Reduce Symptoms of Stress and Depression

Living in a state of good mental health becomes more and more difficult for girls as they approach the teenage years. That's why it is so critical to have sports be solidly in place in a girl's life early on. Just taking the time for recreation can help balance a person's life and alleviate depression. Half of all girls who participate in some kind of sports have higher than average levels of self-esteem and less depression, according to a report entitled "Risk, Resiliency, and Resistance: Current Research on Adolescent Girls." Though researchers are still trying to pinpoint the exact reasons why physical activity is beneficial to one's frame of mind, it's known that a combination of biological, chemical, psychological, and social factors play an important role.

This is how playing sports helped a teenager maintain emotional balance:

> When I manage my time, which I do best when I'm playing sports, I have less stress and do better in school. If I feel overwhelmed with things, it's not a constant, nagging feeling. I don't get depressed to the point where I can't do anything. I know that I can go out on the basketball court and let it all out during a game. Because dribbling a ball and shooting hoops is my passion, I can throw myself into the action and not think about other things. I feel like I can get my head clear and then go home and tackle what I have to do.
>
> —Kathryn, 16, basketball player

Educational Benefits

In general, girls who participate in sports do better in school than girls who don't. This is quite an amazing feat given the practice and game schedules of many young athletes. Nonetheless it is accomplished by setting priorities and making a realistic schedule. When students begin high school, teachers at freshman orientation highly recommend that students get involved with other activities, one of which is sports. It is often interesting that at the end of the academic year when awards are presented, many of the girls receiving academic awards are athletes. Girls don't have to wait until high school to enjoy these benefits. Girls involved in any age-group programs face the same issues of establishing priorities and being realistic about their time commitments. Just make sure that you and your child look at sports the same way that a report from the National Association of Principals does, not as an extracurricular but as a "co-curricular" activity.

Research by Skip Dane of Hardness Research, in Casper, Wyoming, finds the following results:

• The ratio of girls who participate in sports and do well in school is three to one.

- Sports participants take average and above-average classes.
- Sports participants receive above-average grades and do above average on skill tests.
- Student athletes appear to have more parental involvement than other students.
- Once they become involved in athletics, teenage athletes appear to change their focus from the normal preoccupation of cars and spending money to life accomplishments.

Mental Ability and Concentration

It's said that daily exercise can mean the difference between being able to concentrate in school or experiencing difficulty. The American Heart Association wholeheartedly supports schoolteachers in this belief. Healthy children develop a healthy brain, which gains energy from the muscles being stimulated through physical activity. In addition the quick responses called for in sports improve the ability to focus. The play-by-play nature of athletics is a continual source of mental stimulation, forcing players to stay alert for extended periods of time. In talking with many families, parents agreed that learning physical skills helped their daughters focus and stay on task with their homework.

Budgeting Time

While interviewing girls about sports and their schedules, I heard one comment repeatedly: Girls are more motivated to get things done during sports season. When they are off-season, these female athletes often procrastinate doing things because there is no hard-and-fast schedule that they have to stick to. Both students and parents realize that being in sports helps athletes manage their time better. In talking with girl athletes, I've learned that they take a very practical approach to studying—they study whenever and wherever they can, on the bus, on breaks, at home, before practice. Since they know that homework is a priority, and their parents won't let them play sports without good grades, most try to get the job done. This valuable skill has tremendous carryover value for college athletes, who will face even greater challenges as they add extensive travel to their schedule. Going to school and participating in sports becomes their life routine. Even if athletes are not on a sport team in college, they are in the habit of budgeting their time because they know their priorities. And adults who continue to include fitness in their lives are able to do so because staying active, even with a busy schedule, is a habit.

Degrees, Grade-Point Averages, and Dropout Rates

Achieving academic success is important during the grade school years, but it is absolutely essential during high school. According to the National Federation of State High School Associations, a comprehensive study done in North Carolina found noteworthy differences between athletes and non-athletes regarding grade-point averages and dropout and graduation rates. While this survey covered boys and girls, the results are still inspiring and instructive.

	ATHLETES	NON-ATHLETES
Grade-point average	2.86	1.96
Dropout rate	0.7 %	8.98 %
Graduation rate	99.56 %	94.66 %

Leadership

I was reminded of the importance of sports in developing leadership qualities in a conversation with an ice-skater turned volleyball player whom I used to train. Sheila noted that during her middle school years, she was shy socially but could pull herself together for competition. When she went on to high school and changed from an individual to a team sport her freshman year, it was an adjustment. She found herself training with the upperclassmen, who seemed to know and have it all. She admired that. During her sophomore year she was chosen as captain of the junior varsity team. Slowly but surely her teammates came to respect her athletic abilities and her caring, supportive nature. She realized that being a communicator was part of being a leader. Her personal skills peaked in her senior year. She was outspoken, she continued in a leadership position, she became a role model—she was different, a more confident person. But Sheila will tell anyone who will listen that you can't have significant personal growth during one season in sports. It took years of fighting her own demons and watching older girls as role models for her to realize that she wanted to be in charge of her life and help lead others in the same direction.

Planting the Seeds of Passion

Every benefit that we've talked about in this chapter is much more easily attained if girls have a passion for their sport. When they love what they're doing, they stay with it. Oh sure, there'll be some great days and some down days. But on the whole, these young women can see that mostly good things are happening to their bodies and their lives. When girls feel passionate about kicking that soccer ball, shooting hoops, or pitching a no-hitter, that zest transfers to non-athletic parts of their lives. Passion. How do girls discover it in their lives? By having the opportunity to try several sports and the chance to find out where their talents lie.

This is a story written by Brittney, an eighth-grade student, for one of her school writing assignments where she explores her dreams and her passion. She and her dad passed on this story to me and agreed to let me share it with you. What I love about this story is that it's so down-to-earth, so full of energy, so simple in its approach to the value of sports—and filled with the vision of an aspiring athlete.

"Shoot the ball!" my teammates shouted.

Swish. The ball bounces off the court. The crowd grew quiet. I looked at the score: 43–42. The buzzer rings. We won! I made the basket. The audience goes wild again. That was the greatest day I've had in my basketball history.

"Great shot, Brittney!" exclaimed my coach.

"Good job, number 34!" my teammates chanted.

My face must have been red from excitement. And yours would have been too if you were me.

Basketball is the best sport because there is much action, you play many games, and it takes a great deal of exercise. When you play basketball, the game is very fast paced. That means you are always pumped up and ready to play. Girls and guys are very fast when it comes to basketball. That is because the object is to get down the court as fast as you can. The game of basketball always keeps you motivated, also. It makes people happy, so their self-esteem rises. That gets them motivated so they play better.

Most people think the best thing about playing basketball is all the exercise. That's part of it. Basketball consists of a great deal of running. That is a good thing, if you like to run. Even if you don't, though, it helps you get in better shape. Which makes you stay healthy. Working out and practicing basketball will help you get stronger and maintain bigger muscles. How can you disagree with that?

As you can see, there are many things you can enjoy about playing basketball. Now don't tell me it is something you can't cope with. It is very fun. At least give the game a try—you should like it!

If we're doing our jobs as quality coaches and parents, then the young athletes we teach and the daughters we love will feel as much passion for their sport as Brittney.

Starting Right out of the High Chair Makes a Lasting Difference

2

We all know that parents are supposed to begin the learning process in their children by teaching them the names of things, the alphabet, numbers, and colors. But how many of us realize how important it is to throw in a few hops and jumps as well? Nobody questions the value of intellectual education and of getting kids started on their ABCs, but what value do we place on being *physically* educated?

Don't you admire—or perhaps envy just a little—that woman down the street who is smart, has three kids, stays in shape, and has the ability to play tennis or softball in her coed league at work? Chances are her parents encouraged her to be well rounded and they valued physical activity when she was a very young girl. Females can successfully play sports through adulthood if they first learn basic movement skills—like leaping and jumping—and learn them early. So when should such learning begin? Usually around age two is a good time to start. A child may not get the hang of skipping or catching a ball until six or seven, but the earlier you introduce your daughter to some fundamental physical skills, the better prepared she'll be to engage in and enjoy physical activities as she grows.

Pick up any parenting magazine or listen to talk-show pediatric specialists on radio or TV, and you'll find most of them will agree that fundamental motor skills (having to do with muscles and movement) should be in place between the ages of five and seven. Experienced moms and dads, though, say it best. Start your girls early, before they enter elementary school, and do whatever it takes to keep them active so that their primary movement skills are mastered by the time they want to play sports. If paying for recreation programs is a budget buster, go to the park as often as you can and get your girls jumping, sliding, and climbing. Buy "Mommy and Me" exercise videos or join a neighborhood play group—just be active.

An Early Advantage Is a Permanent Advantage

You've probably seen parents who seem frustrated and embarrassed when their child appears uncoordinated or clumsy on the playground or playing field—and maybe your heart goes out to them. Maybe you're afraid of becoming one of those parents. You and your daughter can avoid such disappointments if you take simple steps like showing her how to bounce, catch, or kick a ball when she's two, three, or four years old. The concept of an early advantage being a permanent advantage was presented by educator and author Hiam Ginott. He was the first to fully recognize the value of early training in children. The preschool years, often referred to as early childhood (ages two to six), are the critical time of life when a child is most receptive to developing fundamental movement patterns. Read that last sentence twice. By teaching fundamental movement patterns when kids are preschool age, you will have set the stage for learning future complex, sport-specific skills. Setting the stage doesn't mean going overboard, scheduling lessons every other day of the week. It does mean that you need to provide plenty of opportunities for spontaneous *and* structured play where skills can be developed. However, the single factor that will make the most difference with your daughter's learning of motor skills is the time that you spend with her. Children learn the quickest by watching role models. Later in this chapter I'll provide the help that you need to teach the basic movement skills.

The Benefits of an Early Start

Physical activity is the medium through which children learn about their world. When you provide lots of play activities as well as structured learning, this increases the child's ability to deal with challenges and to master control over her body.

HAVING ADDITIONAL CHOICES

Good basics give your daughter more choices of the kinds of sports she'll be physically able to try out for when she's a youngster. It'll also expand her ability to participate in sport activities throughout her lifetime. If you have spent time with your daughter presenting her with a variety of activities, she will have more choices than the traditional offerings of dance or swim lessons, though both are terrific foundation programs for balance and coordination. If you really want your daughter to have lots of choices, play a variety of ball sports with her.

BEING READY FOR HIGH SCHOOL OR CLUB SPORTS

Children may not know what they will be interested in when they reach high school. For your daughter to have a chance to play high school or club-level sports, early preparation—especially the development of ball handling skills—is critical. Read this loud and clear. We often get balls into the hands of our girls far too late. Begin by getting balls in your daughter's hands as young as age two. Girls need to be able to throw, catch, kick, dribble, bounce, or hit a ball. That doesn't mean she's got to play basketball starting at age five, but she must have the foundation skills needed to play basketball if she wants to make the team. You can't start a sport at ground zero in high school and be successful. And you can't enjoy fully what you're not skilled at doing.

HAVING THE CAPACITY TO ENGAGE IN A LIFETIME WITH SPORTS

As an adult, your daughter may be interested in pursuing a variety of sports and fitness activities. To enjoy a lifetime of recreational activities such as swimming, fitness walking, bowling, hiking, golf, tennis, biking, snowshoeing, aerobic dance, sailing, canoeing, cross-country skiing, running, archery, and alpine skiing, she needs a broad foundation of movement skills and ongoing experience. This is yet another reason to start early with foundational skills and early general fitness activity.

Spontaneous and Structured Play Improves Skills

While play has a purpose, and children need about two hours a day of spontaneous play, some forms of play are more productive than others. Child researchers and educators have identified three kinds of physical play, each important to the growing process:

SENSORIMOTOR PLAY

This is defined as "play that captures the pleasures of using the senses and motor abilities." Girls enjoy using the sensorimotor skills most often seen on the playground—climbing, swinging, sliding, and running.

ROUGH AND TUMBLE PLAY

You're probably used to thinking that only boys play rough. Not so. Girls can tussle as well, left to their own devices. To an outsider it might look as though girls are being aggressive crawling all over each other, but if you look closely, they've got smiles on their faces and they are enjoying the physical contact and good social interaction. This type of play seems to mimic aggression, but the facial expressions are a dead giveaway.

MASTERY PLAY

This is the kind of physical play that helps girls master new skills. When parents spend time with their girls playing activities like catch and ball kicking, it provides an invaluable learning experience.

You as a parent may be asking yourself if being active and playing is enough or if you really have to teach your daughter specific skills. Youth sport expert Dr. Michael Yessis advises parents and coaches alike that "most children will not develop efficient and mature movement patterns without some form of instruction." Please understand that playing with toys and free play are very necessary. But if you want your daughter to be competent, it's important that you spend time with her doing mastery play. In this way she'll gain the coordination and basic skills that will allow her to become successful when she is introduced to sports at the elementary school level. The emphasis here is to encourage structured play *along with* unstructured play. Take a look at how you currently spend your day with your child:

- Do you take an active role in playing with your daughter?
- Does she play outside regularly? At a playground when possible?
- What toys do you provide? Do you include balls and other age-appropriate sports equipment?
- Are you continually trying new activities, new environments?

With just a little effort on your part, you can help widen your daughter's experiences to include such activities as running, leaping, balancing, hopping, jumping, throwing, kicking, and striking. When children enter elementary school, they often have PE only once a week for thirty minutes, so development of fundamental skills at school cannot always be counted on. Because of this, it is necessary for you to support your daughter's physical education as sincerely as her academic education. If physical education budgets continue to be cut, your child will become increasingly more dependent on you to learn about sports, stay active, and become physically fit during her elementary school years. The key is to pay attention to what your child is doing in school.

Mother of Five: "Experience Makes the Difference"

Yesterday I had my special version of a power lunch. That's the kind of meeting where you show up in your sweats and sneakers and spend an hour talking as fast as you can with your friend before she has to pick up the kids from school. We reflected on how we first became acquainted when her daughters rolled and giggled their way through my preschool gymnastics program. We talked about how age three seemed young for her girls to begin "training," but this mom just knew she had to do something, anything, to help direct her toddlers' boundless energy. My friend was quick to add that taking gymnastics lessons was just part of her daughters' early sports experience. Being active together as a family, as often as possible—whether it was to take short hikes or trips to the park or the beach—was a routine, not just a sometimes event.

Now that her daughters are young adults, my friend has had years to reflect on the value of early movement education and consistent family recreation. Unlike many of her other friends' daughters, her girls tried out for and made all of the middle and senior high school sports teams with relative ease. My friend told me that when it came time to try out for sports, it was not such a big deal because the girls were ready, and they were experienced. One of them even received a partial college scholarship as a gymnast.

Without question, this mother was happy with the decisions she had made by making sure that her daughters were physically active and educated at an early age. Not only have her girls experienced the fun and sense of accomplishment that go along with playing sports, but they are also pretty happy individuals. Perhaps sports helped them avoid some of the roller-coaster emotions that teenagers often face. I can tell you she's a believer.

When Should I Start Teaching Motor Skills?

You're probably familiar with the early physical milestones of growing up—crawling, climbing, standing, and walking. What comes next is more important than you think and may easily be disregarded. After walking is mastered in a very controlled way, it's time to take a more active role to help your daughter build her basic motor skills. Why? Because your job as parents is to get your daughters ready for the bodies they're likely to grow into. Because children are starting sport activities earlier and earlier, it's important to get them very comfortable with the foundation skills of movement (also known as gross motor skills) as soon as they are developmentally ready. Chronological age is not the only determining factor, but it is a helpful guideline. Children grow according to their own timetables, and one girl at eighteen months might have a central nervous system that is developmentally more mature than another at age two. It is extremely important that you be very observant of your own child.

When She's Steady, She's Ready

One of the most important things to look at is the way a child walks. Are her steps short? Is her stance wide? Are her arms held high? If so, she's still getting the hang of walking and is not yet ready to comfortably grasp the sports foundation skills. Look for consistent balance when walking before you attempt motor development training. When your daughter is up and running and steady as she goes, you can begin helping her develop her motor skills. The age at which this happens is different for every child, so I can't give you an exact number. Some qualities to look for are a longer stride with arms held down by the sides of the body and the ability to run short distances in control. At this stage in your daughter's development it's time for you to teach her to leap, hop, skip, and jump—and more. But don't panic, you don't need a teaching certificate in physical education. This chapter will map out practical guidelines that will help you get her off to a great start.

As the Brain Grows, So Goes the Child

The most important aspect of a child's growth is the maturation of the brain. During early childhood it develops faster than any other part of the body. The more mature the brain, the greater the variety of tasks a child can perform. Different parts of the brain develop at different rates. This is why some children advance more quickly in verbal skills but may lag behind their peers in gaining physical skills. As the brain matures it can specialize in those particular parts that are used for certain abilities, in this case physical abilities. There are no hard-and-fast timetables, so again, observe your child.

Teaching Movement Skills at Home

Let's lace up those sneakers, grab a spare fifteen minutes, and spend some active time with your daughter. When you do this every day, you'll be amazed at the development that will take place. First, you should learn what to teach and how to teach it. As you read through the following home lessons, you might ask yourself if these movement skills are within your ability and your sports vocabulary. If so, then this section will serve as a refresher course. If not, then the following information will be a primer for both you and your daughter's physical education.

When you're presenting movement skills to your daughter, remember that this is play, not training camp. Take your time and be aware of how often you ask her to do something. Just a few times is plenty. Stop when you see her attention starting to wane and move on to another activity. Also, be prepared to demonstrate what you're trying to teach her. If you feel as though your technical demonstration would qualify for *America's Funniest Home Videos*, just run your recreation program inside the house. Still not comfortable showing your daughter what to do? If she's a preschooler or in elementary school, see if you can get involved with friends or a play group that engages in physical activities, find some relatives who will help you, or sign up for a preschool gymnastics class. Much of what your daughter learns will come about by good old trial and error, so be patient. The idea is to give her many opportunities to improve her skills. Include an extra dose of fun, encouragement, and patience to get the most from each session.

The physical skills that your daughter needs to be able to play sports are called "motor skills" and are divided into three groups. Motor skills are those activities that move the body around from place to place, help the body remain steady while moving around, and guide the hands or feet when controlling sport equipment (such as a tennis racket or soccer ball). I'll provide an age range for each area of skill development. Following are the four types of motor skills.

One: Locomotor (and Locomotor Combinations)

Locomotor skills are those that get the body moving through space. The normal sequence of development is crawling, creeping, walking, running, jumping, leaping, and hopping. Advanced locomotor skills involve combinations of movements: sliding, galloping, skipping, climbing, dodging, and body rolling. For each of the skills listed, I have provided an age range during which you can expect your daughter to do the activity comfortably. A word of caution: Just because other girls her age can hop doesn't automatically mean your daughter will be able to hop. All of these behaviors must be learned, except for running, which develops somewhat automatically—and shows up just as you need your daughter to be by your side instead of halfway across the street!

Two: Stability

Non-locomotor skills are known as "stability skills." They are accomplished with little or no movement of the feet. They are bending and stretching, pulling and pushing, swinging and swaying, and turning and twisting.

Three: Manipulative

Manipulative skills involve handling and managing objects. This type of skill helps to develop eye-hand and eye-foot coordination.

Manipulative skills are bouncing (dribbling and volleying), catching, kicking, rolling, striking, throwing, and trapping (using the sole of foot, leg, or body).

Four: Movement Awareness

There's also something called "movement awareness." Although not considered a motor skill in the strict sense of the word, it is important in developing coordination and being able to sense what's happening around you.

Overall, each group of motor skills contributes equally to the development of your daughter's skills. Inevitably, every girl will develop some skills more rapidly than others, and some girls will progress more rapidly than others.

Sports Equipment for Your Home Program

Most of the items that you'll need to work with your preschooler at home can be purchased at a general merchandise store. Following is a list of equipment for teaching locomotor, manipulative, and movement awareness skills to your daughter.

ITEMS YOU ALREADY HAVE AT HOME
   Towels and facecloths

ITEMS UNDER $5
   Balloons
   Soft sponge ball (three inches)
   Vinyl ball, eight inches (sometimes called a playground ball if it
      is rubber)
   Hula hoop (the smaller the better)
   Jump rope (plastic cover over rope)
   Tennis racket (plastic, oversize)
   Fat bat (plastic, about sixteen inches long)

ITEMS UNDER $10
   Golf club set (plastic golf club and tee platform with balls)
   Traffic cones (twenty inches high; buy two)

ITEMS UNDER $30
  Toddler-size basketball stand with hoop

SPECIALTY ITEMS
  Trampoline jogger (about $40 at sporting goods stores)
  Movement awareness music tapes (look in the phone directory
    under "School Supplies." Audiotapes start around $10, and
    CDs are priced around $13)

Home Lesson 1: Locomotor Skills

Locomotor skills are directly useful in any and all sports and are learned in an ordered sequence—running, leaping, jumping, hopping, galloping, sliding, and skipping. Reminder: Children learn best by watching someone demonstrate an activity. If you can't do it, find someone who can, or become involved in a play group where children are developing the fundamentals.

RUNNING

Immature running occurs after learning to walk. This shows up around eighteen months. Mature running shows up at two to three years of age. And being able to run smoothly appears around the age of five. Running is something kids love to do without any encouragement. So just find a place to do lots of it every day. Since I know you'll be running after your daughter, you get a workout, too, as you get to huff and puff.

LEAPING

(Suggested equipment: three bath towels, a jump rope, two traffic cones)

The ability to leap, an extension of running, means that your child takes off from one foot and lands on the other. This skill may show up before age three. Leaping is best learned after your daughter understands how to go "over" something. Here's a simple exercise: Roll up three bath towels and place them on the floor two or three feet apart from each other. Get your daughter to step over each one of the towels. The first thing she'll want to do is walk on top of the towel, which can be maddening, but keep lifting her leg over the towels one at a time. Once this is mastered, she can learn to leap by going over the towels faster (move with running speed) and a little higher in the air. If you want more of a challenge for her, set up two traffic cones and string a jump rope between them. You can keep "raising the bar" as she is ready to leap higher.

JUMPING
(Suggested equipment: three facecloths, a small trampoline jogger, two traffic cones, a jump rope)

Early attempts at jumping begin with a one-foot takeoff from a surface to a two-foot landing. The mature skill, a two-foot takeoff to a two-foot landing, is developed around two to two and a half years of age. Mature jumping with an arm swing occurs around the age of five. It's likely your daughter has already discovered a great place to jump—the most attractive site in the house—your bed!

The simplest way to introduce jumping is to lay facecloths on the floor and have your daughter jump from one facecloth to another. Once she is consistently steady at jumping from one cloth to the next, take her to the next level by following the same steps as you did for leaping. Set up the traffic cones with a jump rope stretched between them. Again, let your daughter adjust the height of the jump rope.

I know of families who buy a secondhand mattress and throw it on the floor in the garage or somewhere safe to allow their children to practice jumping. Some families use the small trampoline joggers that sit on the floor to build jumping skills. Get one for your daughter and one for you, and you could both get exercise at the same time!

HOPPING
(Suggested equipment: three facecloths)

Hopping, where you take off and land on the same foot, is a skill that's usually developed at around three years of age. Even then it may be a challenge. You can introduce the skill by getting out some facecloths and laying them on the floor in a row. Show your daughter how to hop first. Then have her stand on one foot, hold her hands, and help her hop from one facecloth to the next. Try using the right leg one time and the left leg the next time. Eventually she'll play "hopscotch." Try not to confuse hopping with the famous bunny hop line dance, where you bounce up and down with both feet side by side; that is actually jumping, not hopping. Sorry, fans.

Combinations of locomotor skills, which become fully developed around four to six years of age, are galloping, sliding, skipping, body rolling, dodging, and climbing. These skills are most useful in gymnastics, spirit squads, wrestling, and track and field.

GALLOPING

Galloping is your chance to act like a horse. If you're wondering what part of the horse to act like, it's the legs. This is a step-together-step pattern most often done in a forward motion. Have your daughter lift one leg (we'll call it the lead leg), and as she lifts her leg it will bend as she steps forward. As her lead leg is placed on the floor and takes the weight, her rear leg closes behind the lead foot. Do this in a series across the floor with the same leg leading. If you want to help your daughter get the rhythm, hold her hands while you're moving across the floor. Look for this to develop comfortably around age four.

SLIDING

Kids never miss an opportunity to slide. In summer they slide across the sand into the ocean or a lake. In winter they slide down a hill in their snowsuits. Sliding is also useful in sports. The slide is similar to the gallop except that it is done with one side of the body leading. You can practice this skill with or without music, but in any event, hold your daughter's hands while facing one another and slide across the living room or on the grass outside. Take small steps so she can keep up with you and get the rhythm. She should be able to slide to the left or right side comfortably. Girls do this easily around the age of four. This is helpful in tennis, softball, and basketball, sports where the body has to keep facing a specific direction (where the action is) yet still keep moving. It's considered a transition pattern, where the legs move the body from one skill to another.

SKIPPING

Teaching skipping is sort of tricky. Sometimes four- to five-year-olds can figure it out, but don't be surprised if this skill doesn't show up until age seven. A skip is a walking step forward followed by a hop on the same foot and then repeated on the other side. Learn this by holding hands with your daughter so that she gets the rhythm. Be patient, ever so patient. This is a tough skill to master.

DODGING
(Suggested equipment: a soft eight-inch ball)

This is defined as a sharp change of direction and is an important skill for team sports such as soccer, volleyball, basketball, field and ice hockey, lacrosse, water polo, and skiing. Knowing how to move without colliding into other people or an object is certainly important if your daughter wants to play team sports. Observe how she plays with other children. Does she have problems bumping into them while running? Playing tag and dodgeball (which is nothing more than a form of tag with a ball) are great ways to develop your daughter's dodgeability.

CLIMBING

If you have or have ever had a two-year-old in your house, you know you don't have to teach climbing. In the house, that is. Outside may be different. The jungle gym at the park might be scary. But that's exactly where your daughter needs to be climbing, so stay close by and encourage her. Show her where to place her hands and her feet. Learning to climb comfortably is mostly a matter of doing it over and over again. You'll have to develop a sense of when to stop and when to push through the fear. Keep repeating, "Wow, you are so brave."

BODY ROLLING
(Suggested equipment: three bath towels)

This skill really translates into gymnastic-style rolls. You may notice I use the word *roll* instead of *somersault*. A roll means the body contacts the ground. A somersault is an entire rotation of the body done in the air. Rolls can be taught as early as age two. I was never so glad I had gymnastics training as when I performed my first parachute jump. In our dress rehearsals we were taught by the jump master to bend our knees and roll our bodies sideways immediately upon landing on the ground. I can tell you with perfect clarity that when you are up in the air around two miles, the earth is green and soft looking, but in that last thirty feet, the ground only has patches of green and is hard. Thanks to my gymnastics background, I touched down safely, rolled over my side and up to my feet, and "walked" away from the landing site with a smile.

To teach body rolling, lay two to three towels on top of each other for a safe learning area. Begin by teaching a side roll (it's easier than a forward roll). To roll sideways, have your daughter lay on her back, knees bent up against her chest, hands and arms wrapped across her legs so she will stay in an "egg" shape. Give her a gentle push to roll her sideways so that she rolls over her knees and onto her back again. To teach a forward roll, stand in back of your daughter, have her bend over, and place her hands and head on the towel. You will hold her hips and guide her over onto her back, making sure her head curls under (chin near the chest) so that she does not roll from the top of her head. Her back should be round.

Home Lesson 2: Stability Skills

These skills are useful in most sports. Fortunately they are mainly inborn and can be improved with practice. Any of these skills may be started around two and a half years of age.

BENDING AND STRETCHING

These skills are especially helpful for learning gymnastics, martial arts, and wrestling and for serving in tennis, volleyball, and basketball—and picking clothes up off the floor. Bending and stretching for small bodies can be done sitting on the floor (in front of the TV, if you have to) and reaching forward to touch the toes. Your daughter can have her legs closed together or straddled open. She can also stand with her legs straddled, knees slightly bent, and then bend and reach toward the floor. Stretching of the upper body can be done with your daughter reaching overhead with her arms toward the ceiling.

PULLING AND PUSHING
(Suggested equipment: towel)

These movements are most commonly associated with daily activities. Few of us see our children push their chairs under the table after eating a meal, but we are likely to see them pulling and pushing a dresser drawer open, opening and closing a door, pushing a playmate playfully down the street on a tricycle, or pulling a friend by the arm as they swing around in circles. Watch and make sure they do things with bent knees so that they won't injure their backs—that's a real concern. To teach pulling, use a towel and play a gentle game of tug-of-war with your daughter. Another way to teach her stability while pulling is to have her sit on a towel, still playing a game of tug-of-war, but tell her to keep sitting up straight as hard as she can. To teach her pushing, begin by laying a jump rope down on the floor. Have both you and your daughter stand on one side of the jump rope. Her goal is to push you "over the line" (the jump rope). Your goal is to let her win.

Eventually, pulling and pushing leads to pull-ups (chin-ups) and push-ups. These exercises are often used in fitness evaluation tests and sports conditioning to improve upper body strength. Since it's highly unusual for preschoolers to do pull-ups, my students perform flexed arm hangs by holding their chin over a bar for two to three seconds. Use the bars at the playground or purchase a chin-up bar to install between the doorjambs in a doorway to further develop the pulling skill. For developing a real push-up, have your daughter stand a couple of feet away from a wall and place her hands on the wall at shoulder height. While flexing her elbows, get her to push herself away from the wall while standing up straight.

SWINGING AND SWAYING
(Suggested equipment: a golf club, a bat, a racket, an eight-inch ball)

These actions are the basis for many manipulative skills. The skill of striking involves swinging your arm from your shoulder as in swinging a golf club, a softball bat, or a tennis racket. Have your daughter hit a ball off the traffic cone. The skill of throwing involves swinging her arm from the shoulder as in a tennis or volleyball serve or throwing a ball in softball or water polo. Kicking is the swinging of her leg from her hip as in kicking a soccer ball. The swinging that your daughter will enjoy most is when she is swinging from her hands or the back of her legs on a bar. If you are practicing the manipulative skills (discussed next in home lesson three), you've got this category pretty well covered. Swaying movements are fun to do with music and are most often seen in gymnastics, particularly with the arms overhead, or moving the torso rhythmically.

TWISTING AND TURNING

These are two different actions that involve rotation of the body. Twisting means that your daughter's body parts (usually the shoulders, arms, and hips) move around an axis with a stable base, her feet. Your daughter will twist when she is getting ready to perform a forceful action such as preparing to swing a tennis racket, softball bat, golf club, or field hockey stick or throw a ball. In my toddler classes we practice twisting in a fairly simple way—we dance to music. Do the old "twist and shout."

Turning is a circular movement where the whole body follows the feet. Examples of this kind of movement are maneuvering a basketball or a soccer ball around an opponent. To practice turning, simply have your daughter turn in place until she's made a complete circle. You'll have lots of fun with this when you do it to music.

Home Lesson 3: Manipulative Skills

Manipulative skills, or using equipment, are useful in tennis, field hockey, ice hockey, softball, soccer, basketball, volleyball, golf, baseball, lacrosse, water polo, and bowling—just to name a few. Learners manipulate equipment such as a bat, a club, or a ball. One simple rule in terms of equipment: The smaller the girl, the bigger the surface area of the bat or the racket, the larger the ball, the larger the hoop or target area. Avoid heavy equipment. Put success within her reach all the time. Again, remember that your daughter will learn best through demonstration of an activity. Most important, the younger your child, the more fun you must make the activity.

ROLLING
(Suggested equipment: various-size balls)

Use an eight-inch ball and a towel. This may sound as if you're heading to the beach, but instead just head to the backyard or the family room. Lay the towel on the ground, have your daughter stand about six feet away, and show her how to roll the ball to the towel. If your daughter is under the age of four, she will most likely use two hands and swing the ball from in between her legs. Around age four to five she will be ready to swing her arms from the side of her body to roll the ball. As your daughter's ability improves, use a smaller ball. You'll soon be ready for a family trip to the bowling lanes, sometimes as early as age three.

TOSSING
(Suggested equipment: bean bags, hula hoop)

Tossing is an underhand throw. There are two ways to toss a ball: one way uses two hands (similar to bowling), and the other uses one hand. The goal in teaching your daughter how to toss is to improve hand-eye coordination. Have your child learn this skill by placing a hula hoop on the floor. With a bean bag in one or both of her hands, have her stand several feet away from a hula hoop. Show her how to swing her arm forward and aim the bean bag toward the hula hoop. When her arm is raised, tell your daughter to let go of the bean bag as she tosses it into the hoop. Shifting her weight by stepping forward as she tosses is a mature skill and may come later. Learning the weight shift teaches the use of force. Have several bean bags on hand to develop this skill. You don't want to run back and forth after her every toss. Try not to giggle, but if you get tired of the hoop, use a tall (clean) kitchen wastebasket for a target.

CATCHING
(Suggested equipment: a balloon, various-size balls)

A beginner will catch an object by holding (or trapping) it against her chest. It's normal for your daughter to close her eyes or look away on contact. Begin to teach her catching using a balloon. Stand fairly close (within three feet) so that it's nearly impossible for her to miss. As her catching improves, keep moving farther and farther away. When your daughter is comfortable with the balloon, and you see her eyes watching it (or tracking, as educators say), try having her catch an eight-inch ball. You'll be able to use a smaller ball as your daughter gets closer to the age of four or five because her brain is maturing and with it her vision, which directly affects eye-hand coordination.

BOUNCING
(Suggested equipment: a balloon, various-size balls)

You can begin to experiment with bouncing using a balloon because it moves slowly enough through the air for your daughter to be able to react to it. Watch how she follows it with her eyes and tries to catch it. There is a big difference in reaction here between a two-year-old and a three-year-old. Since this involves eye-hand coordination, as your child grows older her ability should improve owing to the maturation of her central nervous system. When balloon bouncing is accomplished, around the age of three start to use an eight-inch ball. Your daughter will probably use two hands for some time until she develops a faster reaction time. Somewhere around the age of three or four she will master the skill using one hand instead of two—this is dribbling.

Throwing
(Suggested equipment: a small foam ball, a hula hoop)

The art of throwing is certainly a skill to admire. Would you say that the only thing you can comfortably throw is a fit? If this has been a lifelong frustration for you, a skill you still struggle with, get it off your chest. Help your daughter avoid the same fate. By teaching her this same skill, you may also learn something yourself. You can teach your daughter how to throw starting about age two. At this stage her body faces the target as she bends her arm to start the throw. While her arm is moving upward to about shoulder height, she may end up with her hand behind the head. That's just fine. When she lets go of the ball, sometimes her body will turn slightly, or she may step forward. Using a small foam ball and a target, preferably with you holding a hula hoop, have your daughter throw the ball through the hoop. This is a large target, so there's lots of room for error. Move the hula hoop so that no matter where she throws the ball, it goes through every time. Success breeds success, and her enthusiasm for learning this new skill will be clear—you might be ready to give up the activity before she does.

Kicking
(Suggested equipment: a balloon and an eight-inch ball)

Use a balloon to teach beginning kicking. Notice that your daughter will use her toe to kick the balloon. If you can, try to get her to kick with both the left and the right foot. She will eventually determine for herself which is the dominant side. Once she is comfortable with the balloon, graduate to the eight-inch ball. When she kicks it, make sure she runs to get the ball herself. This will be good practice if your daughter later plays soccer. Kicking with the top or side of the foot is a more advanced skill and should be encouraged as the child's skill advances.

STRIKING
(Suggested equipment: a balloon, a small foam ball, a traffic cone, a miniature plastic bat, a miniature plastic golf club, a large plastic racket, a towel)

Place a balloon or small foam ball on top of the traffic cone and have your daughter swing at it with either a bat or a racket. Encourage both one-handed and two-handed striking with the racket. To use the golf club, set up your play space by having her stand on a towel on the floor and hit a foam ball off the towel. You're creating the same kind of hitting area that golfers use on a driving range.

TRAPPING
(Suggested equipment: an eight-inch ball)

Trapping is a way of receiving a ball without the hands. It may be done with the sole of the foot, the lower legs, or the chest. This skill is used extensively in soccer and can be introduced around the age of five. When your daughter is first learning this skill, her main goal should be to stop the ball with her foot. Stand several feet away from your daughter and roll the ball slowly to her, encouraging her to stop it with the sole of her foot. The most difficult skill, trapping with the chest, can be taught by bouncing the ball on the ground and having your daughter lean forward slightly from her hips to stop the ball as it bounces upward from the ground. Take lots of time with this entire concept; it's fairly advanced and is fully developed around age ten out on the soccer fields.

Home Lesson 4: Movement Awareness

Movement awareness means sensing, understanding, and having physical knowledge of what various bodily movements feel like. Consider the following areas when you're evaluating your daughter's aptitude for different kinds of movement.

KNOWING THE BODY PARTS AND WHAT THEY CAN DO

This may sound like no big deal, but children often have a slow reaction to someone giving directions, or they may be unable to coordinate two body parts at the same time. Playing games like Simon says will help you know how your daughter is developing these abilities. Assess her abilities starting around the age of two by watching her as you say, "Simon says touch your knees. Simon says bend your knees. Simon says reach your arms overhead. Simon says twist your shoulders back and forth." This will clue you in on how aware your daughter is of her body parts and what they can do.

KNOWING WHERE THE BODY IS IN SPACE

Knowing where the body is in space in relationship to people and objects and the ability to judge distance is called "spatial awareness." What do you see when you are watching your daughter play? Can she locate objects in relationship to her body? You can play a little game to evaluate her skill in this area. Say to her, "Walk over to the closest big ball," "Run over to the small ball that is farthest away," "Move close to the tallest girl." This skill develops around the age of five and takes time and patience.

LOCATING UP AND DOWN, FRONT AND BACK

Again, here's where the game of Simon says is quite useful. Watch your daughter as she responds to the following: "Simon says put the ball in front of you. Simon says put the ball in back of you. Simon says put the ball down on the floor. Simon says lift the ball up in the air." Play this game around age two and a half to age three. This lets you know how well your daughter understands location and takes instruction.

BALANCING WHILE STILL OR WHILE MOVING

Usually a girl will figure out how to balance standing still on one leg before she will learn how to balance riding a bike. Watch your daughter try to stand on one foot using both her right and left legs. Does she have a sense of how to use her arms to balance herself? It is not enough to tell your daughter to stand still. Balance develops with the maturation of the central nervous system. I often play a game of musical freeze to help girls develop balance while in motion. Tell your daughter that you are going to play some music, but when the music stops she must freeze and not fall down. The mature child (meaning the child whose nervous system is well developed) can move quickly and in control while the music is playing but can also stop on a dime.

EYE-HAND AND EYE-FOOT COORDINATION
(Suggested equipment: a balloon, various-size balls, a hula hoop, a miniature plastic golf club, a miniature plastic softball bat, a large plastic racket; refer to manipulative activities)

Developing eye-hand or eye-foot coordination means developing the manipulative skills that we previously discussed. Eye-hand co-ordination means learning bouncing, catching, rolling, striking, and throwing. Developing eye-foot coordination means learning the manipulative skills of kicking and trapping. Practice these skills with your daughter often. These are lifetime skills, and I urge you to spend lots of time in this area.

RHYTHM
(Suggested equipment: audiotapes)

Rhythm is having a sense of the flow of movement. Sometimes it means being able to repeat a movement following a given tempo. Eventually it means being able to interpret the flow of a particular movement—for example, the swing of a tennis racket. The goal is to establish movement patterns that support efficient motor skills. At age five or six girls will be able to perform simple patterns such as hand clapping, arm swinging, and sliding with the feet. I encourage you to buy children's music and start moving to music with your daughter very early. Or sign her up for ballet lessons.

VISUAL AWARENESS
(Suggested equipment: various-size balls)

This is the ability to perceive and react and can be observed in two different areas: distance perception and figure-ground discrimination. Distance perception refers to the space between an individual and an object. Bouncing a ball to your child gives her time to react, thereby developing the easiest part of visual awareness. Throwing a ball to her is also helpful, but it means she will need to learn to react more quickly. Figure-ground discrimination is the ability to distinguish a form separate from the ground. How do these concepts play out in practical circumstances? If a girl is trying to catch a ball, she must be able to recognize it as different from the sky and the trees and estimate how far away it is at any give time. The faster your daughter can sort through all this stimuli and react, the better. Reaction time increases as the central nervous system matures, even up through the teen years.

AUDITORY AWARENESS
(Suggested equipment: audiotapes)

This is the ability to understand directions and respond. Go to a local teacher's supply store and ask for a nursery rhyme tape that was made for movement education. Often workbooks accompany the audiotapes and will show you what movements to teach. One tape that I work with has great sound effects that prompt certain kinds of activity. When western music plays, we gallop; when slow music plays, we tiptoe; when fast music plays, we jump like mad.

In summary, as girls become more mature in their skills, they will spend less time thinking about what to do and react more quickly. That's what we want—automatic reactions. A mature or efficient skill can appear at any age. But those mature skills will become efficient only through correct practice. That's where you come in. Help your daughter learn the ABCs of sports.

Body, Mind, and Social Skills Grow Side by Side

As you watch your daughter develop her jumping, climbing, and swinging skills, you'll be observing more than her physical traits—you'll be watching her intellectual and social skills mature at the same time. The patterns of psychological behavior that are characteristic of early childhood development are described in the following section. An awareness of these patterns will help you understand some of the behaviors you're likely to see as girls grow through social patterns of play and develop the intellectual skills to enable them to be part of team or individual sports.

Characteristic Social Behavior

How many times have you gone out in the yard and seen your young daughter and her friend playing happily, but not together? You try to encourage sharing, though you might have more success coaxing a cat to swim underwater. Cooperative play comes with physical and social maturation. Here are some typical play patterns that girls display (from beginner to advanced patterns) between the ages of two and five. As always, there are no rigid age guidelines.

- Solitary Play (about two years of age): Your child will play alone and not necessarily be aware of other children around her. Sharing does not come easily, so if you are having a group of kids playing together, have enough equipment so that each child can have her own.
- Onlooker Play: Your child will watch other children play.
- Parallel Play (about three to four years of age): Your child will be aware of other children and play with the same toys in the same ways, but not *with* each other.
- Associative Play: Your child will play side by side with another child, maybe even share toys, but they don't play together as a cooperative activity.
- Cooperative play (about five to six years of age): Your child will play with a shared goal and take turns. This generally starts as small-group play. Around the age of seven or eight, large-group play (with more complexity) such as in team sports is possible. Those girls who seem to be fairly comfortable with themselves will spend more time playing with other children.

Characteristic Intellectual Behavior

Girls will be able to repeat activities only as long as they keep their attention and enjoy themselves. One simple measure equates attention span with age. If your daughter is age three, expect her to be engaged attentively in an activity about three minutes. Individual efforts at building a skill can be repeated up to as many as half a dozen times and then no more. Be ready to change activities frequently. It's also best to give no more than two directions at a time. It's not unusual for a child to forget the directions completely.

Girls will try anything if they think they will succeed. If your child resists a new activity, or shows regular signs of headache or stomachache during an ongoing sport program, she's not ready for what you're trying to introduce. Maybe your child understands the difference between success and failure or other people's reactions to winning and losing. I've seen this awareness begin as early as age three. This awareness depends on how much emphasis is put on winning and losing. Ask yourself, How do I react to winning and losing in my home? How do I react when watching a football game? Though you may not intend to send the "I win, you lose" message, this may be coming across to your child. Does your child cheer and yell with you? Does she think of losing as a bad thing? This may be a harmful message for a young child. Stay alert to your habits.

For all intents and purposes, the preschool stage is when children have no understanding of teamwork. While young girls will sometimes test themselves, they're usually not interested in organized competition. As they're playing, most don't know if they are doing something correctly or incorrectly, if they're meeting a goal or not. They just know they're doing something fun. While they may have some basic skills necessary to do very simple drills for team sports, they do not do well when placed in a game because their intellectual capacity is not mature enough to understand the concept of strategy. They may do better in individual sports, where personal development (the appeal of "I did it myself") is a motivating factor.

When is it time to sign up for team sports? Many communities offer team sports around the age of five. Realistically, productive participation in team strategies will evolve around the age of seven. Before that, your child will only be frustrated by coaching instructions she cannot understand because of her maturational level. For children under the age of seven, having a coach who understands how children mature is very important. A creative team coach will present situational skills in a fun way that leads to cooperative play necessary for team strategy. In short, there's no hurry to get preschoolers onto a team. While coaches may argue this point, educators will not.

Getting Your Child Ready for an Active Adult Life

We began this chapter by stating that your daughter's involvement in physical activity at an early age can be beneficial. Now I want you to look forward to your daughter's future. Picture her as an adult. Wouldn't you be brokenhearted if one day you heard her say, "I wish I could have learned how to do that when I was younger"? Don't you want to give your daughter every opportunity to learn the basic skills now that will help her learn any physical activity she might choose to participate in later? Of course.

I, for example, took up golf much later in life, when I married into a family of golfers. Those first few outings with my in-laws were depressing for an ex-college athlete. A typical round consisted of me using one golf club for eighteen holes and hitting the ball a very short distance—frequently—while my relatives waited patiently for their turn. It was known as "hit the ball and drag Susan." My athletic ego was quite bruised, but I knew I would keep plugging away because I relished the challenge. Most important, this was quality family time. Fortunately, because my life had been filled with sports, I had the desire to pursue learning a new skill that would lead me to enjoy the game. Two years and $2,000 in golf lessons later, I finally "got it." My sister-in-law, who started playing with a miniature golf club as a preschooler, can beat me anytime. Although I've stayed more active in sports over the course of my life, her early advantage is quite apparent. Starting your daughter early with sports will give her an advantage as an adult and will make her more confident to attempt new things.

Here's a quick set of questions for you to answer to understand your own attitude toward sports development:

- Are there activities I don't let my daughter do because I never did them?
- Am I constantly warning my daughter about dangers, or do I teach or show her how to deal with potential risks?
- Do I steer my daughter away from some activities because they're too "masculine"?
- Are there activities I don't want my daughter to do because I had a bad experience?

Your answers to these questions can be very revealing and might make you reflect on how you perceive women's relationship to sports. Your main goal should be to give your daughter lots of opportunities to learn basic physical skills by doing lots of different activities. Spend time playing with her. Take your daily dip into recreational activities where your daughter can move at her own pace, and you will watch your daughter grow to be self-reliant, confident, and physically fit. You're going to be so proud of her—and yourself for putting in the effort.

Understanding Sports Readiness

3

Watching young Olympic teens like figure skater Tara Lipinski and gymnast Dominique Moceanu made a lot of parents wonder, "Wow, how old were these girls when they started?" Many parents assume that unless a child starts to train at the age of three, they'll never master a particular sport. Perhaps your neighbor has already signed up her six-year-old for soccer. There you stand with your six-year-old daughter bouncing all over the house, thinking she's too young to take part in real sport training, but maybe wondering if it's too late to make her a great athlete. While it's never too late to enjoy sports on some level, the more important question is, "Is she ready?"

In this chapter I provide some concrete guidelines that will help you assess when your school-age daughter is ready, willing, and able to participate in particular sports activities. First and foremost you need an idea of what interests your daughter, what she is willing to do, by listening to her comments. Although your daughter may be begging you to let her try something new—like join her first softball team or play her first tennis tournament—such decisions involve many factors.

You can make a big impact by making sure your daughter tries lots of different sports—the more the better, and the easier it will be for her in the future to learn and modify new skills. She will experience the most growth practicing those sport skills for which she is truly ready. Having limited movement experience and a lack of muscle strength will hold your daughter back. Keen observation of your daughter, combined with education about child development and sports readiness development, will help you make an informed decision about when she can start playing sports productively.

When your daughter is at the elementary school level and you're trying to decide if she's ready to play sports, there's more to evaluate than if she's in the right age group. For our purposes, readiness will be defined by researcher J. B. Oxendine. He states that readiness is "a condition of the individual that makes a particular task an appropriate one for [her] to master." Translation: The readiness of a girl to play sports has more to do with your daughter's unique mental and physical abilities than your belief that she is the right age to get involved.

Physical, Mental, and Emotional Readiness

When the Bradshaws signed up seven-year-old Chelsea for soccer, it was all very exciting—a new uniform, a new challenge, and the chance to be with her friends. But within half an hour it was clear that Chelsea's first practice would also be her last. What went wrong? The overweight child had no experience with a group sports activity. It was obvious she couldn't do things at the same pace as her peers. She soon felt hopelessly overwhelmed—and nothing is more humiliating for a child (or, for that matter, a parent).

In the rush to produce wonder kids, children are sometimes pushed into activities that they may not be ready to handle. I'm sure you could name a pushy parent or two who insists their daughter learn to use a computer, play the piano, and speak a foreign language by the time they are in first grade. You probably refuse to carpool with them, right?

No matter how old your daughter is, deciding whether she's ready for a *specific sport* involves taking into account her physical, mental, and emotional readiness. These qualities don't develop independently of each other; rather, they mix and mingle all the time. Sometimes physical growth happens faster than emotional growth. A girl who is taller than average for her age may choose to be with other girls her size. But when she plays with them, she may act more immature than they do, and they may not want to play with her. Or maybe you have an extremely intelligent child on your hands who is so far beyond her playmates emotionally and intellectually that playing physical games or sports with them is a bore.

The point is that your daughter's physical, emotional, and mental abilities need to be taken into account when deciding which activities she's ready for and which she will enjoy most. Let's take a look at these three areas of readiness to be considered during the elementary school years. The key to understanding readiness means realizing that it is determined *ability by ability* in these three main areas of readiness.

Physically Able

Determining physical readiness for sports is not a simple matter, and there are several variables that you should consider. You'll need to address factors both internal and external to the body. Internal factors concern the influence of heredity on your daughter's body type, rate of growth, maturation rate of the central nervous system, muscular strength, and activity level. The environmental factors that affect her have to do with the kinds and amount of physical activity she's used to doing and the basic motor skills she's learned from those activities. Go through the following descriptions and see how your daughter's patterns weigh in.

RATE OF PHYSICAL GROWTH

Maturation of the body, which is controlled by the endocrine system, is referred to as "developmental aging" or "rate of physical growth." Studies show that no matter what stage of maturation a girl is in as relates to her chronological age—delayed, average, advanced—she can still get ready to play and enjoy organized sports. Studies further show that physical growth during the elementary school years happens at a slower rate than during the first several years of life. For the first time since birth, a girl's strength and coordination are not necessarily playing catch-up with her body's growth. But there will continue to be alternating phases of faster and slower growth. Females begin their teenage growth spurt at about nine years of age and peak around twelve or thirteen. Growth in height will usually be completed around sixteen years of age. Early growth spurts do not indicate what a girl will be like at maturity. And a child's rate of maturation is not necessarily a good prediction of sport readiness.

Recommendation: Children who mature quickly in their growth rate often have demands put upon them that are age inappropriate. It's easy for coaches to look at a child who is tall for her age and expect her to do more. Unfortunately, neither a child's mind nor the level of body coordination may be the same as the growth rate. Because of this, you must stay alert to your daughter's levels of frustration while learning sports. While some children are easily frustrated, overt frustration may mean that your child is not ready to learn the skills presented to her. If you suspect that your daughter is delayed in her developmental age, keep her in programs that emphasize sport skill progressions and wait before joining team sports, especially ball sports that require considerable coordination. If your daughter is very mature for her age (height and body mass), she will excel at sports that require speed and strength. However, I want to encourage you not to rush her into competition. There is no hurry. Avoid the temptation to ask her coach to push your daughter in this direction unless she is getting bored.

INHERITED PHYSICAL TRAITS

The physical traits your child has inherited from you have a direct impact on what sports she's best suited for. To get a sense of what kind of physical makeup she may be dealing with, look back and think about how you rated your body and what you could do when you were young. Does your daughter have your height but the same bulky torso as your spouse? Were your legs too long for your jeans? Did you feel uncoordinated when you ran? Did you weigh fifty pounds soaking wet when you were eleven years old? Did you lack the arm strength to play on the bars at the playground? Maybe you watched lots of sports you thought would be fun to try, but when you tried them you felt it was hopeless. How could you know your body type was simply better suited for one sport over another?

Recommendation: I do not want to discourage girls from trying any sport they choose. Just know that participation in some sports will bring them more success than others. The good news is that there's a sport to fit every body. Take an objective look at your daughter's build by considering the following:

HEIGHT AND WEIGHT IN RELATIONSHIP TO HER AGE (CHECK WITH YOUR PEDIATRICIAN):   A girl's weight becomes critical only when it interferes with her ability to enjoy sports for fun or affects her physical fitness. The overweight girl, who is often at the same time underskilled, can find enjoyment and success in a variety of sports, but the starting place will have to be much lower than that for the average girl. Most important, parents and coaches must be alert to higher levels of injury potential.

Recommendation: If your child is overweight, consider sports like swimming and martial arts, which put low demands on the joints of the arms and legs yet develop muscle control. Pursuing activities where children can stay at a basic level is critical to their success. It takes a creative leader to keep kids playing at an elementary level yet still provide challenges for their enjoyment.

BODY TYPE—ECTOMORPHIC (SLENDER), MESOMORPHIC (MUSCU-LAR), ENDOMORPHIC (SOFT ROUNDNESS THROUGHOUT THE BODY): These descriptions of body typing were devised by the research team of Sheldon, Stevens and Tucker. Most girls are a mixture of these types. A girl's body type, or her build, can affect her performance in sports, but mostly at the upper levels of training.

Recommendation: Allow your daughter to go through a self-elimination process in her selection of sports. Slender girls may find less enjoyment in some team sports where there is a lot of physical contact if they do not have sufficient strength to protect themselves. Girls with muscular upper bodies are likely to do well with gymnastics, softball, swimming, and tennis but may need to work hard on flexibility. Girls with muscular legs are likely to do well with soccer, basketball, and volleyball. Girls who are characterized by soft roundness throughout the body will need to gain strength to play sports enjoyably and protect themselves from injury.

SPEED OF MOVEMENT: Does your daughter move fast or slow? Observe your daughter at play to understand how she moves.

Recommendation: The biggest concern is for a child whose general movements are slow. This child can make progress in sports if she has a coach who understands that learning steps must be unhurried. Sports like swimming and martial arts are great places to improve speed of movement. Ball sports may be challenging. Spend lots of time with your daughter boosting coordination and confidence before signing her up for team ball sports.

Genetic Talent

Perhaps a special talent has been genetically passed on to your daughter. Maybe your gift to her was running speed, maybe eye-hand coordination. Some girls may be "wired" for particular sports, or they'll do some things more intuitively than others. While some girls may be naturally more coordinated than others, they all can and must still learn fundamental motor skills.

Recommendation: Get to know what your child's natural abilities are. Explore as many sports as your daughter is willing to try. In this way she is more apt to find the sport that really suits her talents.

Maturation of the Central Nervous System

Don't knock the neurons. The development of the nervous system is key to when your daughter develops various physical abilities. Regardless of how much you play with your daughter or practice basic movement skills, her nervous system will mature at its own pace. The reason for continually presenting age-appropriate skills is to capture that time frame when your child is ready to accept the information. Staying aware of your daughter's rate of maturation will help you in determining her sport readiness.

Recommendation: Know some of the other issues that are affected by the maturity of the nervous system.

- Distance judgment: Throwing with accuracy and catching a ball (eye-hand coordination) often involves more distance judgment than some children are ready for.
- Reaction time: Many sports depend on reaction time. Therefore players may drop a ball when it lands in their mitt because they are too slow to close the mitt. They may strike out by swinging a bat too late. They may also not be able to hit a tennis ball because they cannot swing a racket forward quickly enough.
- Hand preference: As the brain matures, it specializes. Around age five, children become more skilled at handling objects with one hand and will clearly demonstrate right- or left-handedness.

INNATE ACTIVITY LEVEL

Did you have a baby that just wiggled and kicked her legs constantly, or was she able to lie or sit rather calmly? The innate, abiding distinctions that characterize how active your child is are often revealed soon after birth and will remain more or less constant throughout her life. Nevertheless, during the first two to three years of life girls are more active than they are at five and six years of age. By age eight only about one girl in five is as active as the average boy. Keep track of how active your daughter is and at every chance encourage her to take part in fun movement activities.

Recommendation: Seek sports that reflect the activity level of your child. A highly active girl, for example, may be frustrated in a softball or baseball program where she has to stand for long periods of time in the outfield. Fast-moving sports like soccer, swimming, basketball, tennis, or volleyball would be a better bet for her. Recreation classes for dance and gymnastics, and softball programs, usually have varying levels of energy output throughout the practice. These types of sports may be better suited for girls with moderate to low activity levels.

EXPERIENCE WITH PHYSICAL ACTIVITIES

Have you been to the park lately? Have you been spending time at the playground letting your child develop swinging, climbing, hanging, and other similar skills? Has she been playing kickball outside so that she is comfortable with her feet and can make the transition to soccer? Have you been playing any other ball games so that your daughter has the eye-hand coordination to take on softball, basketball, or tennis? Has she ridden on a tricycle or a bicycle? When activities are kept simple and fun, they will become the foundation for her later involvement with sports.

Recommendation: Understand that "in early to middle childhood, experience is a more powerful factor in fundamental motor skill development" than maturation, according to researcher Dr. Steven Aicinena. And the more physical activities you introduce your daughter to as a preschooler, the more she will eventually be sport ready.

PHYSICAL FITNESS

Are you helping your daughter be fit as a fiddle? I'm sure you won't be surprised to learn that the more fit a girl is, the better her chances of success at sports. But how is fitness determined? Many variables are used, but the common measures for children are determined by evaluating these three factors:

- Endurance: (cardiorespiratory) heart and lungs are in good shape; (muscular) muscles are strong enough to move for long periods of time
- Strength: (dynamic) how much weight can you move; (power) how fast you can move a weight, usually your body; (static) how much weight you can hold in place
- Flexibility: movement of the muscles and joints through their full range of motion

Watching your daughter at play will give you a pretty decent idea of where she stands with respect to each of these fitness factors. Some elementary school–age children are currently given organized physical fitness tests at school on an annual basis.

Recommendation: Help your daughter be ready to pass the yearly President's Council on Physical Fitness and Sports Test if it is offered at her school. It is a common measure used within public schools to test fitness and is usually administered to boys and girls by physical education teachers. There are specific goals for each age, measuring the above three specific areas. Your daughter is on the right track if she can perform the skills required no matter if she is six or seventeen years of age. They are as follows:

- curl-ups (measuring abdominal strength/endurance)
- shuttle run (measuring leg strength, endurance, power, and agility)
- one-mile run/walk (measuring heart/lung endurance)
- pull-ups or flexed arm hang for time (measuring upper body strength/endurance)
- V-sit reach (measuring flexibility of lower back and hamstring flexibility)

For more specifics or promotional material, contact the President's Challenge Physical Fitness Program at 800-258-8146.

PHYSICAL STRENGTH

Girls need to be conditioned for the sports they want to play. While most girls peak in their growth rate around age thirteen, they do not peak in their strength until close to fourteen years of age. This truth should be stamped into your consciousness forever: *The stronger a girl is, the faster she will learn.* It's hard to really appreciate how critically important this is until you have two girls in front of you trying to perform the same skill. The weak child will struggle and become frustrated, whereas the strong child will make attempts and show improvement quickly. Girls especially need upper body strength to perform sport skills—hold a softball bat or tennis racket, swim the length of a pool, carry out gymnastic skills on the bars, shoot baskets, and play volleyball.

One young teenager I trained in gymnastics was forced to leave training for a few months. When she returned she expressed amazement at how many skills she had lost because she didn't have the physical strength to do them anymore. It was tough, but she vowed to get herself back in shape as soon as she could. Having experienced what it felt like to be strong, this student didn't like the feeling of not being able to control her body. I wish more girls could experience how great it feels to be strong.

Another benefit of physical strength is that it helps prevent injuries. Your muscles, tendons, and ligaments literally hold you together. The stronger a girl's body, the better it will hold up under pressure and the less prone it will be to injury. Again, one area of particular concern for girls is upper body strength. Professionals in the medical field are concerned that a lack of basic arm strength can cause injuries to the shoulders and arms. Yet if parents help out by buying their daughters a chin-up bar or encourage them to do other activities to help improve arm strength, such injuries can be prevented.

Recommendation: Doing sports is a muscular thing, not a masculine thing. Girls should be educated at an early age that the stronger they are, the more they can do. Resistance exercise training (lifting weights or using fitness equipment) can start as early as sixth grade, as long as it is monitored, and will contribute greatly to gains in strength. Otherwise only the individual's body weight should be used for resistance in the performance of push-ups, sit-ups, and chin-ups.

ENDURANCE

In order for endurance to improve (cardiorespiratory and muscular), coaches must make endurance training part of any given sport practice. For activities that involve lots of running, like soccer and basketball, girls may be asked to do laps around the gym or the field at the end of practice. For activities that involve strength, girls may be asked to do sit-ups, push-ups, and chin-ups. While this may elicit groans from young athletes, developing endurance is definitely worth the effort.

Recommendation: To build cardiorespiratory endurance, go to the park and let your daughter run as long as she can. Just plain running can become boring, so if you have a pet dog or a favorite kite, bring it along. Children can make more enjoyable progress by running with their parents. But they will need some kind of goal to make it a regular habit. Many communities have junior fun runs. Find out what's available in your neighborhood. To build muscular endurance, include climbing structures and have your child hang by her hands as long as she can. Also see if she can lift her feet up to her hands while hanging. (Stand underneath her so she'll be safe.) If there is an overhead ladder or rings, have her move across the length of the equipment. Repeat these activities as long as there is interest and energy to persist without getting hurt.

Mental Readiness

If you have ever stood in front of a bunch of squirming six-year-olds and tried to give directions, you will understand when I say it is nearly impossible to have all sets of eyeballs looking at you at the same time. The frustration factor is enormous both for you and the youngsters, who can't be bothered with rules. Six-year-olds want to play and have fun. When young girls are facing new experiences, their ability to pay attention is limited because there is so much brain activity going on. Young children need a simple set of easy directions to follow. Suppose your daughter is thinking of playing team sports—joining a softball team, for example. Does she have the ability to pay attention while standing for long periods of time in the outfield? Can she understand strategy, think logically, and handle more than two training concepts at the same time? Will she enjoy the challenges that go along with winning and losing? Perhaps your daughter wants to play an individual sport, like tennis. Can she handle the practice and repetition that is necessary to learn basic skills?

The core question is this: Does your daughter's level of mental development match what is required of the sport she's thinking of playing? These questions and many similar ones can be explored in the summaries of mental abilities listed here. Be aware that it's very natural for some capabilities to develop sooner than others.

PAYING ATTENTION AND FOLLOWING DIRECTIONS

Paying attention has a lot to do with screening out distractions and concentrating on the task at hand. This is called "selective attention." It improves steadily with age. In the beginning stages of learning a skill, like hitting a tennis ball or a softball, girls focus on the hit, not necessarily where the ball is going. When hitting the ball becomes routine, young athletes will then be able to think about other aspects of the game like directing the ball where they want it to go and other game strategies. In neurological terms, a pathway is being established from the brain to the muscles by repetition of the sport skill. When the pathway is established, the skill then becomes a reflex action. If a skill can be done automatically, it is considered to be "learned." The action will continue to be a reflex action as long as it is practiced. Learned skills are the goal for all athletes.

Recommendation: To get your daughter started on the road to learning skills, keep these suggestions in mind when you are practicing physical activities. For first and second graders, limit the number of instructions given to two commands. At all grade levels, teach skills by demonstration rather than discussion. Break skills down into small manageable steps. The greater the complexity of the skill, the more repetitions will be needed to accomplish the skill. Better memory skills, and a better ability to follow directions, are exhibited as players gain a greater knowledge and experience with a sport.

UNDERSTANDING TEAMWORK

As girls mature, an interesting development is occurring on two different planes. First, owing to maturation of the central nervous system (development of the brain), girls are learning how to take advantage of and apply game strategy. Second, girls have a deeper understanding of how to solve social problems. The combination of these skills works well together if an athlete is playing with friends and others whom she admires. There is also a troubling contradiction. The older girls get, the more selective they become in whom they will cooperate with on their team. I've often heard coaches say that one team member won't pass a ball to another player if she doesn't like her. Since teamwork is a valuable skill, it is up to the coach to foster working relationships among the team members. Many times this is no small task.

Recommendation: It isn't until the age of seven that girls develop the desire to accept structure and organization. In most cases they are not ready to play team sports with enthusiasm until approximately age eight or nine. This is because by this age they've acquired both increased muscle control and the ability to concentrate.

REPEATING ACTIVITIES THAT SHE PERFORMS SUCCESSFULLY

When girls are absolute beginners, no matter what their age, parents and coaches should make sure that learning steps are small enough to ensure success—in other words, make it easy for the child to succeed. If players are doing something correctly, they'll know it, and they'll want to do it more often.

Recommendation: Parents, coaches, and the girls themselves should notice when there is progress. The more girls are recognized for performing a skill correctly, the more they will want to perform it. For the average girl the desire to refine and improve skills won't show up until the third or fourth grade.

ENJOYING CHALLENGES

Pay attention to the philosophy and coaching style of the program your daughter is involved in. If the emphasis is on the win-loss record for beginners, this will be an unhappy experience for your daughter. When girls begin to understand the difference between success and failure, they start to become very concerned about winning vs. losing and begin to evaluate themselves. Once they understand the dynamics of winning and losing, girls will usually try something only if they think they can do it. Add to this the impact of peer pressure and you have a challenging situation for a coach.

Recommendation: As girls mature, they become increasingly sensitive in social relationships. Adults need to be tactful when dealing with individual personalities and to know how far each athlete can be pushed.

Be careful of a downward spiral called "learned helplessness," however. This occurs when a girl's past failures in a sports activity lead her to believe that she can't do anything. In fact, some kids "know" they can't do some things and are very self-critical. When I am teaching this kind of a child, it takes a long time to bring about even the most modest change in self-esteem. Instead of allowing them to say, "I can't," I try to get them to say, "I don't know how." Then I say, "Oh, okay, I'll show you how." Again, this is a situation that requires finding small steps that girls can master easily so that they can begin to enjoy challenges again.

PLANNING AND PROBLEM SOLVING

Around the first grade, girls are developing the mental ability to plan with others. Between the ages of seven and eleven they should start thinking in a logical manner and considering two or more aspects of a problem. They learn to focus more on facts and relationships and have learned what they must do to succeed at many tasks. Problem solving is a skill used in all sports. Observe your child as she goes about everyday recreational activities. Does she have a tendency to think ahead? How well does she respond to challenges that need to be solved on the spot? Ball sports usually require a quick response to solve a problem. Keep these guidelines in mind as you evaluate your daughter's problem-solving skills:

- Children learn by questioning and doing. Expect girls to ask many questions so that they can understand what they're being asked to do. For an adult, this requires lots of patience to wade through this process. Stick with it.
- The growth of reasoning abilities helps girls grasp the underlying assumptions of an idea. Children learn to apply the logic that they learned in a previous situation to a new, similar situation.

Recommendation: Information is best learned when it is linked with information that players already know. For the early elementary school child, if there is a long period of time between when a problem is discussed and when it will be solved, the child may easily forget the problem. If you are a coach, avoid lengthy explanations.

Emotional Willingness

The most obvious way to know if your daughter is ready for an activity is if she asks: "Can you take me swimming?" or "Can we go to the basketball court?" For girls to be motivated to play a particular sport, they must feel they are involved in choosing it. If the suggestion to play a certain sport comes from them, they are showing a high degree of readiness. There are a variety of reasons why a girl may be motivated to take part in particular physical activities, so it's essential to keep your eyes and ears open. Here are some elements that play a role in a child's emotional willingness to get involved with sports.

FAMILY

The family is the earliest and most important influence on a child's attitude toward sports. If you are not already doing so, involve your daughter in as many different physical activities as you can so that she'll have the sense that sports are a part of life. Help her find something she wants to do over and over again. If a sport is of no interest to a child, she will not actively explore it.

Parents also need to understand that their daughters are capable of tolerating a safe amount of physical stress. There is a difference between being uncomfortable and being injured. Sometimes there will be sore muscles from doing repetitions, and endurance activities will make young athletes tired. But these are all part of the process, so try not to frighten your daughter away from sports by overreacting to minor physical stress. If you're tempted to approach her coach and tell her or him that your daughter looks too exhausted or too uncomfortable to complete the exercises, give *yourself* a time-out. Most important, allow your daughter to take on the same physical challenges as boys of her age. To live a fulfilling life, boys *and girls* need to encounter risks and to know what physical stamina is all about.

Dads and moms must also learn to give up parental control when their children are in the hands of good coaches. For many parents, especially moms, entrusting their little ones to another adult—and giving up the supervisory role for an hour—is a big step. But if you want your daughter to take risks and to enjoy the challenge of sports, go take a walk or get a cup of coffee instead of hovering over her and fretting that she won't be able to make the grade. You might ask yourself, "Whose timidity is being expressed here—mine or hers?"

The importance of parental involvement in a supportive role can't be overstated. Parents need to watch children at play, and every child needs to know they're being watched. It's a big deal. In their minds, if you don't see them do something successfully, it doesn't count. Your kids need your attention and approval. Observe what's going on when they play sports. Notice improvement so you can talk about it: "I saw you trying to throw the ball higher" or "That dive was much better." Your involvement validates what they're doing.

PERSONALITY

The noted psychologist Carl Jung was the first to make the observation that an individual's nature can be observed in the first days of life. At one end of the continuum of personality are introverts and at the other end are extroverts. Most people fall in between these two types of personality.

Accepting your child for herself is very important. Some parents may have such high expectations for their daughters that they hurt them by not seeing and loving who they really are. Sports are a way of communication, and the field or gym is another place where personality type is expressed. The unique attributes and attitudes of a child usually don't change as they mature. Circumstances can have an impact on them, but the more you help your child be true to herself, the better her sport experience will be.

FRIENDS

Most children want to be part of a group and the social aspect of sports often plays a dominating role. The groups of friends your daughter is part of have a big influence on what she is willing to try. If all her friends are trying out for the basketball team, that may motivate even the shyest potential athlete. It is also important to help your daughter foster relationships with girls on the team, especially if they are a new group of peers. Find a way to celebrate the first game of the season. Remember to involve the other girls' parents as well. Maybe you could video the first game and get everyone together for a viewing with loads of popcorn.

MOTIVATION

One trait that requires cultivation and respect is desire. Often desire is more important than natural ability. Many years ago I coached a gymnast who had average skill and a seemingly non-athletic body type. However, she had above-average desire. Her goal was to qualify for the national championships, and her efforts were second to none. Before she graduated from high school she achieved her goal, to the amazement of nearly every girl on the team. I will never forget Dorothy. She taught me a priceless lesson about motivation.

TELEVISION

Never underestimate the power of television to spark your child's enthusiasm for a certain sports activity. Perhaps she's seen gymnastics on ESPN and is now rolling on the living room carpet and dancing around the house. Or she may be inspired by the tennis tournament featuring famous female tennis stars that you tuned in to watch one Sunday afternoon. Such TV viewing experiences can signal the beginning of a passion for a particular activity. Watch sports with your daughter, not just your son.

SCHOOL

School can be the place where your daughter's interest in sports, especially ball games, is first awakened. What's being offered in the physical education program and how it is being presented play an important role in creating interest. How many of us can remember PE classes in elementary school? Do you remember them with joy? Or did you hate them because you were never very good at the sports that were offered? Find out what kinds of opportunities for physical activity are available at your daughter's school—and talk to her about what she enjoys. Be prepared for her to have a possible interest in a sport where only a boys' team is available, and be open to helping her be part of that program.

PLAY STYLE

Is your child more outgoing or reserved? When someone says, "Who wants to try this?" is your daughter the first one standing in the front of the line or does she watch others to see if she is capable of performing the task in question? Faced with a challenge, the girl who knows her body instinctively and what it is capable of will usually have little hesitation about trying something. If your child will try something only when no one else is looking, she may be afraid that she can't keep up with the other children. Girls who are unfamiliar with their bodies and what they can do will move forward cautiously.

If your child will try just about anything, she will do fine in team or individual sports. If your child tends to hold back, find a recreational program that stresses sport skill development, not one that will pit one child against another. This is especially critical when learning team sports. Children are painfully candid with each other when it comes to evaluating ability, so it's best to find low-key situations. Otherwise participation in individual sports may be best for her style.

Progressing Through the Stages of Sport Readiness

There are also three stages of sport development. Some girls will move through these phases very quickly. Others will need to go at a more relaxed pace. Once you have a sense of your daughter's physical, mental, and emotional growth pattern, you'll be able to guide her toward the kinds of sports for which she's best suited at this time in her life. There's no need to rush things by putting pressure on her to get to the stage you envision for her. If you want her to stick with sports, sports have to be a pleasurable experience and the sport of her choice. Nobody can be happy doing something they don't yet have the skills to do. Give your daughter a chance to discover her talent no matter what her age. Keep in mind that I didn't find my passion until I was fifteen years of age. And when I did, there was no stopping me.

First Stage: Sport-Related Basic Skill Development

It's been estimated that up to 49 percent of school-age girls may not have the basic skills they need to participate in the sport they're playing. There's good news here, however. The elementary school years are the best time to begin the mastery of fundamental skills. Most girls will accomplish basic movement skills if they are given a sufficient number of opportunities to practice these movements, as I stated in chapter 2. Following is a list of fundamental motor skills and descriptions for how they should be performed in a mature fashion. *Skills are mature when they are repeatable, efficient, and precise.* This can occur at any age. Ideally these skills are accomplished by the beginning of elementary school. See how your daughter measures up against these guidelines.

OBSERVE SKILL MATURATION

- Running: Look for efficient arm movements such as straight forwards and straight backwards motion with a forward body lean.
- Hopping: Check to see that hopping can be done on either foot.
- Leaping: Arms should move opposite each other, and she should be able to leap fairly high in the air.
- Jumping: Watch for height and distance. Do the arms reach forward forcefully on the takeoff? Can a jump and a full turn of the body in the air be landed with control? Can the child jump rope? With an even rhythm?
- Body rolling: This is generally considered a safety skill as a way to recover from falling. Being able to roll from a fall and move back onto the feet signals control and awareness.
- Dodging: Watch for reaction time—how quickly the child gets out of the way of another person or a thrown ball. Is she quick to react?
- Rolling a ball: Can a ball be rolled with the body slightly crouched down? Is one foot in front of the other? Are both hands holding a ball on one side of the body, partially flexed? Can a ball be rolled with one hand while looking at the target?
- Balancing: Can control be maintained while running, jumping, throwing, kicking, catching, bouncing, dodging, and striking? Is the child able to adjust to changes in speed according to the action on the field?

Commonly, a preference for using the right or left hand or leg (dominance) is established by the elementary school years. Be aware that handedness for writing or eating does not have anything to do with a preference for the kicking leg, throwing arm, or turning direction.

- Bouncing: Can a ball be bounced with one hand and caught? Using one hand, can a ball be bounced repeatedly? It's best if this can be done with either the right or the left hand.

- Catching: Are the elbows partially bent? Is one foot in front of the other? Do the hands move forward to catch a ball in a cupping manner? Can a ball be caught while jumping through the air?
- Kicking: Can a ball be kicked with the kicking leg swinging freely from the hip and bent at the knee? Is the support foot beside the ball when it is kicked, and do the arms move opposite each other? A ball should be kicked with the top part (the "shoelaces") of the foot.
- Striking: Can this skill be performed with the body turned so that one shoulder is in the front and one in the rear? Is the elbow flexed or straightened according to the demands of the sport? Can a sidearm swing pattern be performed? Does the weight shift from the rear foot to the front foot as the strike progresses?
- Throwing: Does a throw display the body turned with one shoulder in the front and one in the rear? Is the elbow of the throwing arm flexed at 90 degrees? Does the weight shift from the rear foot to the front foot as the throw progresses? Can a ball be thrown while jumping through the air? Is there understanding of how to be more or less forceful depending on the particular action called for on the field or in the gym?
- Trapping: Can the sole of the foot be used to trap a ball while it is traveling on a diagonal pattern? Can the ball be trapped while running? Can the ball be trapped with the chest?

In the early years of elementary school, generally kindergarten through third grade, girls are not interested in things that require complex coordination. Throwing and catching with accuracy is harder for them than you imagine. If you're thinking about signing up for any sport that uses a ball, brain maturation is central to reaction time. In sports where this is important (softball, tennis, basketball, volleyball) the younger girl is at a disadvantage. The older the child, the quicker the reaction time and the ability to coordinate complex movements.

OBSERVE SHIFTS IN THE WAY SKILLS ARE LEARNED

As children grow through the elementary school years and the first stage of sport readiness, there will be three significant shifts in how they learn physical skills. Know that these shifts are not entirely age related.

- The first shift is characterized by the use of visual information rather than just touch or sense of body position.
- The second shift normally involves using several senses to learn a skill. No longer will a girl depend on using one sense at a time; instead she will combine feeling with seeing and hearing.
- The third shift occurs when girls are able to make finer and more advanced distinctions about what they've felt or seen or heard. Parents or coaches will see great improvement in a girl's coordination. Her basic skills will start to take on a look of maturity and will become refined.

After the third growth shift, the basic skills should be comfortably in place, and your daughter will be ready for sport-specific skill training.

Second Stage: Sport-Specific Knowledge

Believe it or not, during late childhood, around fourth to sixth grade, girls are not so different from boys in terms of athletic ability. They have developed their strength and coordination, have improved their running speed and reaction time, and are now ready to refine their skills. It's no longer enough to just kick or throw a ball or hit it with a racket or bat. These activities should now take place with an eye toward results. Young athletes can now think about putting a spin on the ball, or speeding up the delivery, or batting more accurately. In other words, they are ready to fine-tune their physical and mental abilities so that they can begin to engage in strategy.

When you are helping your daughter choose the sport she wants to try, know the athletic requirements of a particular sport and keep in mind these four factors.

EASE OF LEARNING

Every sport is made up of essential fundamental skills that players must learn in order to participate satisfactorily. Most sports may be learned with moderate ease. Observe your daughter to know if she seems to grasp athletic concepts comfortably or if she needs a lot of time to process information.

Recommendation: All children learn by observation, so make sure that you, the coach, or another player shows your daughter what to do regularly. This will have to be done more frequently with lots of patience with a child who has difficulty converting coaching information into movement.

STRENGTH REQUIRED

When evaluating your child, make a distinction between upper and lower body strength. Upper body strength includes the arms, shoulders, chest, and back. Can your daughter perform climbing, swinging, throwing, and hanging activities with relative ease? The stomach and back muscles hold the torso together. Can your daughter do a sit-up with bent knees? Can she lie on her stomach and arch her back so that her arms and legs lift off the floor? The same for lower body strength—the thighs, calves, and feet. Can your daughter run and jump with little effort?

Recommendation: People often say to me that they think their daughter is too big for gymnastics or too small for volleyball. Relative size is not the issue. The real concern is to make sure that your child has the ability to manage her own body weight. Children with good upper body strength will have a better chance of enjoyment and success at softball, gymnastics, tennis, basketball, and volleyball. Children with good lower body strength will find enjoyment and success with soccer, roller skating, figure skating, running, and cycling. The stronger a girl is, the faster she will learn. However, a moderate amount of strength will allow your daughter to do most sports at a passable level.

RISK OF INJURY

Somewhere along the way, every child will suffer an injury through sport activity. The idea is to avoid placing your daughter in a situation where the potential for serious injury could occur, considering her size, weight, and strength for the sport she wants to play.

Recommendation: Strength plays an important role in reducing injury because muscle is a stabilizing factor. In contact sports, children should be playing with other children of relatively the same size and weight, or the smaller child will be subject to injury. Besides strength, skill level also affects the possibility of injury. Many parents want their child to play in high levels of sport so that they may learn from better players, but if the child does not have the skills to move up, you are only opening up the possibility for physical *and* emotional injury. Last, too much repetition of strenuous motions will result in overuse injuries. Temper your own goals and watch practice to make sure that the coach is not overloading young athletes.

SKILL AND COORDINATION LEVEL

To know if your child has basic levels of eye-hand and eye-foot coordination, review the manipulative skills in chapter 2.

Recommendation: Children with good eye-hand coordination will enjoy and may be successful at volleyball, tennis, basketball, softball, golf, field hockey, and tennis. Children with good eye-foot coordination will enjoy and may be successful at soccer, figure skating, in-line skating, roller hockey, dance, and cross-country running.

I have listed below the traditional sports that are found in high school, with an analysis of the sport requirements. For analysis of other sports, visit the Web site www.lifetimetv.com/WoSport/gogetfit.

	EASE OF LEARNING	INJURY RISK	STRENGTH	SKILL/ COORDINATION
Basketball	Moderate	Moderate	Moderate	High
Field Hockey	Moderate	Moderate	Low	Moderate
Golf	Moderate	Low	Low	Moderate
Soccer	Moderate	Moderate	Moderate	Moderate
Softball	Moderate	Moderate	Moderate	Moderate
Swimming	Moderate	Low	Low	Moderate
Tennis	Moderate	Moderate	Moderate	Moderate
Track and Field	Easy	Moderate	Moderate	High
Volleyball	Moderate	Low	Moderate	High

A word of warning: If your daughter seems to be struggling in a particular sport and not having fun, help her to get back to basics by brushing up on fundamental skills. Spend time with her outside of practice. Once she feels more confident, she'll enjoy herself more. There is always the chance that even with modest improvement your daughter may not want to continue the sport. There's no big mystery here. Girls don't want to do something that they are not good at.

Third Stage: Specialization in Specific Sports

This stage can take place as early as sixth grade but is more likely to begin around junior high or middle school. It evolves during high school. By this time girls will have chosen to play their favorite sport and give it their all. Some very talented girls may choose to be multisport competitors in high school, playing different sports in each season.

Following is a list of the top eleven most popular sports offered for girls in secondary school programs, according to the National Federation of State High School Associations. Adjacent to each sport is a list of the basic skills necessary to participate in that sport. If your daughter hopes to make the high school team, she will need to perform these skills at a mature level. Transfer of abilities may then occur to the specific sport skills that are desired. If a girl has not accumulated enough basic movement experiences as a youngster, she will run into a barrier (and maybe a crushing blow to her self-esteem) when she tries out for a particular high school sport team. A frequent comment made by the teenagers I interviewed was that they wished they had started sports earlier than in high school, so that they would have had a better chance to make the team. *It is my belief that we do not get balls into the hands of our girls early enough.* You will notice on the following chart that more than half of high school sports are ball sports.

	LOCOMOTOR	NON-LOCOMOTOR	MANIPULATIVE
Basketball	Running	Bending	Bouncing
	Jumping	Dodging	Catching
	Sliding	Stretching	Throwing
		Turning	
		Twisting	
Track and Field	Body Rolling	Turning	Throwing
	Jumping	Twisting	
	Leaping		
	Running		

(continues)

	LOCOMOTOR	NON-LOCOMOTOR	MANIPULATIVE
Volleyball	Jumping	Stretching	Striking
	Running	Turning	
	Sliding	Twisting	
Softball	Jumping	Bending	Catching
	Leaping	Dodging	Striking
	Running	Stretching	Throwing
	Sliding	Turning	
	Body Rolling	Twisting	
Cross Country	Running		
Tennis	Jumping	Bending	Bouncing
	Running	Stretching	Striking
	Sliding	Turning	
		Twisting	
Soccer	Jumping	Bending	Kicking
	Leaping	Dodging	Throwing
	Running	Turning	Trapping
	Sliding	Twisting	
Golf		Stretching	Striking
		Turning	
		Twisting	
Competitive Spirit Squads Special Category: Advanced Gymnastics	Tumbling		
Cheerleading	Jumping	Turning	
	Leaping	Twisting	
	Running		
Field Hockey	Leaping	Bending	Throwing
	Running	Dodging	Trapping

LOCOMOTOR	NON-LOCOMOTOR	MANIPULATIVE
	Stretching	
	Turning	
	Twisting	
Swimming	Stretching	
	Turning	
	Twisting	

Whatever your daughter's stage of sports readiness, give her the chance to be successful at the activities *she* chooses. Be supportive and let her know that trying hard, learning new skills, and enjoying herself are what sports are all about. Remind her that everyone progresses at her own pace and with practice.

Respect the fact that each stage of sports readiness is a time of growth and learning, a time for enjoying successes as well as making mistakes and discovering what doesn't come easily. Most important, encourage your daughter so that she will continue to be enthusiastic about sports throughout her life.

Creating a Lifetime Enthusiasm for Sports

4

You've just picked up the day's mail, and one of the pieces is your local recreation activities guide. You flip through pages of class descriptions and finally spot an activity you think your daughter—and you—will enjoy. Next you select the day, the time, and the session and phone in your registration. Voilà, mission accomplished. Or is it? You've made a selection based on a current interest. But what about making a selection based on lifetime possibilities?

When I read the sports section of the local newspaper, I find articles written and competition results published representing all ages, levels, and kinds of athletes, not just the pros. There are community sports photos of children on age-group teams, results of junior college and four-year institution tournaments, information about who won the masters fifty and over race, announcements about camps, notices about adult leagues, and updates regarding international competitions.

What's the point of all this? You will find when you explore the current sports scene that there is an awesome array of opportunities, whether you are age five or fifty-five. Any one of the dozens of offerings that exist might be the sport where your daughter shines if she has a chance to give it a try. Think about looking beyond the community recreation guide for your sport choices. Following is an exploration of the lifetime progression of recreational, competitive, and leisure sport offerings. My hope is that you will select and enjoy some sports with your daughter that have the potential to become lifetime activities for both of you.

Youth Sports

Community service programs that offer youth sports are a mainstay almost everywhere. Typically, your sport choices will be based on traditional activities like the ones listed below. I have also included some nontraditional activities, since young women are getting involved in more and more kinds of sports. These offerings will vary from region to region. If a sport is a college or Olympic sport, you will be able to find a junior age-group program someplace in your geographic area.

There are several organizations across the United States that manage competitive and recreational sports. Check out the following Web sites for basic information.

- AAU (Amateur Athletic Union): 407-934-7200, www.aausports. org
- The Boys and Girls Clubs of America: 404-815-5700, www.bgca. org.
- YWCA (Young Women's Christian Association): 212-273-7800, www.ywca.org
- YMCA (Young Men's Christian Association): 312-977-0031, www.ymca.net

No matter where your daughter's interests lead her, take the advice of physical educators. Provide her with a multisport background. This is the best approach for up-and-coming athletes and lifetime enthusiasts.

TRADITIONAL	NONTRADITIONAL
Basketball	Beach volleyball
Dance	Bike racing (BMX)
Gymnastics	Bowling
Ice-skating	Curling

(continues)

TRADITIONAL	NONTRADITIONAL
Martial arts	Cycling
Soccer	Equestrian
Softball	Field hockey
Swimming	Figure skating
Tennis	Golf
Volleyball	Jumping rope
	Lacrosse
	Racquetball
	Rock climbing
	Roller hockey
	Roller skating
	Sailing
	Scuba diving
	Skateboarding
	Skiing
	Snowboarding
	Surfing
	Table tennis
	Track and field
	Water polo
	Waterskiing
	Weight lifting
	Wrestling

Enrichment classes offered through your community services programs are great places to experiment with short-term sessions and find out what your daughter's interests are. Most girls are willing to try something new, especially when they know there is a time limit to the commitment.

High School

The following sports offerings represent the kinds of sports that are found in high schools across the nation. Not every state will offer every sport on the list, and many will vary by geographic location. You probably won't find kayaking in Kansas, nor will you find rodeo in Rhode Island. But there are plenty of choices for your daughter, and by knowing what's available, you'll have plenty of time to prepare her for a place on the high school team if that is her desire. The National Federation of State High School Associations compiles statistics about girls' participation in athletics. Their Web site is www.nfhs.org, and they can be reached at 816-464-5400.

Archery	Judo
Badminton	Kayaking
Baseball	Lacrosse
Basketball	Pentathlon
Bowling	Riflery
Canoeing	Rodeo
Competitive spirit	Skiing
(cheerleading)	Soccer
Crew	Softball
Cross-country	Squash
Dance/drill team	Swimming and diving
Decathlon	Tennis
Equestrian	Track and field
Fencing	Volleyball
Field hockey	Waterpolo
Football	Weight lifting
Golf	Wrestling
Gymnastics	

To be prepared for high school sports, girls need to have at least a couple of years' experience in the sport they wish to pursue. Depending on the sport and what state you live in, the tryouts may be a formality or highly competitive. If you live in an area where there are lots of club programs (non–school sponsored, sport specific organizations that offer multi-level, especially elite, training year round), athletes with club training will have a heavy advantage when it comes to tryouts. Sometimes girls who have the physical qualities required to play a sport well—height for basketball, strong legs for cross-country running or skiing—but little or no experience will fare well at tryouts, but don't count on this situation. Being physically fit will go a long way toward helping girls make a team.

College

To play sports at a four-year institution takes considerable effort. If your daughter wants to extend the competitive life of her favorite sport, she'll need to have a solid high school or club background. Expect to start the selection process in the junior year of high school. If a girl's skill level is not such that she can qualify for a college team, often there are club programs on campus that she can take part in. Also know that some junior colleges have tremendous programs for athletes who are not ready for Division I (high-level) or Division II (intermediate-level) sports play. Many junior colleges are reliable feeder programs for the NCAA (National Collegiate Athletic Association) or the NAIA (National Association of Intercollegiate Athletics) system. It is not unusual for a girl to get experience at a junior college level before playing at higher levels—that is, at a four-year college. On occasion, girls improve to such a degree in a sport that they can secure an athletic scholarship. For specific information on colleges that field the sport your daughter is interested in, you can reach the NCAA Web site at www.ncaa.org and by phone at 317-917-6222; the NAIA can be reached at www.naia.org and by phone at 918-494-8828.

STANDARD	EMERGING OR FUTURE SPORTS
Basketball	Archery
Cross-country	Badminton
Fencing	Bowling
Field hockey	Equestrian
Golf	Ice hockey
Gymnastics	Squash
Lacrosse	Synchronized swimming
Rifle	Team handball
Rowing	Water polo
Skiing	
Softball	
Soccer	
Swimming and diving	
Tennis	
Track and field	
Volleyball	

College athletes often take more than four years to finish their education. This will vary by institution and by the sport level at which the athlete is competing. I, for instance, had to go to summer school to meet my graduation requirements. This is usually due to the fact that athletes often take a lighter academic load during the competitive season, so be prepared for this possibility.

International Olympic Sports

Being able to qualify for the Olympics is a dream for many athletes. But should your daughter have that dream, the sport she chooses will place her in either the Summer or Winter Olympic Games. The Olympics are held every four years for both the summer and winter games. However, they now alternate Olympiads every two years. For instance, the next Winter Olympic Games will be held in the year 2002, the next Summer Olympic Games in 2004. For most Olympic sports, female athletes must be fourteen years of age. To get detailed information, go to the Web site at www.usoc.org.

SUMMER
- Aquatics
  - Diving
  - Swimming
  - Synchronized
  - Water polo
- Archery
- Athletics (track and field)
- Badminton
- Basketball
- Canoe/kayak
- Cycling
  - Road
  - Mountain bike
  - Track
- Equestrian
  - Dressage
  - Jumping
  - Three-day event
- Fencing
- Field hockey

WINTER
- Biathlon
- Bobsled
- Cross-country
- Curling
- Downhill skiing
- Figure skating
- Freestyle skiing
- Giant slalom
- Ice hockey
- Luge
- Nordic combined
- Short track
- Ski jumping
- Speed skating
- Snowboarding

(continues)

SUMMER	WINTER

SUMMER
  Gymnastics
    Artistic
    Rhythmic
    Trampolining
  Judo
  Modern pentathlon
  Rowing
  Sailing
  Shooting
  Soccer
  Softball
  Table tennis
  Tae kwon do
  Tennis
  Triathlon
  Volleyball
    Beach
    Indoor
  Weight lifting

Training for the Olympics involves a phenomenal commitment, both for the athlete and for her family. There are pros and cons to this highly personal decision. It can draw families together to support the aspiring athlete, or it can disrupt family relations with constant travel and above-average financial outlays. It can create a lifetime of opportunity following the experience, or it can create a hole in a person's life when the competition is over. Emotional planning is just as important as physical training. Knowing what I know about the Olympics today, if I had to do it all over again, I would do everything in my power to be an Olympian. But there's always the Senior Olympic Games.

Senior Olympics

This national program has both Summer and Winter Olympic Games. People may participate as competitors when they reach age fifty. The starting point for athletes begins with competition at local games that are held every two years. These meets are the qualifiers for the state championships, which are held every two years. This is followed by a national championship that is held every two years.

Events vary from state to state but include sports like basketball, cycling, golf, alpine skiing, bowling, ballroom dancing, and archery. For those women who still have a competitive spirit floating around in their soul, this is a great way to scratch the itch. Plus, you always have a goal to work toward.

Lifetime Activities

The number of people fifty-five and older who exercise frequently increased dramatically from 1987 to 1996. According to a report by American Sports Data Research, there was a 75 percent jump in seniors who sought to keep in shape, at the very least, by working out at fitness centers. For myself, I believe that exercising allows me the strength and stamina to take part in other lifetime activities that I still enjoy, like golf, swimming, cycling, skiing, and tennis. Here is a sampling of some of the more common activities adult women can choose to participate in for fun and friendship.

Archery	Hiking
Aerobics	In-line skating
Backpacking	Martial arts
Badminton	Orienteering
Basketball	Racquetball
Bowling	Rowing
Canoeing	Running
Climbing	Sailing
Cycling	Shooting
Dancing	Skating (in-line, ice)
Diving (scuba)	Skiing–cross-country, alpine
Equestrian	Soccer
Fencing	Softball
Field hockey	Swimming
Figure skating	Table Tennis
Frisbee	Tennis
Golf	Walking
Hang gliding	Water aerobics

It is important to realize that if you are going to instill in your daughter a lifetime enthusiasm for sports, you will want to understand both your expectations and hers.

Know Your Expectations

In the rush to produce amazing kids, children are sometimes pushed into activities that they may not be ready to handle. Be able to truthfully answer the question "What do I want for my daughter?" Can you accept her just having fun? Are you thinking that she has talent and needs to get an early start so that she won't miss anything? As you take a serious look at your expectations, here are three thoughts to keep in mind:

- Be realistic. A five-year-old child, for example, has been walking with consistency only a little over half of her life. No matter how talented you think your daughter is, there's no hurry to enroll her in multiple programs or schedule private lessons.
- Understand that all children can be successful at some level. Children really enjoy sports when fundamental fairness exists—that is, when they're placed in a group reflecting their level, where they have a chance to participate.
- Go back to your own experience in youth athletics. Were you too intimidated to try out for basketball because you were afraid of constantly getting bumped and bruised? Was your experience with swimming lessons disappointing because everyone learned faster than you? Did you go to cheerleading tryouts only to see that all the other girls already knew how to do a back handspring? You can certainly learn from those experiences, but stay open to your daughter's interests. She may become a crackerjack swimmer with your encouragement.

The guiding concept should be to let girls try a number of activities so that eventually a selection is made that matches the personal and physical makeup of the child. Trying lots of activities provides a broad range of skills in which children have confidence. The more skills, the greater the level of confidence.

Know Your Child's Expectations

"What really interests my daughter?" Does she enjoy doing things on her own? Is the companionship of friends an important need of hers? The answers to these questions can give you partial clues about whether your daughter should try team or individual sports.

For team sports, the pressure to perform is spread around the team. It is not focused on the ability of one person. Team sport people are energized by what is going on around them socially. Noise and activity energize them. Often a coach who is demonstrably enthusiastic both with voice and body language is just right for them. The conditions of play are always changing, and it's exciting. Those who participate in individual sports may prefer to be the center of attention. They want to be the cause of their own success or failure. They can endure solitary training.

When children play, it is possible for them to be interested in many kinds of activities. They should try lots of them. Experience is the best way to find the sport that will be your daughter's passion. Everyone likes to perform and practice activities that excite them. When "the activity" comes along in your child's life she'll let you know, and you'll see it. The chosen activity that is right for her now may be all wrong when she is more mature, but it is the journey through sport that is important. Sport is physical activity, and regular activity helps girls to enjoy a full and healthy life.

Shopping for Recreation and Competition Programs

5

During my childhood, recreation programs were something we took advantage of mostly during the summer months, when we didn't have to go to school and our parents wanted us outside in the fresh air. The big summer event in my community was to buy a badge that allowed you to swim and use the changing facilities at Crystal Lake. I doubt my mother ever did little more than ask the neighbors where to sign up and then give us some treasured cash to purchase the badge. Shopping for children's recreational activities via the phone directory, let alone the Internet, wasn't the norm as it is today. Nowadays many families schedule multisport recreational instruction throughout the year, changing sports from season to season.

Competition, for me, was reserved for races at the playground on the Fourth of July and high school, when you finally got the chance to be on a team. Today girls don't have to wait for high school to be on a team (although much to my amazement, many still do), and the number and variety of competitive sports that are available are no longer confined to what's offered in high school and at holiday events. Year-round offerings at recreational centers include such varied activities as soccer, gymnastics, softball, volleyball, diving, cheer-leading, tennis, martial arts, swimming, and basketball. These are among the standard choices for families. Participation in competitive sports now starts as early as age six for novice players and goes up to elite levels with teams that journey across the nation. I remember being so thrilled when, as a freshman in college, I had my first plane ride to a tournament. I thought I had hit the big time.

Whether your daughter is interested in training for one particular sport or just wants to have some fun after school or during vacation, this chapter will help you sort through and compare the various programs available in your area. Choosing the activities that are most suitable for your daughter requires more than just flipping through the Yellow Pages or surfing the Net. There are some key points that will guide you through this screening process and enable you to ask important questions when you're interviewing program representatives. Remember, it's all about choosing the sports program, coach, and activities that your daughter will benefit from and enjoy most.

Evaluating Recreation Programs

First, determine your daughter's stage of development. She may be in the discovery stage, and you would like to find an activity that might interest her and that she can enter at a novice level. Maybe you want to encourage her in an activity in which she's recently shown some interest. Then again, you may have a daughter who needs a high-powered program to galvanize her spirit. Nowadays your choice of recreation programs runs the gamut from low-key introductory classes to competitive traveling teams. Depending on where you live, you'll find national nonprofit organizations like the YMCA, community recreation centers, and club programs that offer specialty training. Know your options before making your choice.

Where to Look for Recreation Programs

Look for a quality recreation program the same way you would look for a good doctor. Check with your friends who have enrolled their girls in sports programs. Call your local chamber of commerce to find out if they have any recommendations. The Yellow Pages of the phone directory is a good source for locating programs. Try these listings:

- "Recreation Centers"
- "Youth Organizations and Centers"
- Individual sport instruction (such as "Gymnastics," "Swimming," "Martial Arts")

The front section of most telephone directories usually includes "blue pages" or something similar that list neighborhood parks, and these parks may host some outdoor activities for children.

Another good source is local parenting magazines. Monthly publications will carry advertising for an array of programs.

Check the sport section of your local newspaper for youth notices.

Be sure to consult your local school district or your local elementary school for recommendations.

Following are some of the organizations that offer children's athletic programs.

NATIONAL NONPROFIT ORGANIZATIONS

These organizations can be found in most states. I have included phone numbers and Web sites to make your search easier.

YMCAS (888-333-YMCA, WWW.YMCA.ORG)/YWCAS (212-273-7800, WWW.YWCA.ORG): Programs offered through these organizations typically have an excellent assortment of age-appropriate programs and very reasonable rates. They are represented in ninety-seven countries around the world and offer special summer camps as well.

BOYS AND GIRLS CLUBS (404-815-5700, WWW.BGCA.ORG): Providing "The positive place for kids," the Boys and Girls Clubs' mission is to create an encouraging and supportive environment for children. They work very hard to make their programs available to all children in the community and strive to help families who have financial difficulties. Rates are modest, and their program offerings vary from community to community.

GIRLS INCORPORATED (212-509-2000, WWW.GIRLSINC.ORG): Girls Inc.'s goal is "Inspiring all girls to be strong, smart, and bold." Girls Inc. aims "to make sports an integral part of girls' lives. Through a three-program series, girls learn how to feel less vulnerable and more powerful, how to be both cooperative and competitive, and how to discipline their bodies and their minds." Programs are set up according to ages (six to eight, nine to eleven, and twelve to fourteen) and stress motor skill development up through individual and team sport training. Girls Inc. has more than one thousand sites nationwide that cater to after-school, weekend, and summer activities.

AMERICAN VOLKSSPORT ASSOCIATION (210-659-2112, WWW. AVA.ORG): "Promoting health, fun, and fellowship through noncompetitive walking and sporting events for everyone." This little-known organization had its origins in Germany. It is a great starting point for families who are looking for some activity with a low level of commitment and low cost. From coast to coast they organize hikes covering various distances and journeys. Families may have a choice of biking, hiking, or swimming. Trails are selected for safety, scenic interest, historic areas, natural beauty, and walkability.

Look for local listings for these organizations in your community newspaper, on the Web, or in your neighborhood recreation guide.

COMMUNITY OR CITY PARKS AND RECREATION PROGRAMS

Every community offers recreational activities for children of all ages. Contact your local town or city hall to request a brochure and to get on their mailing list. Each community will have its own offerings. Depending on how well funded a program is, there are usually three different enrollment periods—summer, winter, and spring. The fees are reasonable, and there is usually a good range of choices. Many now have their own Web site where you may register electronically.

THE PRIVATE CLUB SYSTEM

A combination of entrepreneurial effort and increased interest has led to the growth of private club programs that offer training on a year-round basis. These are private or non-school-sponsored leagues. Private clubs are operated by small-business owners who typically were athletes themselves. Generally only one sport is being taught at the facility, and it is ongoing year-round. The teachers in private clubs are usually high-level, experienced, career professionals. The major emphasis is on competitive training, with a variety of levels offered to accommodate beginners through advanced. The coaches are generally familiar with teaching students at different learning levels and can adjust to individual learning styles. If you and your child are sincerely interested in "training," the private clubs are the way to go. This is especially true if your daughter wants to represent herself or her high school in league and statewide competitions.

Club programs tend to have higher tuition rates than community programs operated as nonprofit organizations. Know what your money pays for. Does it cover salaries, uniforms, field rental fees, insurance, tournament entry fees, travel, and referees? Will you have costs beyond tuition? Most programs should have this in writing. In cases where an athlete with tremendous talent is not able to afford the fees in club programs, I suggest that you ask the director if any financial assistance is offered.

PUBLIC SCHOOLS

Many public schools face budget problems that often have an impact on non-academic programs like physical education and after-school athletics. Because of this, you should not depend on your daughter's school to fulfill her recreation requirements. The only way you'll know what's happening at your daughter's school is to ask her and observe the programs being offered. Find out how often PE is being taught, who is teaching it, how much of the class is spent being active, and if the activities encourage all children to take part. If PE is being taught only once a week, I recommend that you look into some additional activities for your child. In some school districts, after-school programs are organized by the school itself. Some districts hire private contractors to come on site and offer after-school programs.

What to Look for in a Recreation Program

You've scanned the Internet and the Yellow Pages in search of the kinds of programs available in your community, you've talked to your friends who have daughters and gotten their suggestions, and most important you've discussed this decision with your child. Now you have to make a choice for her. Making a knowledgeable choice means taking specific factors into consideration. No matter how anxious your daughter is to wear a uniform, make sure you understand the philosophy and procedures of a particular program. At the introductory levels, the major emphasis needs to be on improving fitness and teaching sport skills and downplaying competition so that every girl learns how to play.

Before you spend time and money, become informed about the following areas. Each program will have its own style and feeling, and your job is to make a good match between your daughter and the program.

FACILITY

Watch out for overemphasis or underemphasis on the facility. It's great to have a beautiful training center, but make sure the staff are every bit as engaging as the property. It's wonderful if the place is attractive and modern, but cleanliness and safety are the priorities.

BASIC PHILOSOPHY: LET THE GOOD TIMES ROLL

You know how you feel when facing another boring workout. Well, young girls are even more insistent on having a good time. The only thing they have on their minds is enjoyment—pure and simple. Most want to be active, probably with their friends, and have moderate challenges. Make sure you and your daughter observe classes (or practices) to see if the participants seem to be enjoying themselves. When families come in to watch my gymnastics classes, I always invite the prospective child to join us. Prescheduling a trial class where the child gets a chance to participate is the best way for a girl to know what is expected of her and to test the waters of that program.

SKILL LEVEL AND AGE APPROPRIATENESS OF THE ACTIVITY

Programs should be offered with enough skill levels or ability divisions to allow girls a realistic chance to learn new skills. It is also important to have defined steps that signify skill levels. Some sports, like swimming and gymnastics, have more defined levels than others, and it is relatively easy to assign students to their respective classes. Other sports like basketball and soccer usually depend on tryouts to place girls in the correct group for their age, ability, and size.

Make sure you ask about the content of programs to know if the activities are age appropriate. The younger the child, the more the program should be oriented toward sport skill development. The older the child, the more appropriate it is for her to prepare for competition. Often registration is scheduled by grade level in school or a child's age group. It's not unusual to find introductory levels scheduled as coed for young elementary school children.

EMPHASIS ON SKILL DEVELOPMENT

Most girls should be building basic skills (as outlined in chapter 3), up through the third and fourth grade, no matter what sport they're pursuing. When they're part of a developmental squad, sport skills should be emphasized over competition, as these skills must become second nature. If you want your daughter's skills to progress more rapidly, try spending some time with her at home. Please remember to spend that time in a pleasurable way, or it will only be time wasted and may turn her off from sports altogether. I can't emphasize enough how important it is to have a solid foundation of motor skills before going on to play team sports, since team sports require the use of strategy. No child can pay attention to *how* to play a game if all her attention is on *what* to do.

PARTICIPANT-TEACHER RATIO

These ratios will vary from sport to sport and program to program. The most important thing to keep in mind is that beginners will need a smaller participant-teacher ratio than high-level players, as this enables them to focus on skill development. Intermediate to advanced participants, especially in team sports, can tolerate up to fifteen players per coach. Your best bet is to observe individual programs and determine if the children are being well served. Experienced coaches with good organizational skills can handle a higher participant-teacher ratio than beginner or disorganized instructors.

PARTICIPATION BASED ON A LEVEL PLAYING FIELD

In order to make sure that girls play at their level and interact with other players at their level (team or individual sports), an evaluation day may be scheduled before the start of a seasonal program. Ordinarily this is a mass skill testing session for all the participants. Following the skill evaluation, appropriate groupings will be established, and practice times assigned. If your daughter does not have a good experience at this tryout, ask if one of the coaches would be willing to meet with her on a one-on-one basis.

AMOUNT OF PLAYING TIME AND SIZE OF PRACTICE AREA

Every girl should be able to play during every practice, and all players should be scheduled an equal amount of time on the field of play. The more active girls are during practice, the more likely they are to acquire skills and become physically fit. Especially for younger elementary school girls who are still developing strength, stamina, and coordination, the following should be taken into consideration:

- A smaller time frame of play than standard regulations
- A smaller area of play than standard regulations
- Girls need to be moved to different playing positions frequently to gain a wide variety of skills
- For individual sports, there needs to be enough equipment or play area for girls to have a basic workout and not spend time sitting around.
- The more organized the coach, the better the practice will be.

By the time girls are eight or nine years old, if they are physically fit, they should be able to play for a longer period of time using a larger practice area.

A MOTIVATION AND REWARD SYSTEM THAT VALUES EVERYONE

Make sure the participants are given some kind of recognition. It's okay to ask ahead of time if the girls will receive acknowledgment for their efforts. This helps to make sports an attractive part of their lives. At the very least, every girl should go home with good memories, if not with passable skills. Conscientious coaches will find something positive in each player that can be valued. Before making your choice, ask if any of these items are awarded at the end of a session:

- Participation certificates
- Attendance awards
- Trophies for personal bests, most improved
- Recognition for best sportsmanship

Program directors are responsible for ensuring that staff members support the mission statement of the organization. Though the wording will vary from program to program, the number one goal is usually to create situations where girls have the chance to be appreciated for their efforts, a chance to succeed and become confident. With proper research you can feel confident, too, that you've found a program that is a good match for your child.

GAME-TIME PHILOSOPHY FOR BEGINNING COMPETITION

It is up to the leadership of any given program to establish a minimum amount of game play for each girl. Ideally each child should play every time there is a match or game. For team sports, it's best to rotate girls through various positions to allow them to expand their skills and eventually find out where their talent lies.

The goal of an organization should be to keep the league teams even so that any given team is not obviously dominant during the sports season. Some programs do not even keep track of a win-loss record. Also, there should be no team championships or rankings for beginning levels. This helps to keep athletes and coaches focused on skill development.

At the lower levels, coaches will often officiate games while continuing to instruct players. This gives the girls the opportunity to continue learning on the spot—putting in place the essence of what education is supposed to accomplish.

STAFF

Coaches come in a wide range of ages and skill levels, from interested high school students to trained adult professionals. Instructors need to be sensitive to the special issues that concern girls who lack previous sport experience—shyness, lack of physical strength, anxiety trying new skills, fear of failure in front of their friends, and lack of assertiveness. Look for the coach's ability both to be supportive and to encourage girls to face challenges. I have outlined in chapter 8 the skills a coach should possess to have a positive influence on players and athletes. Make sure your daughter's coach measures up.

Recreation Alternatives for Teenagers

I'm addressing teens specifically because they have the least amount of options available if they don't make the high school team or are not good enough for private club teams. Yet this is the age group that needs the most options. To stay healthy and occupy their time after school, teenagers also need structured activity. What kinds of activities are suitable for teenage girls who want to be physically fit but may not wish to pursue sports? Some successful programs have been developed by the secondary school system. Following are three possibilities that might work in your community.

LAST PERIOD FITNESS AT HIGH SCHOOL

One high school coach I interviewed set up a special program for girls who were not on a team. She set up fitness and sport training to run the last period of the school day. It was a win-win program.

The goal of the class is to use a variety of training and conditioning activities and techniques to insure a well-balanced workout program. The curriculum is designed for each individual to participate in a program for health, wellness, and fitness; to develop measurable improvement in each student's strength, aerobic capacity, and flexibility; and to offer the opportunity to participate in sport-specific activities. Because this program is offered during the last period of the day, the girls get a PE class credit. See if your daughter's school offers such an activity.

LUNCH PERIOD INTRAMURALS

In this lunchtime program, students check out equipment so that they can play in the gym. This is a terrific concept, but like anything else, it requires cooperation from the staff at the school. The girls need supervision in the locker rooms (that means a woman needs to be on duty), supervision to check out equipment, and supervision in the gym.

LOCAL HEALTH CLUB PARTNERING

Some schools have an arrangement with their local health clubs. For a fraction of the regular cost, girls can work out and get in shape as part of the PE program. This involves being committed to a specific period of training. What a great link to lifetime fitness! Call around and see if this is an option for your daughter.

Evaluating Competitive Sports Programs

When your daughter's talents and interests have outgrown recreational programs, you will probably want to investigate competitive sports. When that time arises, you'll need to research the market

pretty carefully. Involvement in competition is usually not encouraged for girls earlier than age seven. However, this is changing, as ev-
idenced by the young competitors in the recent U.S. National Jump
Rope Championships. The youngest was six years old.

Before we examine the specifics of competitive sports programs,
I want to say that it's important not to let competitive sports take
the place of free play activities like bike riding or in-line skating.
These unstructured activities are as valuable to a child's social and
physical development as scheduled classes or specific sports training. Free play keeps girls active, and though skills are developed in a
random way, when neighborhood activities are combined with organized sports, the benefits are tremendous.

With that said, if your child is to have a successful experience
with competitive sports, you need to honestly assess her abilities, interests, and temperament. You may see your child as advancing rapidly, but does she belong on the Olympic track? Maybe your daughter
can have a great deal of fun being the best at beginner and intermediate levels of sport play. Here are the key points to consider when
evaluating the decision to play competitive sports:

- Does your child have the basic skills of the sport?
- Does your child have a passion for the sport?
- Does your child have a realistic opportunity to succeed?
- Does your child have your commitment to help her succeed?

It's possible that you may have two daughters whose attitudes
toward competition are very different. Here's what one mother had
to say:

> As mother of two girls, ages ten and thirteen, so much de-
> pends on what they're looking for from sports. Five years ago,
> we got involved with recreational sports on a lark. I believed
> it was good to stay in something even if they never really ex-
> celled at a sport. It was a precaution for later years. Now I see
> so much of it is listening to your child. One daughter wanted
> a highly competitive place where she thought she would find
> the best coaches and they would treat her in a respectful way.
> My other daughter has different, more relaxed aspirations. I
> came to realize that their motivation is critical, their talent,

their work ethic. The main thing is to observe and be aware.
Get the input of your children. Get involved.
—Sherry, mother of two girls

Taking all these factors into consideration, it is still impossible to know how your daughter will react once competition begins. The public display of skill for all to see and critique can be overwhelming. Certainly competitive sports can be a very positive experience for a girl. When a coach stresses assertiveness rather than aggressiveness, and when parents and children put competitive sports into the proper perspective, valuable life skills can be learned.

Where to Look for Competitive Sports Programs

When you are looking for a competitive sports program, many times your budget will determine where your daughter gets to play. Some public schools will have no- or low-cost programs. Private clubs will have moderate to expensive monthly schedules. If your daughter is just getting started in a sport, you may choose to keep your costs down until she and you are ready to make a stronger commitment. Remember, just as in any other purchase, in most cases you get what you pay for.

MIDDLE SCHOOL

Across the country, sport offerings vary widely in middle schools. Some schools can afford to offer PE programs only during school hours, and many of these will be coed. Usually, the traditional array of sports will be taught—basketball, softball, track and field, and soccer. If a school district has the money to hire staff and furnish transportation for an after-school intramural program, you're in luck. I suggest contacting your local middle school (if your daughter is currently in elementary school) to know what the opportunities are for her athletic education outside PE classes. If they are limited, private club programs may become invaluable, as a bridge between middle and high school sports.

Middle school can be a place where girls develop their competitive sports skills. In some enlightened communities senior high school squads schedule a training day at a nearby middle school. Varsity players may come and talk to younger girls about high school sports and even conduct a sports clinic. The benefit of this interaction is that future high school students form a connection to the school, thus easing the eventual transition. In many communities girls find out about high school sports too late, and they miss deadlines to register for tryouts or aren't prepared when the time for tryouts comes.

HIGH SCHOOL

The top ten most popular high school sports are basketball, track and field, volleyball, softball, cross-country, tennis, soccer, golf, swimming and diving, and spirit squads (cheerleading). Since high school is frequently the first place girls have a true sport experience, representing their high school on a sports team is a big deal. It is not only a social milestone, for some it is a personal turning point. It was for me.

If a program is all-encompassing, girls can join a team at the entry level as freshmen with tryouts held in the spring of a girl's last year in middle school. Sometimes tryouts are held in the later part of the summer, other times in the fall. Either way it is a much easier transition to high school sports if there is a freshman program. At this entry level coaches try very hard not to cut anyone from the team. Sadly, too many high schools cannot afford a freshman program, which translates into there being too little opportunity for girls.

The next layer of competition is the JV (junior varsity) level, which is the feeder system into the varsity program. This is the stage where players are judged by skill level. Only so many girls can be part of the team, and often both parents and girls face an additional dilemma: whether an athlete should play school sports if she plays and competes for a private club. The question is whether girls who train only on a seasonal basis earn a place on the school team when they may be competing against girls who train year round. The truth is, it may be too difficult.

High school coaches want parents to remember what high school sports is all about: it's about getting the most kids as possible involved in activities. But parents who put money into club programs may have a hard time separating private club programs from high school sports mentally. Sometimes parents of club athletes are very assertive and opinionated about how the high school program should be run. Attitudes can become even more aggressive when parents believe their daughter has a chance to get an athletic college scholarship.

SUMMER SPORTS CAMPS

Choosing a reputable summer program takes some investigation on your part. When you look over the promotional materials, try to get a sense of what happens at a particular camp. Try not to be put off if there is an activity that doesn't match your needs. The basic program may still have merit. Here are some things to consider when evaluating summer camp choices. The older your child is, the more she will want to have input into the discussion, especially if her friends or teammates are trying to make a joint decision.

- What are your "must have" features? Are they present?
- What are the qualifications of the staff? Most camps are taught by college students with guest appearances by professional coaches.
- As you review brochures and videos, is the emphasis on the beauty of the facility, or can you see if the campers are having fun? Are the counselors interacting with the athletes?
- Is there a good mix or sport training and purely recreational activities? Are some activities restricted to certain age groups? What are elective activities?
- Does the camp have a registered nurse on site?
- Is the philosophy of the camp clear? It should be in writing.
- Is this a residence or a day camp?
- How many hours a day are spent in training?

My first experience at a summer camp was as a counselor and gymnastics coach during my college years. I loved being in my sport environment every day, helping girls reach their potential. It was heartwarming to see not only an increase in sport skills, but growth in friendships and decision making. As coaches we were role models for sport development because the girls could watch us work out. They could see that we struggled and achieved, or struggled and fell short. There was certainly plenty of time for those crazy, zany special events at night to keep the experience balanced. Frankly, some of my closest lifetime friendships were made at camp, and hopefully your daughter will have the same opportunity to develop lifelong pals. I will always remember those days, because the staff really made an effort to help girls grow and to help them forever remember their camp days.

PRIVATE CLUBS

Refer back to the private club description under recreation programs if you need to refresh your memory.

COMMUNITY AND CITY PARKS PROGRAMS

Recreation programs offered through your community can be great for an introduction to competitive sports. Be prepared to find traditional offerings—soccer, softball, basketball, swimming, martial arts, dance, and tennis. Most programs offer sports on a seasonal basis, so it's possible to try a few different activities over the course of a year. Sometimes participants are requested to bring their own equipment, like a tennis racket and a can of balls, for example. Usually the emphasis is on fun and enjoyment. But depending on the region of the country, these programs may be highly competitive as leagues battle one another, community against community.

What to Look for in a Competitive Program

Once you have arranged to visit a facility and have your daughter evaluated, you'll need to get some nitty-gritty questions answered: what are the number of training hours, what is the cost, what is the length of the competitive season, what are the qualifications of the staff, and so on. Here are the main areas you will need to understand and the particular features that are relevant.

TRAVEL TIME

Is the level of the athlete high enough to warrant substantial travel? In general, the higher the level of the athlete, the more reasonable it becomes to travel a long distance. If you have a talented girl with a keen interest for a particular sport, it can be important to get proper training in the early stages, and this may involve more frequent travel for greater distances. I suggest you tell your daughter that when she reaches an advanced level of training, you would be willing to drive a longer distance for her to have better coaches. You certainly have to consider other family members, the dinner hour, and homework.

FACILITY

The most important factor is safety. Having a well-lighted area with the floor or ground being evenly surfaced is number one. The equipment should be in good repair and meet industry standards. There should be enough equipment or playing areas for athletes to spend their time on the field of play, rather than sitting on a bench as an observer.

NUMBER OF TRAINING HOURS PER WEEK

This will determine your daughter's level of commitment. The higher the level of skill she wants to master, the more motivated and committed she will be. But the number of training hours she commits to will affect more than just her; it will affect the whole family. Consider these questions:

- How many hours a week does your daughter need to spend on homework?
- How much time do you have per week to be away from home?
- Are you both prepared to eat dinner in the car?
- How does the schedule in question affect other family members?

Practice schedules are proportionate to the age, skill, and fitness level of the child. Beginners may practice three to six hours a week. Intermediates practice six to nine hours a week. Advanced players practice between twelve and fifteen hours a week. While this may not be representative of all programs, it can be used as a guideline.

STAFF: QUALIFICATIONS, TEMPERAMENT, STUDENT-TEACHER RATIO

Watch the way a coach deals with girls on an individual basis. You want someone who talks to the girls in a positive fashion. All girls should be treated in the same way, no favoritism and no belittling individuals. This is not an easy assignment. Coaches may shout in the heat of the moment, especially during a match; but when it's over the coach must be able to connect with each girl no matter what kind of game or competition she's had. Observe the coach in action to find out if she or he is solidly grounded by a sense of fairness. Sit in the bleachers and see if there is any apparent domination of some girls on the team, including their telling the coach what to do. If the coach allows the most vocal or talented players to frequently have their way, the other teammates will learn that hot shots can simply push everyone around.

Having the choice of a male or female coach doesn't happen very often, but there are pros and cons for each gender. Sometimes it is easier for girls to talk to a woman than a man. Other times girls like a man if he's been a player himself and can show the girls what to do. But if a woman coach is athletic and has the sport skills that girls want to learn, this can be extremely empowering to young girls.

Ask about the participant-teacher ratio. Anywhere from six to eight athletes per coach is an acceptable ratio for individual sports. Team sports will be determined by the size of a normal playing roster.

Another area of concern is the personal background of the coach. Find out how long the coaches have been at a program. The longer the better. Check to see if the staff is first aid and CPR trained. When your daughter is practicing at a community facility, you can always ask the director if a background check has been done on the staff person working with children. Should your daughter train in a program where the person in question is both the coach and the director of a program, go to the local authorities if you want to have a background check carried out. You can never be too safe.

TRAINING FEES

Paying for sports lessons is no different from paying for piano lessons. The higher the level of training, the better the instructor, the higher the fees. Some programs will ask for monthly payments, some for quarterly payments, some will want payment up front for the season. On occasion, some programs have youth scholarships. It doesn't hurt to ask.

INDIVIDUAL GOALS VS. TEAM GOALS

Finding a program that will take your daughter as far as she wants to go can involve considerable research. How high can the coach take the girls? Do you want to train for national-level competition or do you want your daughter to compete on a level at which she is comfortable? In other words, do your daughter's individual goals match the team goals as set out by the coach?

LEVEL OF COMMUNICATION

Ideally all parties involved want open lines of communication. Parents want to know what kind of progress their daughters are making, and the girls want to know how they're doing in practice. The head coach should make parent and student communication a regular part of the program. If the instructor has not made it a priority to stay in touch about an athlete's progress, you are well within your rights to make regular phone calls. This is no different from what you would expect from a school teacher. Whether done over the phone or informally after practice, staying in touch is a key element in coach-parent-player relations. Sometimes coaches focus so much on training that they forget parent relations are just as important.

AMOUNT OF PLAYING TIME VS. SITTING ON THE BENCH

How much time your daughter spends on the field of play depends on the philosophy of the coach and the competitiveness of the program. Coaches will always be confronted with the dilemma of making a decision about who will represent the team during a tournament. In the best of all possible situations, there will be a balance between a desire for a winning program and an athlete's right to participate. Find out the coach's philosophy ahead of time. There are times when a coach will not be aligned with the philosophy of the program. Go to the director if it works against the best interests of the child, or ask the coach directly for a meeting.

FUND-RAISING REQUIREMENTS

Most private club programs as well as public and private schools involve parents in fund-raising, so be prepared for more involvement than just driving to and from practice. Most programs have booster clubs that work together to develop a budget and recommend ways to raise funds. Find out what is expected of you beyond the tuition payment.

Playing up—Moving up the Competitive Ladder

How do you know when your daughter is ready to take on the demands and rewards of higher levels of competition? How do you know she is ready to "play up," as coaches say? The answer shows up in one of two ways, or maybe both. One clue is that your daughter will ask you if she can do more. You may hear comments like "It's too boring," "It's too easy." Another indication is that the coach will suggest that your child is ready to move up to the next level. Whichever the case, your next step is to have a long talk with your child about what it means to be on a team. After that, schedule a parent-child-coach conference. As a private club coach, I always get together with the child and her parents to answer questions and uncover any hidden issues. Commonly, the next step is to invite the child to team practice and agree on a trial period, after which there will be another family conference. This of course varies from sport to sport, so talk to parents in your neighborhood or to the program directors so you know what to expect. Even after the trial period, there's still the experience of the first competition to anticipate. There's nothing worse than driving home from a meet with a crying child who finds out that competition is not what she thought it would be.

Playing up means your daughter can remain in community recreation programs and advance to traveling leagues; she may leave the community recreation center or her high school team and enter club programs with rigorous competitive schedules. Here are two stories that reflect two kinds of competitive experiences. One is a success story, the other is one of disappointment. Both describe reality.

In junior high I was very shy and never very competitive. But all my friends were trying out for the high school basketball team and they wanted me to join them. So I did, and I ended up making the team because I was tall and could run. Once I got on the team, it was really my coach who got me interested in basketball. She was always there for me, encouraging me a lot since I didn't know anything. She was very concerned on a personal level with all the girls.

Club basketball was a whole new story. The coach was very demanding, and it was not what I was used to. He yelled at us to get us going. He challenged us to step it up to the next level. At the end of every practice we would get in a team huddle and say, "I'm a better player than I was yesterday, but not as good as I will be tomorrow." He stressed individual improvement on a daily basis. That was new to me because I was new to basketball. Just to think that I could get better on a daily basis was really encouraging to me.

—Heidi, 15, basketball player

One of the reasons I tried out for high school cheerleading was to have fun. When I got to be a member of the varsity squad, practice was completely different from what I saw as an outsider just watching. Nobody got along very well, and the girls were very critical of each other. I couldn't understand why everyone wasn't just helping each other. For them every-thing was about competing. I used to think, What does it matter if you get first place if you can't get along with any-one? *I used to go home crying and tell my mom I didn't want to do it anymore. Eventually I had my mom call the coach for me. As soon as the phone call was made, I felt relieved but was left with very bitter feelings. I knew I was a winner for quitting because in my own way, I was able to get my life back and not put myself through the pain anymore.*

—Cheryl, 16, high school freshman

The moral of the first story:

- Girls have to want to compete, with themselves and against oth-ers. At the high school and certainly the club level, a fair amount of tough-mindedness is required. This athlete was able to work past the demands of the coach, because he was supportive.

Of the second story:

- Teammates have a huge influence on one's enjoyment of the ac-tivity. The basketball player could rely on her teammates to bring her through the tough times, but the cheerleader could rely only on backbiting from the other girls on her team. Had her team-mates been on "her side," she might have enjoyed the experience more.

The transitions in each of these cases may have been a little smoother if each athlete had gone to a practice before they tried out for the program. Most important, your daughter has to handle her own dilemmas. These may be tough words for some parents to read, but this is important to prepare teens for adult years.

Girls on Boys' Teams

Ten years ago the issue of girls being on boys' teams did not exist. Today expanded opportunities for girls make this situation a possibility. Depending on whom you talk to, you will get different answers. Most medical doctors agree that when puberty arrives, physical differences in strength and size between girls and boys are significant. These differences become apparent in team sports in particular. Physical educators who have to deal with student athletes are usually very aware of the need to separate the sexes on a day-to-day basis.

STRENGTH IS ESSENTIAL

When tryouts are held, girls will be expected to pass the same fitness and skill tests as the boys. The best thing a girl can do to help herself be ready is to be very strong. For girls this means improving upper body strength. If your daughter sticks with the basics like chin-ups and push-ups, that will be a large step in the right direction. Strength training for young athletes is a relatively new field, but the use of rubber tubing is getting more and more popular. Consult aerobics or fitness professionals for specific exercises. Always get recommendations, and evaluate professionals before you start something new. The goal of strength training is not to bulk up, but to have the strength necessary to handle the demands of a particular sport.

BE OPEN TO THE BENEFITS

During the interviews that I had with female athletes and their parents, and by reading news stories regarding girls playing on boys' teams, I found positive comments. Girls who grew up playing sports with boys seemed to be very confident. Girls expressed that the interaction made them more competitive. So if your daughter wants to be more competitive, this is one way to approach it.

Here is one adult athlete's experience with coed sports.

As a parent coach now, I look back to when I was elementary school age and I got to play with the boys. They would pick me to play with them because I had the skills. I got to play basketball with the boys because I got started early. The combination of an early start and playing with boys gave me a great start. And eventually I ended up playing college basketball. With the boys it is very competitive. Maybe the boys could outrun me, but I could shoot baskets.

—D.J., parent-coach

Parenting the Competitive Athlete

What do you want for your daughter? This is an important question to ask yourself when approaching competitive sports. Be honest with yourself. Is it important that she be on a winning team? Is it important that she have a coach who will really push her? Is it possible you're pushing your daughter into a program she never wanted to be in from the beginning? As a parent, you must be able to separate your sports feelings from your parental feelings. In other words, the message to your daughter must be your unconditional support no matter how much progress she makes. When your daughter experiences an individual or team loss, you will need to stress her efforts, to help her discover what she did well and has learned out of the process. There will be times when you feel your daughter isn't going anywhere. Take into consideration that this may be a period of time when her skills need to mature. You've got to encourage your daughter to keep going at her own pace and achieve. This is especially true during growth spurts, where there may be dramatic body changes. Equally important is to help your daughter learn to handle tension in a productive way. We are all different in how we handle tension. Some girls thrive on the tension of competition. Some find the tension inhibiting. The more confident a girl feels about her skills, the more likely she is to be successful. Your job is to help her remain calm, make sure she gets to warm-ups on time, prepare her clothing, and be there to listen—not to discuss game strategy, that's the coach's job.

You will know your daughter doesn't want to play competitive sports if everything seems to be overwhelming for her, if there are suddenly more injuries or accidents than usual, if she's crying in the car, or if she frequently says, "I want to spend more time with my friends." Coaches don't always see the same girl you see riding home in the car after practice. Talk with the coach if those rides home are getting emotional. And keep listening to your daughter. You are a sounding board.

Investing in Your Daughter

Introducing children to a variety of competitive sports rather than specializing too early has a beneficial long-term impact. Here's a little-known and intriguing fact that supports this position: As the race for international sports domination became more intense several Olympiads ago, Eastern bloc coaches discovered that their standard approach to training had limits. While they were able to produce quick initial results by having young athletes specialize at a young age, the children showed little improvement beyond a certain point. After much scrutiny, the specialization approach was replaced by a thorough and balanced early youth sport and physical education program. Only after children had been through this broad-based kind of training did they begin their specific competitive sports training. Why? Because these sport professionals came to respect the enormous contribution that a broad background in sports provided. The young athletes who engaged in a variety of athletic activities prior to specializing brought with them a range of abilities and problem-solving skills. And their performances topped those of athletes who had focused entirely on one sport. I must say I agree wholeheartedly with this philosophy.

Here are some thoughts from a mother of a gymnast who has learned to take a very balanced approach to her daughter's competitive sport activities. A key point—this mother has come to realize that her daughter is of average talent, has a good but not fierce competitive attitude, but most important has developed life skills that will aid her in the academic, personal, and business world. Not bad.

What do I want my daughter to get out of competitive sports? I didn't have a firm opinion when she started, but everything that is good about my daughter today is due to participation in competitive sports. She's self-disciplined, self-confident, and focused, and she doesn't need a lot of direction. Give her a task and she can complete the assignment. Also, sports has become such an awesome environment to build social skills. She has learned to speak out when she has to and can be quiet when it is important. She knows when it is time to work and time to have fun. She even carries out assignments at home without supervision. I see that she has a lot of stick-to-it-iveness, knowing that anything that has to be learned takes repetition. Her confidence has grown, and that helps, especially since she is a small person. She's found what she's good at. If she feels like she is attaining her goals, that's OK with me.

You can push your daughter, but if she just becomes defeated, you've pushed too far. Some kids thrive under being pushed, and their parents want to keep the pressure on. This works when a child is really competitive. It's rare, though, but it's best if one parent keeps balanced and does not push.

—Sherry, mother of two girls

Using Player-Friendly Language

6

When I first started to pay serious attention to how I talked to athletes I was coaching, I was startled by what I was hearing myself say to children. I had just finished college, and I didn't hold back anything when I was giving instruction. "Where's your drive? Your attention to detail? Your passion?" I asked them routinely. Looking back to the start of my teaching career, I realize I was fortunate not to have been fired by my employers.

Adults who coach kids are, in a sense, among the most powerful people on the planet. Whether professionals or parent volunteers, they have the potential to catapult star athletes toward performances that will enthrall thousands. They can develop skills and attitudes that'll last a lifetime. Or . . . they can injure the ego in such a harmful way that the athlete has second thoughts about keeping sports in her life.

Whichever the case, coaches or parent coaches almost always mean well. But sometimes they forget they're working with unseasoned emotions as well as unseasoned bodies and that young people need pep talks, not bullying. The difference between training that builds up and training that tears down is mostly in the parent's or coach's vocabulary.

Unfortunately, the most visible role models in sports are the professionals we watch on television. There, million-dollar-a-year players accept verbal abuse from million-dollar-a-year coaches, or vice versa, all in the name of fame and glory. But those are accomplished adults, and even some of them don't accept harsh treatment very well.

In this chapter I'll suggest ideas for evaluating what you say and how you say it as you work with girls on a team or at home. You'll be supplied with specific ways to turn your words into powerful tools of motivation and inspiration, whether you're a parent or a coach. You'll also learn how to help girls become aware of and possibly eliminate some of their own unproductive statements that may regularly show up during practice. My goal is to help you take the negative emotions out of communication, and substitute a calmer, more supportive, and effective approach.

Training in sports is hard work. I want to remind you in the sincerest way that athletes need respect for their efforts.

Start Listening to Yourself

Chances are that if you're volunteering to coach in your community, you have some background in the sport you want to instruct. Perhaps you're not a coach, but a parent who has only the best intentions of helping your daughter with her sports skills. Even if you know how to teach the specific skills, you may be at a disadvantage if you don't know how to teach using player-friendly language. Your communication skills should be equal to or better than your sport knowledge. When girls leave practice, they want to go away with two feelings—happiness and a reasonable sense of accomplishment. For them to do that requires that your voice and your attitude be on their side. This may take huge amounts of self-control on your part. You'll truly help girls make breakthroughs when you can reach into their minds and their hearts. This is a tall order, and having communication skills in place to make this happen takes time and practice. Begin by taking an honest look at what you say and decide if you're truly committed to giving girls one of the best experiences of their lives. Then, changing the way you express yourself will come more easily.

Here's one fairly typical situation. If you are a coach, picture yourself at practice getting ready for a big upcoming tournament that will qualify your athletes to go to the next level. The girls seem to have forgotten the strategies that will help them score as a team. You can't get across the gym or the field fast enough to let them have a piece of your mind. They see you building up a head of steam. Your players feel terrible already because they know their game is not coming together. Now they have to listen to a verbal tongue-lashing too.

I have an extremely vivid mental picture of myself doing this to one of my athletes at a national gymnastics competition one year. We were warming up on the floor exercise routines, and my gymnast's tumbling was going from bad to worse. Down to the last few minutes before we had to compete, I went charging over to "fix" the problem. It was hilarious. I went around the mat one way to talk to her, she went the other. This cat-and-mouse game went on for a couple of minutes until she could no longer avoid me. I fixed the problem all right, just not the right one—me.

Do you ever listen to yourself using negative phrases? Unfortunately, I have heard many coaches using them too many times. Ask yourself . . .

DO THESE NEGATIVE COMMENTS COME OUT OF MY MOUTH?
"You did it wrong again."
"What's the matter with you?"
"I told you to do it till you get it right."
"Are you deaf? Didn't you hear what I said?"
"You're running like you have a piano on your back."

Sadly, such words may be very familiar to many girls. These are among the most common phrases used to express irritation by novice or unthinking coaches and parents. And they hurt. I once knew a ten-year-old with a passion for soccer who spent more time on the bench than on the field. Her skill level was so low that she couldn't be depended upon to receive the ball or return a kick. Her teammates knew she wasn't very good and would appeal to the coach not to let her play in critical games. In agreement, the coach would tell her, "I can't depend on you because you have no clue about what you're doing yet. I'm going to substitute in somebody else." It wasn't very long before the girl quit the team. Fortunately she tried another sport and a new set of teammates who didn't put her down.

This coach may or may not have made the right decision to have her sit out during critical games, but using hurtful words to communicate with an already discouraged child was not the right way to handle the situation. She already knew she wasn't as good as her teammates, but she would have felt much better if the coach had given some thought about her feelings and said something like, "You're getting stronger, and when we play this team next year, perhaps you'll be ready to give it a go," or "I know you've been working on those kicks, and we'll find a spot for you when the time is right." In either case—or in a dozen other ways—the coach would be giving the same message: The child had more work to do before she'd be ready. But by choosing his words more carefully, the coach could have avoided giving her that sinking feeling of failure—and the possibility of turning her off to sports forever.

DO I TAILOR MY COMMENTS TO EACH INDIVIDUAL?
Remember that each girl is different. Some are more sensitive than others. Your child or the girls on your team have different ways of responding to the information you give during training. If you're committed to helping each girl be the best she can be, you're going to have to address each one individually. Some girls can take it when you say, "You're going to have to give a better effort." As a coach, some tough-skinned team members may even argue with you. Others will say nothing because they're the kind who might say ten words in two years. One clue that you're using the wrong verbal strategy is when a girl gets teary eyed and has to go to the bench to calm down. In some cases you had better be ready with some emotional first aid.

HOW DOES A GIRL REACT WHEN I CRITICIZE HER?
The minute you comment on your child or athlete's efforts in a negative way, she will react: she may glare at you or react as if you're talking about not *her* play, but somebody else's. The moment you take time to draw a breath, she'll protest strongly, telling you, *"I'm trying my best."* Notice the reactions your words elicit: Can you see

the exasperation on a youngster's face? Is the overall mood of a team pessimistic at best? If so, you're at a standoff. The greatest sin is to verbally go after one girl in front of the other athletes. The child who is being criticized is embarrassed and will retreat or lash back at you. Believe me, the onlookers will be wondering when they'll be next in the line of fire.

Do I Bring More Than Equipment to Practice?

Every day before you leave the house, as a responsible person, don't you check to see if you've got your watch, your wallet, the keys, and some cash? An even greater sense of responsibility applies when you step out on the field or walk into a gym to coach your teams or bring your daughter to practice. Coaches, in addition to your whistle, clipboard, and equipment, do you bring along your encouraging attitude, your empathy, and your positive vocabulary?

Your words speak louder than you think. If you frequently feel extremely frustrated after a practice, it's likely that your frustration is obvious to the players and parents, too. At your core, you have to be there for your daughter, for your athletes, and not yourself. Girls will accept what you have to offer as a coach or a parent when they understand that you are there for them and accept them as people with feelings.

You need courage to admit that you could be instructing your team or giving your daughter tips in a more positive manner. One of the things that made me question my use of language was that I was losing interest in teaching. I didn't feel particularly great about what I was doing, and I was becoming increasingly bored. It occurred to me that if I was going to continue teaching, it had to be fun for me or it would be awful for the girls. I had to do more than just constantly point out what they were doing wrong.

Then it dawned on me that if I chose to, I could be more than a coach. I could be an educator, a mentor. I realized that many of the delightful, animated girls I had in front of me would probably not be doing cartwheels when they were forty years of age. But if I was doing my job right, they would have the memories of happy times doing cartwheels in the gym in their youth. They would take with them a positive attitude, an approach to problem solving, the habit of persistence. I resolved that whether I had a girl in front of me for five minutes or five years, I would do everything in my power to make a positive impact on her life.

I decided to take a look at what I was saying on a daily basis. Was I offering encouragement? Was I making the girls feel bad because they couldn't do what I wanted them to do in class? Did I create an environment where girls couldn't wait to come back for the next lesson? What kind of feedback was I getting from the parents of my students?

When you're coaching girls and trying to get your daughter on the right track, they want to trust that you won't let them get hurt emotionally; for young women emotional support is key. They want to trust that you want the best for them. Girls should never have to hear rude or foul language. Talk to them as you would want someone to talk to you.

Training Yourself to Use Supportive Language

You've got your work cut out for you teaching children, but it can be less stressful if your principles and procedures are in place. The overriding principle in your approach has to be that girls enjoy themselves as they're learning new skills. The procedures have to do with the basic ways you encourage or stimulate a child so that they believe they have a reasonable chance of accomplishing what you are asking them to do.

Research indicates that 85 percent of athletes will improve their performance if you work with them in a positive manner and give them precise information they can use. Further, it has been shown that girls will respond favorably to praise in contrast to boys, who respond to competitive challenges and extrinsic rewards. Sometimes knowing the right thing to say to inspire and motivate your team members or your daughter requires training on *your* part. This section will offer specific phrases you can use when you're at home, in the gym, or out on the field to replace any verbal habits that are not useful and turn kids off.

BITE YOUR TONGUE BEFORE YOU SPEAK

It takes a while to learn the habit of thinking before you speak. If you feel something negative just has to come out of your mouth, blow hot air, grunt, whistle, do anything but speak. Think carefully about what you want to say before you say it. When you're able to

stay focused on telling players what you want them to do and how
to do it, you'll make the process less emotional and you'll notice a
positive change in how your child and your athletes react.

USE ONE NEW PHRASE A WEEK

As you go through the material in the following pages, you will
find many phrases that you can use to shape the way you talk to
your daughter or the girls on your team. Pick one phrase a week for
a particular situation that you wish to change, and work it into your
speech. When I'm training new coaches, we work on verbal communication as much as sport skill building so that they understand
these are companion skills.

DARE TO DO A DAY WITHOUT "DON'T"

We Americans seem to have an unconscious affinity for negatives.
Watch or listen to advertising. Potential customers are often urged
to make buying decisions through use of the word *don't*. "Don't forget" . . . "Don't be late" . . . "Don't delay."

At work and at home, too, we continually tell people what we
don't want them to do—and hardly ever communicate what we *do*
want them to do. If you think I exaggerate, here's a challenge: Try to
get through a single day without starting a sentence with the word
don't. I dare you! It's tougher than you think. I discovered that sentence patterns are built into us as strongly as any other habit, and
you have to really want to make a change to create a new approach.

When overuse of the word *don't* became clear to me, I resolved
that my first order of business was to eliminate my habit of starting
sentences with "don't." Some months into this decision I began to
realize the enormity of the project I had taken on. The challenge I'd
created for myself was almost as difficult as learning a double somersault. When I felt a "don't" ready to leap off my lips, I had to force
myself to remain silent while I fashioned a sentence that started
with something other than the word *don't*. I had to tell my students
what I wanted them to do, not what I didn't want them to do.

USE "INSTEAD" TO REDIRECT THE ACTION

What a great word. Instead of using "don't," use "instead." Look at
the possibilities for using this word to redirect action during unproductive moments.

- The nonproductive way: Don't run with the ball like that.
The productive way: Instead of running with the ball like that, try this.
- The nonproductive way: Don't swing the racket with the face open.
The productive way: Instead of swinging the racket like this, keep the face like this to get topspin.
- The nonproductive way: You can't kick the ball like that and expect to get a goal.
The productive way: You could kick the ball with the side of your foot instead of the top of your foot.

STRESS SUCCESS

You don't ordinarily find Coaching or Parenting 101 offered at your local educational institutions. So how do you know what to say if you haven't had a good mentor? If your motivation is wanting girls to be successful, start by telling them that. Here are some positive phrases you can use to encourage and motivate your daughter and your athletes:

- If you come to practice wanting to improve, you'll be successful.
- If you straighten your arms, you'll be successful.
- If you keep your eye on the ball, you'll be successful.

Your specific piece of advice can be anything, but I always use the tag line "you'll be successful." This phrase must be used over and over until your players understand that you are on their side and you want them to achieve mutual goals. Most important, you want to build into their spirit the desire to achieve. Eventually your female athletes will accept the climate you're trying to create and they will *ask you* what they need to do to be "successful." When they do that, you have taken a giant leap toward patterning goal-oriented speech—yours as well as theirs.

Take this approach one step further by making long-term suggestions, such as the following:

- If you perform five successful backhands, you can go on to the next level.
- If you make twenty successful shots in a row, I'll let you try something new.

- If you weight-train for two months before the season, your additional strength will be a key factor in your success.
- All you have to do is fifty successful hits in the batting cage and you are done for today.

MAKE ROOM FOR "IMPROVEMENT"

Obviously one of the main aims of coaching is to improve performance. This is where an encouraging approach can be incredibly effective with young girls. Instead of going right to an attack mode, try using phrases such as the following:

- I could see you were trying to make an improvement.
- It looks as if you understand what to do. But maybe your body is moving too fast for your mind to make improvements. Let's slow it down a little and try again.
- I bet you'll improve if you just try . . .
- You seem to have a basic understanding. If you want to improve and have a more advanced understanding, you'll need to pay attention to . . .

SAY GOOD-BYE TO RIGHT AND WRONG

While you can't eliminate a girl's frustration, you can reduce her guilty feelings. Do this by being nonconfrontational and nonjudgmental. It's important to avoid "loaded" words. Instead of describing an action as "good" or "bad," or "right" or "wrong," use words like "correct" or "incorrect."

A typical learner will ask: "What did I do wrong that time?" I usually reply, "You didn't do anything wrong, but what you did was incorrect." This puzzles them mightily. After several months of using this tactic, I found that my routine paid off. Lo and behold, they actually started asking me, "What did I do incorrectly?" (I must admit that I spent a substantial amount of time coaching their vocabulary, too.) When I first heard this from one of my gymnasts, I knew I had made a breakthrough—one of those phenomena teachers pray for. I had changed my way of communicating and changed my students' vocabulary. It never occurred to me that this would happen. Yet there it was, two positive changes for the price of one.

In my own teaching, I have observed that it takes several months to install a success-oriented vocabulary. If you're a coach reading this, it's wise to tell the athletes' parents what it is you are trying to accomplish by your choice of vocabulary. At the very least, they can support you; at best, they can try the same approach at home.

TRY HUMOR

When things are looking pretty discouraging and skills are just not coming together, it's time to lighten up. As a parent, you'll certainly be faced with some time in the car when you need a major mood change. Ask your daughter or your athletes in a kidding way:

- "If we had this on instant replay, how would it look?"
- "We're ready for television, right?"
- "Should we start all over again and pretend this just didn't happen?"
- "What do you mean you can't do that? Even my grandmother knows how to do . . ." (I generally say this when I'm with young elementary school children.)

What humor brings to a situation is the reality that we're all human and we all make mistakes. Children need to be encouraged not to take things too seriously. And I want to persuade *you* not to take things so seriously. Parents, coaches—remember our girls should be doing things for themselves, not us. There's plenty of time for intensity as girls grow into young adults. This does not mean they shouldn't pay attention to detail, but when girls are making the effort to stay active and healthy, why increase their chances of developing high blood pressure?

Encouragement Breeds Success

Here are some suggestions for creating a more supportive and success-oriented environment for your children and athletes. Never underestimate the power of an encouraging word. Girls especially are motivated by pleasing their teachers. The most enjoyed and admired adults are the ones who make girls feel good about themselves and motivate them to bring out the best they have to give.

GET A HANDLE ON WHAT'S WORKING

Identify any step in the right direction. Find something your child or athlete is doing right, however small it might be, and then build on that. It's human nature for hope to inspire movement and for movement to eventually bring progress. Play to this tendency by using phrases such as these:

- I saw you make a positive change.
- You were really trying your best today. (Or, That's the best I've ever seen you do.)
- Wow! Remember three weeks ago when you didn't know how to do that?

BE ENTHUSIASTIC ABOUT REACHING GOALS

To create the desire to achieve, you need to keep your athletes' or your child's (and your own) enthusiasm sky-high. Again, your words and your tone of voice will be the key. Try phrases like these:

- You are so close to hitting the ball every time, it's unbelievable.
- If you could just fix this one little thing, you'd love it.
- You're going to really enjoy knowing you can do that any time you want.
- You will be so proud of yourself when you get your first goal.

Another phrase I use frequently is "Be a go-getter, not a giver-upper." Sounds corny, but it works. Anyone can give up, I remind them, but it takes someone special to hang on and work things out.

ACKNOWLEDGE WHEN A GIRL "GETS IT"

Accept that understanding happens on the inside before it happens on the outside. "Getting it" precedes doing it. When your daughter or one of your athletes says, "I get it," share in their enthusiasm. Accept that getting a new understanding of a concept is progress. If I could turn this paragraph into a flashing light, I'd do it because this idea is critical. Letting girls know that you recognize they've made a jump in the learning process—regardless of how well they're able to put that understanding into action—reinforces their learning. Remember, breakthroughs don't always show up immediately in the form of a physical change. It takes time for muscles to develop new patterns, and even more time for muscle memory to take effect.

- Last week when we worked on this, you didn't understand. Today you're talking like you get it.

- I can tell by the questions you're asking that you're getting the idea.

TAKING THE "FAIL" OUT OF FAILURE

If, despite your and her best efforts, your young athlete is frustrated by lack of success, move on to something else and come back later to the skill she's having trouble with. When people are on a downhill slide, they tend to stay in the groove of the unwanted habit. Meanwhile, remain nonjudgmental, stay calm, acknowledge that you see she is stumped, and offer loads of encouragement. Let her know you're not saying things just to boost self-esteem, but to keep her interest level high and maintain her faith in herself.

- Maybe we need to go back to some fundamentals.
- If you don't see me getting upset, there's nothing for you to get upset about.
- I can see you're having a hard time. Back off for a few minutes.

PRAISE, THEN MAKE SUGGESTIONS

Happily, you can offer constructive criticism and still let your child or the athlete know you recognize her effort. I often start my comments with a positive statement, then address the area that needs to be changed or developed. For example:

- Cindy, you did a terrific job of spiking that ball. Now we just need to fix your strategy of where to place it.
- I can see you've got the idea of how to swing the racket. Next, let's get control of your position so your swing can be stronger.
- You had sensational power in that kick. It's time to really focus on your technique so the ball will go where you want it to go.

When you make corrections or ask for changes, make sure that you address only one area at a time. It's nearly impossible to change two bad habits simultaneously.

Helping Girls Talk Friendly to Themselves

Part of using player-friendly language is to help girls learn to talk to themselves in a friendly way. By helping your daughter or your athletes change the way they talk about themselves, it helps them change the way they look at themselves, and maintaining a positive self-image is key to young girls. It's a tough road to improving performance when all a girl can say about herself is, "I'm terrible," or, "I can't do it right," or, "I'm never going to get this." That's the time you've got to hop in and equip the player to change *her* vocabulary. As soon as I hear those kinds of comments, I say, "First of all, you're not terrible, and second, I see you're having a tough time." It's no different from helping a child who's lost a pet. First, recognize the pain; then move down the healing path.

All champions develop the ability to look at a situation, analyze it, make a new plan, and put it into action. They learn that it is a waste of time and energy to focus on limiting self-talk. To make girls champions in their own way, we've got to help them get rid of disabling thoughts by redirecting their language. Depending on the age, level, and sensitivity of the girl I'm working with, I use anything from tender loving care to tough love to reshape language thoughts.

There are times when girls say the most maddening things. You may find yourself using every bit of patience you can muster just trying to stay calm. What follows is a typical list of the expressions girls use during training and some recommendations on how to deal with their language patterns.

"I CAN'T"

Your response:

- Say, "I believe you," and send the player back to the end of the line or to the bench. The athlete eventually works her way up to the front of the line again. I again ask her to attempt the skill, always letting her know I will help. If she still says, "I can't," she gets the same response from me. Eventually the student tires of this game and asks for help. Meanwhile I instruct the girl to say, "I don't know how to do that," instead of, "I can't." It's important that you accept that a team member or student may not know how right now—but let her know that you'll help her learn.
- What do you think is holding you back?
- Do you feel like there's something you don't understand?

"THAT'S NOT FAIR"

Your response (stay calm):

- That may be true. What do you think is fair?
- Not true. (Then explain why.)
- If you have a group issue (instead of a personal issue), work on getting consensus from the group.

"THAT'S TOO HARD"

Your response:

- You're right, it is hard. But I'll do everything I can to help you make it happen.
- That means we haven't worked up to that level yet. When you make improvements, you probably won't say that.
- Have you tried that yet? Let me help you. I want you to be successful.
- I felt that way too when someone asked me to do that for the first time.

"I DON'T CARE"

Your response:

- Are you getting pressure from home to do this?
- Is there something bothering you? (Take her off to the side so that you can talk about it.)
- Is there someone on the squad [in the class] you're not getting along with?

"I DON'T WANT TO DO THAT"

Your response:

- I hear you don't want to do that, but does that mean you're tired, embarrassed, or scared?
- I know there are times when you just don't want to do it. Sometimes you need to do it for your teammates.
- This is a necessary skill to make the whole thing happen. If you choose not to learn this, you may not be ready to play/travel with the team.

• I want you to be successful, and I'm sure you do, too. Did we move you up a level too fast?

"I'M AFRAID"

Some children are just plain afraid to take chances, while others have a very high tolerance for risk. Age seems to have little to do with this. I've seen five-year-olds climb a twenty-foot rope with little hesitation while some older kids hold back. You can only guess what girls are thinking, so let me share with you some strategies to help deal with fear.

• Choose your bravest or most enthusiastic players to go first on any new activity. That can give courage to the more fearful ones.
• Peers frequently have more influence than the coach. If you've got a particularly timid student who's slowing down the whole group's progress, try burying your pride and backing off. You may be pleasantly surprised at the change that occurs in your absence. Give the peer process a chance to work.
• Help the child picture the balance between risk and reward. You can help them see why they sometimes need to be bold. For example, you might say: "When you learn this, you'll have reached your goal of going to the advanced level."
• Many times fear arises because fundamental skills have not been solidly learned.

Your vocabulary in dealing with risk and fear should vary depending on the ages of the child involved. Over the years nothing has become clearer to me than the fact that you've got to deal with this issue on a case-by-case basis. Here's the kind of talk I've found useful in helping girls over the fear hurdles:

APPROACH FOR AGES THREE TO SIX:
• I know this is a little scary. But I'll be right here to help you. (If they remain frightened, back off and reintroduce the skill later.)

APPROACH FOR AGES SIX TO NINE:
• I can see that you're scared. Why don't you go do [another activity] and then come back?

- Are you afraid of getting hurt? Tell me your feelings and I'll try to help you with them.
- Let's think for a moment: What will happen to you if you do this?
- Watch how I help [name] get through this.

APPROACH FOR AGES NINE TO TWELVE:
- Let's back up. Is there something you don't understand, some part I can help you with?
- If you're scared, that may be your body's way of telling you you're not quite ready.
- What do you think we should do?
- How can I help you get through this?
- What's the worst possible thing that could happen?

Use Your Words to Inspire Your Girls

Deciding to change the way I talked to my athletes made a huge difference in the way I felt about myself as a coach. I found out that if you keep communicating with girls in a way that lets them know you're on their side, they'll continue to come back to your program. I know some coaches don't believe that communication goes beyond the explanation of strategies and skill development. But no team can last without some sense of mutual respect, a goal that's eagerly pursued, and some inspiration.

This chapter has been all about communication. By using the strategies we've discussed in this chapter, you'll be creating an environment where you help girls challenge themselves to learn and grow. When you leave behind negative ways of training athletes, you'll serve them in a way that brings out the best in them and rewards them according to their accomplishments. You'll make it fun for yourself and fun for your players. What more can you ask?

Exercise the Mind Along with the Muscles

7

What do you want your daughter to get out of playing sports? Believe it or not, parents usually answer with a statement that has more to do with personal growth than athletic skills: "I wish my daughter wouldn't give up so easily, I want her to be able to stick with an activity." "I hope my daughter will become a little more self-disciplined." "I wish my daughter wouldn't be so shy, that she would be more assertive." "My daughter drives me crazy with the way she wastes time, I wish she would learn to get on a schedule." The personal qualities that are important to parents and are lifelong assets to a person are grown through sports participation in the day-to-day, practice-to-practice, game-to-game schedule. Girls are stimulated to exercise their minds by learning to take risks, by continuously making decisions, by emphasizing self-discipline, by budgeting time, and by having to cope with losses. This is the greatest opportunity outside of the home to help girls cultivate personal skills that they can use on and off the playing field. Whether girls are running up and down a soccer field or shooting hoops, they can frequently view sports as a struggle between themselves and their rivals. Yet the real task before parents and coaches is not to emphasize winning, but to help girls realize that the actual battle is within themselves.

I'm not going to say that sports builds character. I will tell you up front that there is precious little definitive research regarding sports and the moral development of athletes, and expert opinions vary widely. What I can say is that sports can help develop personal skills if parents and coaches choose to go beyond teaching just athletic skills. The environment in which sports take place is *the* critical factor. When a coach develops a *mature* coaching philosophy, his or her underlying goal is to instill productive personal habits (not just something you do, but something you embody)—so that girls can say to themselves, "I am self-disciplined, I can make decisions quickly"— then young athletes are really exercising their minds along with their muscles. Ultimately, just as a good swing with a tennis racket becomes second nature, *essential personal skills can become automatic.* The longer athletes participate in sports, the more they learn physically *and* mentally.

Decision Making

Decision making is a daily exercise in the home, at work, or while playing sports. The ability to make quick decisions and follow through is often what differentiates the person who is great from the person who just does well, whether on the playing field or in a professional field. The greatest gift we can give our daughters is the ability to know the difference between goal-oriented and tension-relieving decisions. A tension-relieving decision provides only immediate relief from a problem without considering the long-range implications. A goal-oriented decision is one that calls for planning and a step-by-step approach.

Begin with Cooperative Decision Making

Developing decision making in sports should begin in nonpressure situations. First teach the progressions of learning various skills, then let the athlete help decide the course of the training by giving input about what skills need the most improvement. Because people are more likely to cooperate in activities they help to plan, it's important to hear their opinions. Athletes also feel they are part of the decision-making process if a coach takes time to ask either an individual or the team as a whole, "What do you think you need to work on in these next few practices to get ready for our first competition?" Best of all, being part of the process shows girls how to take into account specific factors, how to weigh them, and how to evaluate the potential results.

Build the Skill of Thinking on Your Feet

Thinking on your feet in a real situation is another decision-making skill playing sports helps to develop. Many actions in sports are reflex reactions, but decisions such as where to kick, hit, or throw a ball require some strategic thinking on the move. One of the great benefits of being involved in physical activity is that it constantly forces girls to make decisions involving safety or strategy, with barely a moment's notice. During any given practice, girls are called upon to make dozens of snap decisions. Having to deal with the unknown regularly helps girls learn to make the best of what comes their way. As one student said in an interview, "You can plan all you want in your life, but things can change. The point is, how will you react under pressure?" The outcome of these choices is usually neither divine nor disastrous, but somewhere in between, where learning can occur.

Having the ability to deal with a situation on the spot is a tremendous asset. As a small-business owner since the age of twenty-four, I have had many opportunities to interview potential employees. One of the key things that I look for is the ability to think on your feet. Since I don't have time to do my job and somebody else's, I look for a person who has sound judgment, who can make a decision and move forward. Making effective decisions and making them quickly is a useful and highly regarded skill. This personal skill is a dominant trait of leaders. While not everyone is cut out for leadership, people can certainly lead more functional lives without being subject to decisions by others that are not in their own best interests.

Apply Problem-Solving Methods

In order to train girls to think for themselves and solve problems, ask questions instead of giving commands. A very simple way to teach children to solve their own problems is a method used by academic teachers to great success. Try this approach for young elementary school children: Ask your daughter or the girls on the team an "either/or" question with the desired answer in the question.

"When you missed hitting the ball, were you looking at it or looking someplace else?" I suggest supplying choices and asking the students to choose the response they think is correct. This makes training a mental as well as a physical exercise.

When posing more complicated questions, give the players enough time to think of an answer. Make sure to word your question so that the players can give a short answer. When you get a response that isn't correct, keep refining the question you are asking. To simply ask if there are any questions or if everyone understands can produce blank faces, especially in younger children. Whenever girls give the correct answer, say something like "Now you're getting it." *Always* give feedback.

For older elementary school girls, you can ask more open-ended questions, provided you have educated them along the way to know what the proper technique is for a particular skill. For example, you might ask, "Was that done correctly?" When I am teaching students to do a cartwheel using a demonstrator, I call attention first to what the arms are doing and then the legs. I continue using a player for a demonstration several times, and then I ask for observations about individual aspects of the skill. For any age group, however, I use the word *situation* instead of *problem*. I never ask the girls what the problem is; instead I ask them what they observed in that particular situation, because for girls the word *problem* carries some connotations that illicit a defensive reaction. The problem becomes a personal confrontation, and girl athletes lose sight of the situation at hand. The word *situation* takes the sting out of a coaching statement and helps the girls stay focused. Boys tend to be desensitized to the word problem and accept that form of address.

Also, be sure to ask more than one child for the answer to a question before you tell them what the correct answer is. This gives more players the opportunity to exercise their minds. Train your players to observe themselves in action by asking questions like "Did you see your kick go sideways or straight ahead? What would be the best thing to do next time?" I find that this questioning technique requires a great deal of patience. The girls can get frustrated because you won't give them the answer, but hang in there. This method teaches them to observe, come up with working concept, and most critically, deal with a situation when you are not there.

Help Girls to Evaluate Their Own Progress

Getting young athletes to think about their progress is an important long-term process. For a girl to be aware of how she's performing at any given time requires practice in self-evaluation. Essentially your goal is to get each of them to make corrections in the areas that need changes. Always have girls start with what they think they are doing correctly, then identify the areas that need improvement. Design your questions so that the girl's answers will be fairly short. Here are some simple ones to try:

- Did you see what happened when you . . . ?
- Did that work when you tried it that way?
- What would happen if you . . . ?
- Can anyone be helpful to Anna and give her a suggestion on what to do?

Another approach involves having the girls keep a journal. They can write down two or three things they think need improvement. That forces them to focus on building skills in areas of weakness. Usually this method leads to improvement because players are evaluating their own stumbling blocks. If you think journals are not the way to go, try asking, "What do you think we need to work on?" at the beginning and end of each practice—and listen to what each girl has to say. Sometimes you will be in a team meeting with girls, or in a parent-child discussion, and a girl will say, "I think the problem is . . ." As one coach said, at least she's thinking, even if her ideas weren't exactly on target.

Focus on the Age Group

Remember to adapt a series of questions for the particular age group you're working with. Obviously a four-year-old will require a different set of self-evaluation cues from that for a preteen.

Ages Two to Six

Focus on only two choices, the correct way or the incorrect way. Ask them:

- Was that safe or dangerous?
- Should you swing the bat higher or lower?
- Did that look okay or not okay?

AGES SIX TO NINE

During this period, you can train girls to observe themselves and others. For example:

- I want you to watch Jackie's arms. When she did that, was it helpful?
- How is Debbie going to make that work?
- What do you think happened that time?

AGES NINE TO TWELVE

The girls are now mature enough that you can start to place the burden of learning on them. For instance:

- If you want to do A-B-C, what do you have to do first?
- Could you feel your leg straightening out when you wanted to keep it bent?
- What would you like to accomplish this time that you didn't do last time?

Good Sportswomanship

Teaching a child to be a good sport begins with placing her in an age-appropriate program. If she's in over her head, all she will learn is frustration instead of how to deal with occasional setbacks. If you are thinking of signing your daughter up for a competitive program, also get ready to have a family discussion about the ups and downs of participation. Deciding what to say can be based on the interactive play you have already observed as your daughter romps with her friends. Does she get upset if things don't go her way? Does she cry or just pout? In other words, can she handle the "you win some, you lose some" philosophy?

Once your daughter joins a program, let her know that if she's enjoying herself, trying hard, and improving her skills, she's on track as far as you're concerned. Also, no surprise here, emphasize that losing graciously is part of playing sports. It's normal for her to feel disappointed when her team loses, but talk to her about shaking it off and looking forward to the next game. I tell my athletes they always have another chance to play better. You might ask your daughter to think about what she did *right* during the game and what kinds of skills she can practice for next time.

Is Your Daughter Picking up Bleacher Creature Habits?

Too many parents forget that children learn social behavior from their moms and dads. Be a good example when it comes to sportsman/womanship. If you're up there in the bleachers yelling obnoxiously at the referee or at a coach because you feel a wrong call was made, will your daughter learn to be a good sport? One successful Little League program I read about had a rule regarding parents making loud, offensive comments during a game. The first time a parent made such a comment, he or she got a warning. If it happened again, the child of the offending parent would be suspended for two games. This rule worked beautifully, making the bleachers a setting for encouragement rather than a roost for rowdy parents.

Try these strategies during the competitive season to help your daughter stay on balance emotionally. And remember the positive vocabulary discussed in the last chapter.

- Keep pregame pressure in perspective. It's ridiculous to impose a professional tone on recreational games. Comments about winning the league game can intimidate an already tense child.
- Teach your daughter to be a gracious winner. It's not sportswomanlike to make the losing team feel bad by making belittling comments.
- Try offering little rewards. If your daughter shows a good attitude three games in a row, you will take her out to lunch at her favorite spot.
- Steer her efforts and thoughts toward building the skills she'll need to be a winner. If you are watching a game together, you could point out the skills that contribute to winning.
- Have clear consequences for losing your temper. Ask your daughter what her opinion is about someone who is out of control. When watching other athletes, see if you can point out to your daughter what a player did to keep her cool.
- Help her accept responsibility for team performance instead of blaming others.

Coping with Not Making the Team

Here is an anonymous story that I found on the Internet written by the mother of a high school basketball player. As she watched her daughter travel down the rocky road of competition, this mother discovered that her daughter was a true superstar when it came to persevering and learning to cope. The mom admitted that her own view was colored by the fact that she had never played sports herself. But she slowly began to realize that her daughter's love of basketball was a profound expression of who she was. The game became much more than a hobby for her daughter. Here is that mother's story:

Watching my daughter practice and noticing how she responded to the coach's praise was an eye-opener. Her inner drive showed up in a way that made me understand I was witnessing something terrific happen in terms of my daughter's growth. I knew she realized that her skills were only good enough to be on a feeder team. But instead of spending her savings on a much desired stereo, she decided to sign up for special training at an athletic club so that she could improve her skills. I finally understood that this was someone who believed that hard work would help her meet her goal—making the high school team.

Team tryouts were agonizing, extending over a period of days. Every practice another girl was cut from the group of candidates. Yet when the day of the first game arrived, in marched my jubilant daughter in her new sweatsuit. I was stunned and knew that no matter how much or how little my daughter played, she was a winner. What a life lesson: Work hard and meet your goal. It couldn't have been planned better. But incredibly, when the first game was over, she was cut. After a tearful session with me at home, she resigned herself to go back to the lower feeder team, knowing that this was just another bridge to be crossed, not a river without a bridge. She kept an eye to the future when she could attend a college and play with a team that was a better match for her. Until then she would continue improving her skills during her senior year. It was simply a matter of loving the game and being able to play.

Wouldn't you love to have a daughter like that?

There are no magic words to get athletes through major emotional crises. Besides providing unconditional support, here are some positive thoughts to help your daughter deal with emotional setbacks.

- What do you think you could do differently to prepare for next time?
- Are there other factors you don't know about that might have caused your not making the team?
- You are an asset to any team. Maybe it's the team's loss in not having you.
- This is not who you are, it's just what you do.

Coping with Competitive Losses and Poor Performance

It's not easy to deal with a tearful daughter whose team has just lost the tenth out of ten games in a row or who struck out every time up a bat. All you want to do is hug and reassure her that she did her best and that there's always another chance. As you drive her home and listen to her sobs, all you can do is grip the steering wheel with grieving hands. Here are some guidelines to steer you through the rough waters of defeat:

- Let your daughter spend some quiet time by herself after a difficult game. This will give her time to calm down before you try to talk to her.
- Find something that went *right* during the game and mention it.
- Ask if your daughter felt good about her performance.
- Prevent your daughter from speaking unkindly to or about another teammate who may have had a bad performance. Get her to think about how this player feels: "Don't you think Cindy feels awful?" In a similar vein, never allow your daughter to put down the other team just because team won. Make it clear that her team had a better game that day.
- Bring your daughter's attention to any incorrect referee calls that went in her favor.
- Help her to understand that the officials are doing the best they can. Yelling at a referee won't get that person to change his or her mind.

- Convince her that playing her hardest weighs in as success.
- Find out if your daughter learned anything new that she can use the next time she plays.
- Make sure that your daughter's expectations of herself are realistic. Help her to understand that even the pros have bad days.
- Keep in mind that a parent's reaction to losing is not wasted on a child. Keep your own emotions in check so that your daughter can never point you out as a bad example.
- Give your unconditional love.
- Make sure your daughter understands that recreational sports are not her only focus.

Risk Taking and Mental Toughness

If I had a nickel for every time I've heard a child say, "I can't," I would be a wealthy woman. Negative patterns are learned early in life, as any preschool teacher can tell you. According to author/speaker Brian Tracy, "Every child comes into the world with only two fears: One is fear of falling; the other is fear of loud noises." Since children are born fearless, they have to be taught what to be afraid of. What have your children heard you say? "Don't go skateboarding, you'll get hurt. Don't climb that tree, you'll fall. Hockey's too rough for girls." Instead of forbidding your daughter to try potentially risky activities, I suggest that you evaluate them carefully and see if your daughter can handle them, perhaps with your guidance at first. Show your daughter how to deal with things she hasn't tried so that she won't get hurt. After all, life is all about facing challenges.

Growing a gutsy girl is not for the weak willed. You need to help girls stand up for themselves by standing up to your own fears as a parent or a coach, even if this isn't part of her nature. You may even gain some nerve yourself. Developing new, risk-taking habits starts by changing old ones.

One habit too many parents fall into is trying to rescue their children before they have had the chance to try something on their own. If the parents step into a situation too early and too many times, girls will not be tested in a rigorous way, and they won't know if they can meet new goals. Prevent your daughters from living with rationalizations, such as "I could never do that." Here are the basic concerns that fuel their fears:

- Fear of failure: This is the greatest fear of all. To combat this fear, you need to teach girls that failure is part of learning—and that if we didn't fail, we'd never acquire advanced skills and new ways of doing things.
- Fear of criticism: Critiquing a player without having them feel threatened can be accomplished when you use player-friendly language. We just finished a whole chapter on how you can make that work, so flip back to it if you need to. However, do try to get a sense if there is something going on beyond the normal reactions. As a coach, you may need to talk with the parents if you suspect something more than the usual concerns is going on.
- Fear of what other players will think: Whether your daughter is in individual or team sports, not performing her best and having "everybody watch me" can be humiliating on and off the field. As one of my athletes said to me of her playing ability, "That's all they thought I could do," even though she knew she had more to offer. Tell your daughter that she's not alone. You might even recount some of your own experiences to let her know you've been there and you know how it feels.

Emotional Risk

The only way anyone can realize his or her full potential is to take risks. Starting at the early elementary school age, you need to help girls make the connection between reaching goals and taking risks. Start by setting little goals with little risk. The goals may not be met, but the point is to establish a pattern of attempting new behavior or new activities. Regularly talking about risk and reward will eventually condition your daughter to think in these terms automatically. You have to keep saying, "If you don't try, you'll never know if you could have done it."

Efforts made by parents and coaches to manage emotional risk really can pay off when they are sincere and unwavering. Witness the testimony of a high school student who was able to stabilize her feelings with regard to the reward-risk concept:

> *After failing twice before to make the team, I had just come back from my third year of attempting to earn a place on the high school varsity show cheer team. I knew I was better than many of the other girls trying out. All year long I had been*

practicing my tumbling skills and making my jumps higher. I felt good about what I had done. I just wanted to prove the coaches and other girls wrong. But in the back of my head I felt the risk I was taking because the past two years I had tried and not made the team. I had been crushed every time I didn't make it. But I knew I would keep trying because I desperately wanted to make the team.

The next morning, the list of girls who made the squad was posted outside the girls' locker room. My name was not there. I went to talk to the coach to find out what went wrong. Although I didn't think I had been evaluated fairly, having been in sports for several years gave me the inner strength to talk to the coach. At least I tried. When I started sports I was shy, but I built up my confidence and my belief in myself because my gymnastics coach outside of the high school gave me confidence to go on.

—Kelly, 15, high school senior

Let Her Be the One to Communicate with the Coach

Perhaps you can relate to this scenario: Your ten-year-old daughter is not one of the stars players on the team, but she makes some progress and seems to enjoy participating. Halfway through the season, however, she's on the bench more often than on the field—and now she's ready to bail out. She's so upset about her lowly status that she breaks down in tears every time you suggest that she talk to her coach. What's the right thing to do? Do you call the coach for her? Do you encourage her to talk to the coach at the next practice? When you've got a sobbing child in front of you, the choice can be an emotional one.

Communication skills come into play in nearly everything we do, and playing sports is no exception. You'll be helping your daughter learn how to express her thoughts and feelings if you let *her* try to handle any problems that may arise between her and her coach. Depending on her age, you may need to accompany her when she approaches the adult in question; but try not to be too quick to rescue her. Standing up for herself and voicing her concerns are skills all young women need to learn. How can you help? You can have her practice with you what she'll say to the coach—so that she'll be prepared to face an adult. Perhaps even writing something down might help. And you can certainly let her know that you support her. With a younger child, you might even want to go with her and say to the coach, "[Name] has something she would like to talk to you about." Whatever happens, make sure that you control your own emotions, and intervene only if the situation turns sour.

PHYSICAL RISK

One of the greatest challenges girls have to deal with in life is learning to face fear of injury. That's not to say that boys don't have these concerns as well. When girls learn how to manage their bodies in a variety of challenging situations, they can face the possibility of injury with less fear. Little by little they add more daring feats to their collection of skills. Through attempting *controlled* risks repeatedly, people who take chances with their bodies learn to become mentally tough. You are ultimately responsible for your child's safety, and you will have to be clear about when to let go of *your* inhibitions and when to place limits on your daughter. The U.S. Naval Academy, now boasting an 11 percent female population, requires women to participate in sports every semester and recently has added boxing and wrestling to the curriculum. One female cadet, Jamie Humphrey, says, "Direct physical threat really helps build your confidence." Why? You know what to expect of your body and your mind. These cadets exemplify what girls are capable of and act as role models for those girls who wish to develop in these areas.

Depending on the age and skill level of the girl athlete, you must provide varying opportunities to take physical risks and succeed. Beginners need a 90 to 100 percent chance of success, intermediates need a 50-50 chance of success, and advanced players will try when there is a limited or perhaps even an almost impossible chance of success. These percentages are based on my observations of working with girls, so while they may not be exact, they'll give you a working range.

When I think back to many of the sport injuries I have seen in recreational gymnastics, most of them are a result of accidents, rather than a girl taking a high level of risk. But here's an inspiring and dramatic story about an athlete who knowingly took a huge physical risk. I was a witness to this event as a spectator in the gymnastics arena at the 1996 Olympics in Atlanta, Georgia.

For many people there is a kind of pain that can go as deep as any physical injury—it is the pain of knowing that you [may] have stopped just short of excellence. Such was the pain that confronted 1996 Olympic gymnast Kerri Strug. In the women's vaulting finals, the first of two vaults caused her to injure her ankle to the point where she was in pain and seriously questioning her ability to perform a second vault. Yet the prospect of losing the hotly contested team gold medal was far more painful than the prospect of further injury. Knowing that the team title meant everything, she chose to work through the pain and perform a spectacular second vault, and assure the team medal. She was carried off the podium for all the world to see. It wasn't long before the cries of child abuse were heard, since many people felt that Kerri's coach forced her to do the vault, thinking only of gold. When questioned by the critics, Kerri said, "I'm eighteen years old. I can take my chances."

Had I been Kerri's coach, knowing the athlete's capacity for accepting risk, I would have allowed her to make her own decision. If I were the competing athlete, I would have summoned up every ounce of my strength to do what I had trained so long and hard for. At the international competitive level, athletes have the passion and the conditioning to reach deep inside themselves and go to the edge.

Keep these ideas in mind when a player is trying to take risks and work up to a higher level of performance:

- If you challenge girls to achieve goals that are far beyond their level, they won't be able to develop courage, only fear. Make sure that your daughter or the girls on your team are not doing too much too soon.
- Embarrassing girls in front of their friends, parents, and teammates by intimidating them with words like "Don't be a chicken" is nonproductive.
- Instead of turning a cold shoulder to your daughter when she balks at doing something scary, talk about it and find out where her fear is coming from. Most fear comes from inadequate preparation.
- Giving your daughter too much help is a surefire way to make her

believe that she can't really do it on her own and that she doesn't have to work through the problem. Phrases that can help her include the following:

I know this is hard, but I'm here for you.
Let's work on getting a picture in your mind of you doing it right.
I saw you try to do that all by yourself. Good job.
How can I help prepare you for this situation?
I know this has to make sense before you do it, so let's talk
  about it.

Self-Discipline

Participating in athletics is all about self-mastery. The benefit comes when you feel in control of your mind and body, you feel confident. Developing the personal strength to start and stick with an activity, to achieve a goal, is a lifelong journey for which sports can prepare you. One good reason to keep athletics in your life is that it puts you in a situation in which you must be disciplined. Being self-disciplined usually means that you are productive. What college doesn't look for a disciplined student? What employer doesn't look for a productive employee?

Positive Self-Talk

Getting up the nerve to believe you can do something often starts with the way you talk to yourself. When done in a constructive way, it is called "positive self-talk." A noted speaker and author, Dr. Dennis Waitley, calls this kind of optimistic approach "positive self-expectancy." He notes that when the mind and body habitually envision going for the best, the body will move toward its best, or whatever goal is set by the athlete. When you find yourself in one of those tough conversations where your daughter keeps putting herself down, you have to redirect how she sees herself and find a goal she thinks she can move toward. Ask her questions; for example, "Can you see yourself acing a serve on the tennis court?" Find out what she can picture herself doing.

Putting girls in different sport situations allows them to eventually find a setting in which they can make self-talk work successfully for them. It may take a few years, but here is how it developed for one athlete:

Especially with ice-skating, I defeated myself because I didn't have the self-confidence. I was nervous, and in my thoughts I put myself down because I was too tall. But I knew I had the skill, and I wanted to try to make myself a better competitor. After competition, I'd be angry and very disappointed in myself, and I wanted to take the failure back. I'd come home and say, "I know how to do it. Why do I always fail?" I felt like a failure and got really depressed. At the time, I didn't think I was making myself think that way. But as I look back, I was. When I changed sports to basketball, I often relied too much on my teammates because I didn't think I could do well. I would always give the ball away. I didn't want to accept the blame, and I didn't want the glory. Then I really started working on my skills. I didn't want to repeat the past of just crying after competitions and talking down to myself. Now failure just means that I tell myself to go on to the next game and try even harder. I take the blame more in stride and tell myself, Keep going, you're going to make it.

—Shannon, 15, high school freshman

Why do girls put themselves down? Perhaps it is the message about what is expected of them. Remember, it is typical of many parents and our society to expect boys to be good at sports as well as courageous and persistent, but many people do not have the same expectations for girls. Girls have to overcome this barrier, while boys generally root out this path and live up to expectations. When assertive sports-related behavior does not come easily to a girl, it's easy for her to have doubts about her capabilities. Over time, that can be a drawback as she struggles to improve her sports skills. The message needs to come across loud and clear that it's OK to expect girls to be proficient at sports as part of their growth. Therefore, girls need to be taught how to talk to themselves in a positive and constructive way in order to ask and expect more of themselves. Fortunate is the girl who is self-motivated, for she will likely be more assertive. Yet even the self-motivated girl still needs to know how to reassure herself that she is doing a good job.

You can encourage your daughter to give herself positive messages by teaching her to erase negative self-talk and come up with something more supportive:

- I don't know how, but I will do my best.
- I'm better than I was four weeks ago.
- I am just facing a temporary setback.
- I can do better next time.

Keep telling your daughter that how she talks to herself will determine if she moves to the next level. Remind her how far she has come and that you're proud of her. Most important, be a role model and keep defeating words out of your vocabulary.

Goal Setting

Goal setting is another way girls can learn to discipline themselves. When I am coaching girls, I frequently ask them, "What goal are we working toward?" Or provide that goal: "If you do ten cartwheels today, I bet you'll reach your goal of learning a round-off." I'm forever trying to get girls to think about what small goal they can reach right now. I've found that it's the moment-to-moment goal setting that makes the most impact. I'll bet I say the word *goal* fifty times during a practice. Typically coaches say, "Did you swing the tennis racket at hip level that time?" But if you were to say, "Did you meet *your goal* of swinging the tennis racket . . ." you will add a more powerful incentive. Get girls used to hearing the word *goal*. I mostly work with short-term goals, because setting long-term ones is often unrealistic for early elementary school children. Make goals small and attainable. The more frequently girls can set goals themselves and have a chance of meeting them, the more they'll feel ready for the next challenge.

Time Management

Budgeting time well is another aspect of self-discipline and another personal skill that playing sports helps girls develop. What is every parent's dream come true? Having their children do homework without a major hassle. It's amazing how most athletes, with additional demands on their lives, usually turn out to be good students and the best time managers. They know that their parents will demand that homework be done if they want to play sports. Many young athletes either do their homework after school and before practice or they do homework after practice. Sometimes girls just fit it in whenever they can, which is fine if they have discipline.

Over time, the habit of doing extracurricular activities and homework as a way of life becomes a stable pattern. For this athlete, the daily expectation was unquestioned:

> *The life I knew was go to school, then go to the gym, then do my homework, then go to bed. That was normal for me. I got used to the routine. I think I was lucky at a young age to get into the habit of budgeting my time. It was easy for me to continue to do that as I grew older.*
> —Amanda, 21, college graduate

If possible, let your daughter set up her own routine of when she can do her homework—before or after practice or a little of both. You can help her determination to stick to her own schedule by supporting her in the following ways:

- Have her clothing ready for each game and practice.
- Make sure you get her to practices and games on time.
- Have her write down her schedule and put it on the kitchen bulletin board or refrigerator.
- Tell her when you'll have time to help her with her homework when necessary.

By helping girls in these ways, you show support and belief in their athletic abilities. It is also a specific way to demonstrate team effort, here between parent and child. Girls need all the input they can get to develop team-building skills. When girls are helped to stay focused, they are less likely to spend undue amounts of time drifting off into phone conversations, going to the mall, or watching television.

The more your daughter participates in planning when to do various activities in her day-to-day life, the better she'll be able to manage her time as she grows older and is out of your reach. Not only will she be learning an invaluable life skill that will keep her focused, but she'll be a sought after commodity at work and in her community. You've probably heard the expression "If you want something done, give it to a busy person." Now you know why.

Teamwork

Learning to cooperate with others to develop a cohesive unit, a team, is an ability that young athletes usually develop when they participate in organized sports. Developing this social skill takes hours of playing time and a coach who makes it a priority. Depending on the family background of the players, some girls will have a harder time than others putting the basics of teamwork into practice. In some families both parents are present and a child sees parents working as a team. But this isn't always the case. In the same vein, a child may have many siblings, and they are used to sharing space, responsibilities, and time with their parents. Or a child may be alone in a household, used to having things go her way, and has to learn to share all of life's details. Players who are firstborn in their family may be used to lording over younger sisters and brothers. Those who are the youngest in the family may be accustomed to fighting for their own space. Family dynamics affect how girls respond to pressure, how they compromise, how they support their teammates, and whether they rebel, confront, or remain silent when they're upset about something. Get to know your girls if you are a coach, and you may better understand why they respond the way they do.

Girls are very much relationship oriented, and that can work both ways—for the team or against the team. When girls enjoy and respect each other, you will have a cohesiveness unlike any association you've seen with boys. However, if girls are not relating well to each other, they will not play with each other, literally. If you're going to have an effective team, you'll need to pay attention to the group process, for it may very well be the major cause of team losses.

As a parent, try these positive steps to encourage a sense of team spirit in your daughter:

- When you're watching sports on TV, point out examples of teamwork.
- After a game, ask your daughter what she did to contribute to the team.

- Offer praise right away when you see your daughter working for the team: For example, "I heard you say, 'Nice job,' to Ashley. That was really supportive of you."
- Never put down another player in front of your daughter.
- Help develop the idea that when you have a better relationship with teammates, you are better able to help your team. Members will accept comments from each other when they are given in a friendly way.
- Keep reminding your daughter that she'll meet people her whole life who won't be team players. She won't be able to control the content of their character, but she can speak up and encourage them to be part of the group.

Areas of Concern

I usually don't like to point out negatives, but some behaviors are never in the best interests of the group. When you see players displaying any of these characteristics, you've got to nip it in the bud immediately.

- Horseplay: Making jokes or fooling around at inappropriate times distracts the group from the task at hand. Let girls know that there will be time for jokes at the end of practice. Another thing to watch out for is pushing and shoving. This is just plain dangerous, and your players need to understand that without question.
- Name-calling: This can happen when your back is turned at practice or off the field, where the news about who said what to who gets around quickly. If you can identify the girls involved in this behavior, take them aside separately and see if you can find out what's at the bottom of their ill will. If you don't know who is involved, have a group meeting and say to the girls, "We don't seem to be playing like a team. There's seems to be some ill feelings out there. Did you know this is causing us to lose points?" Usually I try to put the burden of the problem on the girls and ask how they can fix this situation.
- Withdrawing: If you see a girl withdrawing or depressed on a regular basis, either she is not learning the sport skills or she is not fitting in socially. Plan to spend some time with her to draw out her concerns. If you aren't getting anywhere, then go to her parents. But try to solve it with the child first. That way they won't feel

you are a traitor. For the time being, she must know at least that you, the coach, is on her side. Communicate with the whole team, state what you observe—for example, that not everyone is getting the ball passed to them. Let them know that this means the whole team isn't as effective as it could be.

- Constantly raising objections: When you're constantly being interrupted, ask your player if the issue needs to be handled now or if it can it wait until later. If the girl insists on airing her concerns at that moment, get input from the other players and ask what her peers think. Believe me, they will tell her.

- Dominating behavior: If you have a player who insists on her own way, gives orders to other girls, and constantly interrupts when you are giving instructions, you need to discuss this individually with her. It's likely that her teammates have already started ignoring her orders, but you still need to address the problem. On occasion, this behavior arises when a girl feels inadequate. Discussing this with her has to be done delicately—no finger-pointing.

- Not giving 100 percent: It's great when everyone is working toward the same goal, but when teammates are not giving 100 percent, the committed players find that they have to take up the slack on the field or the court. This causes tension and resentment. One player told me, "You need people who want to be there. You wish other people would give their all. You find these kinds of people in nonsport activities, too, like committees at school. They never ask, 'What can I do to help?' There are times when I go up to my teammates and say, 'Hey, we all have to give something if our team is going to be successful.'"

Voicing Opinions and Tolerance

Tolerating others' attitudes, beliefs, and feelings is an everyday matter of concern on or off the field of play. If females are to be equally respected to males in the workplace, they must develop communication skills that are straightforward. For coaches, dealing with the behind-the-scenes issues are one of the most prevalent and ongoing concerns. Attitudes about play tend to be divisive; for instance, some players will value the win, some will value just getting to play. Unfortunately, girls tend to talk behind each others' back and tend to gossip more about their ill feelings toward another person. Boys, on the other hand, tend to be very direct with each other, verbally and physically, and get it out of their systems. In order to promote harmony and teach players how to reconcile disagreements:

- Point out common ground. What are the things that are working well in terms of teamwork?
- Get your players used to having opinions discussed briefly, to the point, and getting a consensus. Maybe they agree to try one solution for a certain period of time, then review the results. I tell my athletes that if they can't come up with a solution themselves, they'll have to accept my decision. You can be sure no one wants to do that, so give them a specific time frame to work things out. It's best if the idea comes from the players rather than you.
- Encourage quiet girls to speak up. If only a few girls are volunteering opinions, make sure that you, as the coach, ask quieter players to contribute—"[Name], I was wondering what you think about that." When some players feel as though they're not being heard, that will break the team spirit in a flash.

The Power of Peer Guidance

One thing that's true about parents and coaches is that we're sure we have all the answers. We believe that if we just explain something long and hard enough, we'll get the message across to our children and players. But is there another way? There is, and it was shown to me by one of my sympathetic and alert ten-year-old students. I was trying to help a girl learn a somersault in one of my gymnastics classes and was getting nowhere fast. Suddenly another student came over to me and said, "I bet she's scared. When I was first learning that, I didn't like it at all." Then she followed up her comments with a few suggestions and a demonstration for my frustrated and near tears little student. For whatever reason, I actually kept my mouth shut and let the two girls try to work out the problem. They did.

When I realized how powerful this peer demonstration was, I couldn't get out of my own way fast enough. I began using peer helpers as much as possible. Whenever I'm at my wits' end (or hopefully before I get there), I now ask girls in the training group if they can explain to a confused teammate how to do something. For simple skills, this works easily. As the girls approach higher levels of training, you will have had to spend some time making sure they know *both* the skill techniques and the proper communication skills that you have hopefully taught them. If you're a parent in a playground situation, you can use the same peer helper technique by picking a demonstrator from the group, a child who already knows how to do what you're trying to teach. Because the sense of camaraderie is so important to young girls, peer help can be an easy and effective way to communicate.

Persistence

"Hanging in there" and "never giving up" are ways of describing one of the most valuable traits a person can possess: persistence. Persistence is probably responsible for creating more success stories than any other personal quality. To master an athletic skill, coaches and parents must continually create an environment where players are willing to persist and practice—over and over and over again. This willingness to try and try again happens when the training steps along the way are small enough to ensure that the player sees success regularly.

Translating the concept of persistence into action can be approached in a variety of ways. My strategy is to make learning a "numbers game." While most young athletes think of numbers only in terms of scoring, I often use numbers to get the point across about persistence. For example, I know from experience that it takes approximately three hundred trials to learn a back handspring for gymnastics. Every one of my students learning this skill knows that in order to eventually reach that magic number, it is best to try it twenty-five times each day before she leaves the gym. This is also in keeping with reachable goals through small steps. You may have to use number of ground strokes practiced, number of baskets that are shot, or whatever suits your situation. By educating girls about this numerical approach and following it steadfastly, girls will understand that if they keep at it, they'll reach their goal.

Coaches and parents can also motivate girls to persist by visualizing a picture of what a specific achievement looks like and how it will feel. This is nothing new, but it is not used nearly enough as it could be for training. When the image of a goal is constantly kept alive and is associated with some reward that is meaningful for a particular person, its magnetic pull will work slowly and surely to bring about the desired result. People move in the direction of their dominant thoughts. Communication with your daughter about sports participation should focus on the rewards, not the obstacles, if she is to persevere.

- Help your daughter collect pictures of her role models and put them up where she can see them frequently.
- Have her write out her goal, very simple and short, and put it where she will read it every morning and night.
- Find ways to reward persistence, perhaps buying her a new glove when she makes it to every softball practice.
- Provide small rewards for achieving small goals, large rewards for achieving large goals.

Here is my own story that demonstrates the power of persistence in my life:

> The Olympics was out of reach for me as an athlete owing to my late start in competitive sports, but I never gave up my desire to be involved on the international level somehow. When I found out that the 1984 Olympics were to be held in Los Angeles, a little flame was lit in my soul. There was no question in my mind that I would do whatever it took to get to see the Olympics. Some people might think that selling a successful East Coast business and most of the household furniture might be a little extreme. But I had always wanted to live in Southern California, and this gave me the perfect excuse. In 1980 my husband and I packed up two cars and a trailer and took our dreams on the road.
>
> Somewhere around the beginning of 1982 I called Los Angeles directory information and asked if there was a phone number for the Olympic committee. Fortunately there was. I soon reached the personnel department and was told that if I wanted a volunteer job, I was to send my name in on a postcard. If I wanted a paid position, I had to send in a résumé. What did I have to lose? After that I called every few months to see the status of my résumé. Nothing. Then in the summer of 1983 a fellow coach invited me to be a volunteer at the Olympic gymnastics dress rehearsal. I was there in a heart-

beat. My friend assured me that my name would go on a special list of volunteers to be considered for the official event.

Months went by and my frustration grew as I waited for the Olympic committee to call. And one day they finally did. My husband took the call and told me I had an interview the following Tuesday at ten A.M. What a rush! Driving to the interview was as nerve-racking as any balance beam routine I'd ever done. When I arrived at the personnel office and filled out the job application, something seemed out of order. The secretary interviewing me became impatient with my ignorance. I had to tell her I didn't know exactly what I was applying for; I had just showed up for my appointment. She stated firmly that I should follow her. I was praying that it wasn't out to the parking lot. After interview number two, in which I had a short discussion with a man who also said, "Follow me," I was even more confused.

I walked into a room where there were five people waiting to greet me. By now the perspiration circles under my arms were about to connect like the Olympic rings. It was at this point that I realized they weren't talking just about a summer job. They were offering me the position of sport coordinator— director of the Olympic Gymnastics Competition—and asked if I could start in ten days. I was thrilled and overwhelmed at this chance!

On Monday morning, October 30, 1983, I walked into the converted airport hangar in Culver City as an employee of the Los Angeles Olympic Organizing Committee. Three thousand miles and three years after leaving New Jersey, my dream had come true, bigger and bolder than I ever could have imagined. If anyone had ever told me that turning cartwheels as a teenager would one day give me the chance to be a part of the Olympic movement, I would have thought them crazy. Extraordinary things can happen to ordinary people who persist.

As a thirty-year veteran of teaching gymnastics, I have seen thousands of girls come and go. Some can manage constant challenges, some fall apart. What most often distinguishes those who succeed from those who give up is the willingness to persist. If your daughter is in competitive sports, ask yourself how well she employs persistence to handle these situations:

- Getting used to a new team and a new coach: Does she enjoy the sport only if she has a particular coach or teammates?
- Dealing with an injury: Does she stop going to practice or does she go and work on the things that she can do?
- Coping with a losing streak: Can she put it behind her and focus on improving her skills for next season?
- Handling new challenges in general: Does she tend to be excited or worried?
- Comparisons: Is she realistic and focused on bettering her own performance, or does she become discouraged if a teammate is consistently better than she is?

What can you do to strengthen your daughter's persistence? Certainly you can remind her how far she's come since she first dribbled a basketball or scored her first goal in soccer. You might recount for her the specific ways in which her practicing has paid off. In my experience, though, persistence usually is tied to an athlete's enjoyment of, even passion for, the sport. The more your daughter loves getting out there on the field or gymnasium floor, the more likely she is to stick with it.

Strong Muscles, Strong Mind So Combined Are the Tools of Self-Reliance

The most valuable benefit of sports participation is the development of the personal skills that we've been exploring in this chapter. If your daughter can learn to weigh her options and be decisive, solve her own problems and be a team player, communicate effectively and be a good sport, take risks and be persistent . . . she will be well prepared to take charge of her life as she grow into a strong, self-reliant woman. Even if she never picks up a tennis racket or hockey stick after graduation from high school, she will have learned how to interact cooperatively with others, how to deal with her leaders and people with different points of view, and how to have faith in herself. By giving your unconditional support as your daughter learns these personal attitudes and skills, you'll be assuring her of a healthy advantage in the game of life.

What It Takes to Coach Girls

8

Most families are led to believe that the person who coaches their child chooses to do so because he or she has the devotion and the credentials. But as a parent you should also know the background of this person who will spend so much time with your child. In community recreation programs, a child can be involved anywhere from one to more than fifteen hours a week with an instructor. On the elite level, girls may spend as many as twenty-four hours a week training with their coach. Given that possibility, it's a good idea for parents to know an instructor's qualifications. What if it's you who wants to coach? What do you need to know? Whether the person is a professional or volunteer parent coach, he or she needs to have the technical, managerial, and, most important, social skills to make your child productive and happy. Having the right qualifications is essential, but before you make any commitments, have an honest chat with yourself. For your sanity and the children's happiness, it's critical to be clear about what motivates you.

Do You Have a Philosophy That Serves the Child?

The "going for the gold" attitude infects many full- and even part-time children's coaches. No wonder, since it's almost impossible not to be influenced by the ongoing media attention paid to winners. Let's face it, professional athletes are paid to win. Then there's college sports. How teams place over the course of a season affects in some measure the reputation of a university or college program and the jobs of the coaches—no win, no job. At the high school level, athletes and parents are eager to earn scholarships and want college recruiters to be reviewing their sport skills. At many levels, money and sports are intimately tied together. But where in this whole equation are the interests of the child addressed?

Understand the Interests of the Child

Always keep in mind the idea that experiencing joy is essentially what girls are interested in when they're physically active. Whether girls are engaged in "play" activity (the need for movement) or "sport" activity (the desire to achieve and compete), it's got to be enjoyable on some level. Coaches and parents need to distinguish between the two approaches so that children are supported in the way that best suits them. There will be times when a girl may be in a program only because her friend is there or because her parents want her there. Ask yourself if you can be content to coach girls with those attitudes. Occasionally there will be a few elite players with the skills and temperament to handle advanced training. But to pin your hopes and your ego on coaching even a few "stars" probably isn't realistic. Be prepared to deal with all kinds of needs and interests. Girls' needs will range from the desire to be part of a team to enjoy the social nature of being with other girls to truly wanting to achieve sports skills and the glory of winning.

Focus on Player Development

It changes your coaching perspective when you can ask yourself at each practice, "What are the players doing well today?" A great coach will have a specific constructive comment for every girl about her effort when she leaves the field or the gym. Being supported in this way can mean the difference between players staying with a sport experience and avoiding it altogether. The younger the player, the more coaches need to weigh personal worth development against sport skill building. Whether a player is unskilled or experienced, athletes perceive these comments as valuable reflections of their relationship with the coach. When you make it your goal for your players to progress at each practice (even if it's just instilling a new thought or getting a shy player to speak out for the first time), you're demonstrating that a child's time at practice is time well spent.

Your team can have a very mediocre season record, but if your focus is on player development and fun, the girls will come back next season. Player development requires that coaches make sure everyone plays and gets equal attention. It means acknowledging ways that a player has been contributing to the team effort as well as reaching a personal goal. Tell your players that you know there will be times when they mess up or forget skills, but their best effort adds up over time and makes a difference. If you're trying to help players get better every week, they'll know it and in turn will enjoy and value the time you spend with them.

Never Put the Win Ahead of the Player

There is a place for winning as long as athletes are prepared physically, mentally, and emotionally to handle it. We discussed sports readiness extensively in chapter 3. Some girls will feel the need to achieve through sports later than others; some may never feel it. What is always true is that the process of learning should be emphasized above the product of winning. This is particularly so when you're coaching beginners. In local recreation programs, where some 85 percent of coaches are parent volunteers, an emphasis on winning may discourage young athletes from staying with a program for the long run. Studies show that girls who drop out of sports often complain, "It's no fun anymore," or, "I wish my coach would quit yelling at me." Girls reported "there was too much pressure" as a higher ranking reason to quit sports than did boys.

The story that follows is about a coach who learned the hard way a lesson about the pitfalls of putting winning above participation:

> One of the male basketball coaches who works for our rec-
> reation program decided to substitute out a poor player dur-
> ing a recent match and bring in his daughter so that the team
> could win. After the game, he felt bad about what he had done
> to the weak player because he realized he put the win ahead
> of the girl. He went over to her house and apologized to her

that night. He knew that if he was going to live with himself,
he had to view the girl as a person first, then a player.
—Jeff, Boys and Girls Club director

Believe in and Assure Personal Growth

Some individuals who coach are fundamentally committed to the dynamic of personal growth. It is awesome to be part of a child's learning process, to help children perform something in a game that they've been doing in practice, or help them to try something they've never tried before. If you can create an emotionally safe environment in which you respect and encourage each player, whatever her skill level, growth will occur. This doesn't come easily. You will have to work through a variety of issues at every practice. Will you be able to handle the full range of normal emotions exhibited by young girl athletes? Along with jubilation when they win, you can expect some other difficult emotions and behavior, like talking about non-sports-related matters while waiting for their turn at play, stubbornness and not wanting to play with someone they don't like, fearfulness, and tears. Can you deal with that kind of emotional roller coaster week after week? If you show your athletes that you care about them as people, that you care about them learning, you'll win their hearts and they'll be more likely to give the sport their all. Once you have prepared them to handle game play and they feel you're there for them, you'll have their enthusiasm for the season.

Do You Have the Technical Knowledge?

If you want to be the head coach, you should know your sport very well. If you don't, give yourself enough time to attend several practices (including other coaches' practices) ahead of the date you're scheduled to start and get some additional training. Also, find out if there are any referee courses that you can attend. This will help you familiarize yourself with the rules. I can't emphasize this enough. If you don't get educated, you'll invite humiliation and make your coaching experience more difficult for you and your athletes.

Perhaps you are a concerned parent who will never coach, but you're searching for a coach for your daughter's community team.

A good place to start is with a local junior college or university program. If there are no higher education programs close by, or you can't elicit the help of local competitive athletes, put an ad in your local newspaper—"Calling all moms or dads who are ex-college athletes." You could even go to practice sessions of adult recreation programs and put out some feelers there. Those recreational adult players should have enough background to know the basic skills and strategies to make a program function. Ideally you would like a coach who knows the skills and strategies that are suitable for the age and skill level of the children under their direction.

Keep Yourself Educated and Updated

It's a good idea to check with the national governing board of your sport to find out if they have a training video, or if there are local, regional, and national workshops you can attend to get educated. Check the appendix in this book for sport by sport information to locate the national governing board. If you want to try your local library as a resource center, look for books and periodicals that are current. Some materials may be outdated because techniques change. In addition to basic sport skill education, find out what accreditation is necessary. Many sports require professional development certification, some annually. They are U.S. Volleyball, U.S.A. Wrestling, U.S.A. Gymnastics, U.S.A. Cycling, U.S.A. Basketball, U.S.A. Bowling, U.S.A. Softball, U.S.A. Figure Skating Association, U.S.A. Shooting, and U.S.A. Skiing. Several sports are still working on a nationally based program that will establish qualifications for coaches.

I remember that when my husband and I first started coaching girls, we attended dozens of workshops to build on the information we already learned as competitive gymnasts. It seemed as if we were traveling every weekend. Today there's no question in my mind that the early education paid off. Understanding information is one thing. Communicating it is quite another. Gaining respect is a whole category unto itself. It takes a long time to be a quality coach.

Where Can You Get Help to Be a Responsible Coach?

Here is a list of organizations that offer training programs that emphasize a coaching philosophy encompassing the mental, social, and psychological aspects of sports. See the appendix for phone numbers.

- The National Youth Sports Coaches Association (NYSCA)
- The American Sport Education Program (ASEP)
- The Program for Athletic Coaches' Education (PACE)

In addition, check with Human Kinetics, a publisher that carries sport-related educational materials developed by authors nationwide.

Do You Have the Necessary Management Skills?

Being able to manage a group of excitable youngsters is not the easiest task. I remember when I first started teaching, I was assigned to an elementary school physical education program. It was basketball season, and basketball was not one of my strengths. Within fifteen minutes of starting a class, my group of children was so out of control and so loud that they could be heard throughout the entire school. It didn't take long for the principal to come charging into the gym and, using a voice that could be heard above a nuclear explosion, gain control. I wondered if anyone could see my body cells liquefying. Lesson learned: Know how to take control.

Class management is the skill most lacking in new teachers. And it is the one that takes the longest to learn. A lot of coaches try to get through to their athletes using fear, yelling, and threats. But with girls your best bet is to be organized and supportive, because girls do not respond positively to threats or yelling. They will play their hearts out for a coach if they recognize that she or he can put a game plan into effect, can make their practice time productive, and can demonstrate authority over players in a nonthreatening and just way. And that's a tall order.

Keep Girls Active During Practice

Getting into a routine beginning with the very first practice will start your team off on the right foot. Activities such as taking attendance, making announcements, calling a break time, and giving a quick review session at the end of practice (which is a great time to point out progress) can be preset. Once this basic structure is in place, you'll want to observe these general guidelines to ensure a productive and enjoyable practice:

- Organize and plan practices. This is your premier function. Determine what drills you expect the players to perform and how much time it will take for each kind of activity. Be sure you specify what strategies will be worked on during this particular practice time. If some girls are sitting on the bench waiting for their turn to participate, they could be doing physical conditioning instead. That too needs to be spelled out. Having things written down on a clipboard not only looks impressive, it's effective as well: the list acts as a plan that can then be referred to by an assistant coach or any of the players should there be questions. If you sense some struggling going on during a practice, just say to the girls, "Do we need a quick [or early] break?" Remember, your goal is to keep the girls focused.

- Tell your players why you are doing certain activities. Just being "told" to do an activity doesn't give players the opportunity to understand the steps in the learning process. Nor does it help them develop decision-making skills. If you want the girls to develop a certain strategy, tell them when to use it and how to anticipate when they'll need to put it into action as well as the steps involved. You want your players to be thinking on their feet all the time.

- Have a clear signal when you want to stop and get your players' attention for instruction. This could be a whistle, a raised arm, or a specific word. For sports that involve balls, it's best to ask the players to put the ball on the floor while you're talking. Otherwise, keeping them focused on you may be difficult.

- Give everyone a chance to play. When you schedule practices, be certain that everyone gets playing time. For team sports, the players should know the circumstances under which they are substituted on and off the field of play. Since practice serves as the foundation for competitive play, coaches must let players know what the game plan is before every match. Then in difficult, heated game situations, the weaker players can make a contribution— and they should. To pull this scenario off successfully, establish a team philosophy whereby "everyone plays" at every practice and at every game. This is one of the most difficult coaching strategies to install. Sometimes you have to convince the parents as well as the children that this is the right thing to do.

Maintain Control by Developing Authority in Your Voice

This doesn't mean you have to yell, but you do need to be heard plainly. I recommend that you observe a variety of coaches and even classroom teachers to know what phrases they use to maintain order and get promote action. Many new teachers I work with try too hard to be nice; they use gentle voices, and the girls just don't pay attention. Also, teachers who frequently "ask" girls to do something instead of telling them to do something are not as likely to get speedy cooperation until a deep level of mutual respect has been established. And for the most part, avoid using "okay?" at the end of your directive unless you're working with a group over which you have a good control. Use this phrase only in the rarest of circumstances. While you may think you are simply making sure you're understood—your players may interpret this as being asked to decide whether or not they want to participate. Your job is to take control, give them caring guidance, and watch them bloom. When you can control your students with just your voice, you can allow for more independent situations. For example, you can assign small groups to go off and work on their own on special drills once you're assured that they'll return to you (as the command center) at your request.

Learn to Manage Your Team One Girl at a Time

Your girls are a group of individuals in addition to being a team. Each one has her own special needs, which you will have to manage one girl at a time. Your girls may have as many personalities as there are planets. Here are some typical personality types to expect:

- The new girl on the block: Some girls are superexcited about playing a particular sport but have no idea what skills are involved. They have a greater need for guidance. To help inexperienced girls get settled, perhaps you could assign a "buddy" or "sister" who could answer what the new player may think are "dumb" questions.
- The underperformer: This is a girl who has been on your team for a long time but has trouble staying enthusiastic and focused. She has the skills but may not be committed. This type of girl needs less technical direction but more emotional support. You'll need

to find out why she's there. Is it for herself or for her parents? Does she need a self-confidence builder? This is also part of your job as coach.

- The superstar: The skilled athlete can be a terrific role model, team leader, and supporter of other teammates. She could also be somebody flying around in her own little world, throwing temper tantrums or prattling on, demanding everyone's attention, with no one listening. Make sure that this person is constantly challenged so she won't get bored. Also, in your attempt not to "spoil" her with too much praise, be careful that you don't deprive her of emotional attention, thereby allowing her to drift and feel abandoned.
- The no-show: Take the time to call if a girl misses a practice and find out if there's a problem.

When a child tells you she doesn't want to practice a certain skill, make an effort to find out *why*. Maybe your attitude has turned her off. Maybe she's physically fearful. Maybe her peers are giving her a hard time. Maybe her body is changing faster than she is able to adjust her athletic skills to meet changes in weight, difficulties with her menstrual cycle, and increased breast and hip size. All of these factors have an impact on self-consciousness and coaches and parents should be sensitive to them. Or perhaps she has troubles at home or at school or just doesn't like that particular activity. Balking at doing a skill can happen at the most inconvenient times and may disrupt practice. If you're lucky, you might be able to deal with it on the spot. You may have to say, "Stick with it for now and we'll talk about it after practice." At the very worst, you may have to play along with the problem and have her sit out. Do you have the interest and energy to find out what is holding this girl back, or are you just going to tell her to tough it out and play whether she likes it or not? If you do the latter, you may be suppressing the love for the very sport you're committed to kindling. Above all, remember who's putting out the effort. *She* is. And her feelings count. She needn't be pampered, but she should be listened to.

Know When to Punish or Redirect Behavior

The goal for every child is to strive for self-management. The goal for the coach is to develop "eyes in back of your head." You have to be very alert and scan your group frequently to get a "read" on the situation so that you remain in charge. Keep the rules short and sensible. Children must know what you will tolerate and what you won't. For example, treat your teammates and coach respectfully; no gum chewing; no wearing jewelry or inappropriate clothing. My favorite rule is, "Never scare the teacher." The girls in my classes know that if they are doing something that scares me, it probably is dangerous and therefore is not acceptable. In any event, dealing with discipline involves two approaches, either you redirect or punish behavior.

REDIRECTING BEHAVIOR

- Use parenting skills. Rather than saying, "I told you not to do that," simply state what the player is supposed to be doing. Ask her how many times she's done the activity successfully. Remind her of her goals.
- Ask the players who are out of line to change the skill they're working on. When you feel you have the group back to a good working mode, you can always go back to the skill you want them to develop.
- Focus your remarks on the unwanted behavior, not the child. With preteens one of the biggest problems is "visiting" with their friends while you're trying to give instructions. If I see a girl talking, I direct my instruction to her. In other words, I can be explaining a procedure and midsentence can say, "[Name], I want you to know that when it is your turn to go on the balance beam, you start training your cartwheel." She will look at me right away, knowing that I'm directing my comments specifically toward her. I find this tactic works much better than constantly telling the athlete that she's not listening.
- Give your players a second chance if you feel that their behavior can be turned around quickly.

PUNISHMENT GUIDELINES

- If you need to punish a child, walk up to her and talk to her directly, rather than shouting across the gym or the field. Get the undisciplined child away from other players so that she does not spread disruptive behavior.
- Be clear that there has been a violation of policy. My most fre-

quently used phrase is, "This is unacceptable behavior." Find a phrase that suits your style. Handle it quickly so that the entire practice isn't disrupted.

- Make the consequences for misbehaving simple and clear. For most occasions and most age groups, having a time-out is sufficient. For team sports you may need to substitute out the offending player and put in another. The punishment should be age appropriate. Young girls should have a short time-out. Otherwise they may forget what's going on, forget why they're on a time-out, or lose interest.

- Never embarrass the child in front of others.

- Have a quick student-teacher meeting at the end of practice. "[Name], I felt like you were having a tough time paying attention today. What's going on?" Or, "Is something bothering you?" Or, "You didn't look like you were having any fun today." Listen to their side of the story. It is critical that the child does not feel threatened. It is important for you to say, "I really want you to be successful [to enjoy yourself, to hit the ball, to learn to run fast, whatever]."

- Schedule a parent, child, coach conference when you feel that a child's behavior is frequently a problem. Behavior problems usually boil down to a few different areas: 1) the child is having a "social" problem with another child; 2) the child is afraid of doing something or afraid of failing because the skills are becoming too difficult; or 3) the child really doesn't want to be there.

- Avoid using physical exercise as punishment. I'll be honest with you. In my opinion, coaches who use exercise as "punishment," such as running laps or doing push-ups, have a lack of management skills. They rely on this traditional approach because most of the time it is effective. Yet if coaches create a fun and productive atmosphere, their athletes usually don't horse around or have behavior problems. This is not always true, but it helps. Punishment that involves physical activity does not contribute to player development. It only turns the girls off to the coach and is counterproductive, since we want girls to *enjoy* exercise.

- Once a child has been disciplined, wipe her record clean. Move forward so that you can get on with the business at hand, which is to learn skills in a happy and productive environment. It will take

a mature attitude on the coach's part not to hold a grudge or let the athlete with behavior problems negatively influence practice.
- Avoid group punishment. Here is an example of an ineffective group punishment.

> *I was refereeing one time where I saw the coach actually stop a game and make his team run laps because he was upset with the way things were going. This coach should have been stopped by the parents, but some coaches can be very intimidating. In this case, the offending coach usually told parents who questioned his behavior, "If you don't like it, go to another program."*
>
> —Tim, parent coach

There are times when your only recourse is group punishment, but this in ineffective at best. Parents need to have the personal strength to take their daughter and walk away from this kind of a program. Too many parents stay and let their daughters, as well as themselves, take the abuse, believing it will eventually pay off in skill development and prestige.

Pay attention to how you criticize girls. Losing your temper, shouting, and taunting can be taken seriously by females and can be interpreted as a personal attack. This means that as coach you will need to tone down your disciplinary voice. Believe me, they'll still get it if you need to reprimand them with a firm voice.

Do You Have the Social and Psychological Skills?

Many of the skills needed to be a good coach are very similar to those needed to be a good parent. If you choose to coach, you will always be part coach, part parent, and part psychologist. This means being a good listener and being observant. Above all, be willing to evaluate yourself. I think it's important to ask yourself, "Would I enjoy having myself as a coach?" Here are some essential qualities and skills that will help you become the kind of coach you'd want to have yourself.

Be Enthusiastic

Coaches can set the tone for learning by their level of enthusiasm. I have to admit, it took me a lot of years to figure this out, but now it is the number one skill I bring to my classes. From the minute I say, "Hi" to the minute my students leave my class, I am absolutely upbeat. The girls under my direction don't need to know that I've waited twenty-five minutes in line at the post office or had to reroute my drive to the gym because the main road is under construction. They care about enjoying their sport, seeing their friends, and improving their skills. Keep in mind that you have to leave your personal dramas behind you when you show up to coach. Your job is to create an environment that allows the girls to expand their thinking and their skills and to feel good about themselves.

Being enthusiastic applies doubly for working with beginners. You've got to let them know that everyone started at the beginner's level. I often tell these athletes, "I was just like you when I started." Stress to them the importance of practice, practice, practice, and that if they do extra training at home, maybe one day they will play like the girls they admire. You've got to help them believe they can reach their goals, and this comes across in your voice as well as your message. The worst thing a coach can do is to write a girl off. If she has overheard you say, "She's never going to be any good," she will take it to heart, and it will be nearly impossible to turn her around under your guidance. Maybe someone else can help her, but not likely you.

Many times I show enthusiasm for progress just by shaking a girl's hand. This simple connection is invaluable and makes her feel terrific. Over time I've noticed that girls with strong handshakes are very self-confident. Teach them a confident handshake, they're going to need it for life. Think of enthusiasm as the motivational fuel for the players' minds.

Catch Your Players Doing Something Right

If you want to be a successful coach in the eyes of your athletes, find something that your athlete is doing right, even if it's merely standing in line properly. There have been times when I've had to rack my brains to think of something positive to say before a girl leaves my class. But try I must. I might say, "I noticed you moved a little faster that time," "You look like you're getting more comfortable with that skill," "I saw you hustle more than I've ever seen before," "You stayed on the field the whole time," "This is the first practice that you did not fall down one time when you were running."

This is nothing more than supporting the notion and the process that success breeds success and that girls are highly responsive to praise. And if you sincerely compliment a child in front of her parent, that is more rewarding than a hot-fudge sundae with a brownie. When you hear a child tell her parent about her accomplishments, you know you are on the right track. However, the ones that you really want to reach out to are the average or below-average athletes. They're the ones who need a little extra boost to stay with a program. Girls who feel happy and productive will keep coming back to your program year after year.

Help Timid Players Come out of Their Shells

The longer a coach waits to help a shy child, the tougher it is for the child to emerge as a productive athlete. It's likely that in her experience she's been allowed to remain on the fringes and not participate and hasn't learned to work through her problems. Sometimes her parents may be quick to rescue her and say, "That's okay, you don't need to try it if you don't want to." If there is any one phrase that I wholeheartedly recommend for parents to leave out of their vocabulary, that's it. Once that phrase is spoken, there may be little hope for the coach to change a child's way of thinking.

We do a deep disservice to girls if we let them believe that hanging back is an acceptable way to go through life. The real world is just too tough—in business, school, sports, and personal life to avoid all conflict and flee from all possible failure. Try these ideas to help a shy child become part of the group:

- Give shy girls lots of time to observe the new activity. Underneath the frightened exterior, they often want to try a particular sport or activity but may not feel that they have the necessary physical skills to be part of the group. For them, the whole process is filled with uncertainty and unfamiliarity. Often when a group leaves an area, the timid girl will try an activity when she is sure no one is looking. Allow her the opportunity to do this.
- Parents, if you know your daughter is very slow to join groups, take her to the activity a few times for her to observe before she actually tries to get involved.

- Place the shy child in individual sports instead of team sports. That way no comparisons will be made in front of other players. After her confidence builds, try team sports if that's the right direction.
- Allow the timid child to pace herself. There's no need to push her too far or too fast. Break skills down into small steps. There's a fine line in figuring out when fear displaces any possibility of learning. Sometimes the complexity of a task creates frustration, which in turn leads to fear of trying anything new. Remember to rely on peer help—have an older girl show the shy child what to do.

There may be a time when a parent simply must leave the area if his or her child is to make progress. Have such parents tell their daughter they're going to leave, and then they must do it without looking back. They may feel they are abandoning their child, but they are really giving her a chance to grow.

Make the Klutz Feel Like a Jock

A child's worst nightmare is always being picked last for a team. For one little girl named Nicki, it happened all the time. She was the team klutz—she knew it, her parents knew it, the coach knew it, and all her teammates really knew it. "I only got to play if there was no hope." Other girls would "make fun of me if I messed up. No one stopped it."

When you have a child who has to struggle for every little bit of progress, you have to take a very careful look at the situation you might be putting her in. I'm going to make a statement that may be unpopular: If one of the girls on your team is constantly feeling bad about her performance, consider talking to her parents about taking her out of team sports, where comparisons are obvious. You might suggest putting her in an individual sport where she can make progress at her own pace. If you are working with a child who just barely muddles her way through a practice, try the steps we've discussed in previous chapters:

- Set individual goals.
- Set attainable goals.
- Let girls know that learning has occurred through understanding a new concept.
- Notice progress.

Another way to help a girl with coordination problems is to improve her physical strength. Stick with the basics of sit-ups, flexed arm hangs, and running. Remember that these activities need to be done in a fun way, and it is always more fun if the coach or the parent, at home, joins in.

Learn to Deal with Tears

Why do girls cry during practice or competition? There is no simple answer, but beyond physical injury, commonly it is a reaction to frustration or fear. Start by accepting that with girls especially, strong feelings will be displayed over a wide range of emotions. It goes with the territory. Here's what some high school girls have to say about the kinds of experiences and feelings that caused them to cry:

> *I was blowing every shot, and I felt like crying because I can't take frustration very well. I told myself that if I kept on like that, I would have no chance of winning. My dad and my coach told me that if I showed emotion, my opponent would take advantage of me. It took me a long time to learn to get myself under control.*
>
> —Heidi, high school tennis player

> *I cry very easily. After a very intense practice, I just crash in the car with my mom.*
>
> —Krissy, high school basketball player

> *Girls on the team would go away crying from practice. We were always told by the coach what we had done wrong. My teammates were the first ones to criticize me. I tried so hard, and I never did anything right. I could tell my mom everything all the time. She was upset that all my teammates cared about was competing. When it came to quitting I had to have my mom call the coach, because I was so upset and crying.*
>
> —Christine, high school cheerleader

> *I cry all the time. When I get frustrated I cry and it doesn't bother me, so I just do it. My coach says not to get frustrated. I had an injured ankle and I was pushing myself, and I couldn't hold it in. After he talked to me, I was fine and kept*

*playing. I don't cry uncontrollably. When I get frustrated I just
cry, and I don't think it's bad.*

—Tricia, high school volleyball

In some cases there'll be girls who need to open the floodgates
and have a good cry. How do you deal with all these emotions? Begin by asking in a concerned way what is going on. First, find out if
there is any physical injury. If not, I usually invite the girl to talk to
me. Not all girls like to tell you right away what is wrong, so use the
following checklist, and by a process of elimination you may discover what the problem is. The question is, is the crying brought
about by frustration or by fear?

FRUSTRATION ISSUES

- The inability to perform the skills that are being trained
- Perceived unfair coaching or refereeing decision
- Losing a game
- Name-calling, fighting between players, cutting in line, not get-
ting enough turns
- Not receiving enough attention by the coach
- Emotionally stretched to their limits

FEAR ISSUES

- Potential for physical harm
- Bullying tactics by a coach
- Nervousness before competition
- Parental reaction
- Entering a new group or a new environment

Here are some more ways, in no particular order, to deal with crying:

- Find out if girls need to step out of play or if they can pull them-
selves together and get back into the game as quickly as possible.
- Have a private meeting after practice or a game.
- Use humor to try to get girls to understand it's not the end of the
world.
- Hold back and see if the girls can work it out among themselves.
- With older, more experienced players, ask them directly how they
think the issue should be resolved.

Do You Have the Safety Knowledge?

Having the necessary skills to deal with potential health and safety problems are essential if you're going to be a coach. Do you have a current CPR and first-aid certification? If not, it's a good idea to attain them. Use your phone directory to contact the American Red Cross or American Heart Association to get the dates and locations of courses held in your area. Training lasts anywhere from four to eight hours depending on the program you select.

In addition to being certified in first aid and CPR, there are other safety issues that need to be addressed regularly.

- The safety of outdoor fields (holes in the ground), and of equipment, should be checked before having athletes start practice or a game.
- Medical emergencies: Carry signed waivers with you at all times so that if there is a serious accident, you can take the appropriate action if the parent is not present. In case of an emergency, have a chain of command. Decide which of your support staff will stay with the injured child (it could be the team mom) and who will remain with the team. The parent's waiver should include information regarding any allergies or special medical conditions the child might have.
- Have a first-aid kit at every practice and game. Carry ice at all times. It is also smart to have feminine hygiene products along with the first-aid supplies.
- Establish an accident report log. This journal should record the date and time of the accident, note how it was handled, and identify what caused the accident. If you ever have a lawsuit brought against you, this is useful documentation in court.
- Decide if children need a physical before they begin an athletic activity. Safety also involves knowing the fitness of each child. If you have a girl who is overweight, has allergies, or has a serious lack of physical strength, it can be noted on a special form.

How Coaching Girls Differs from Coaching Boys

With girls there is always a mixed agenda—the social and the athletic. Getting these two approaches to square with each other is every coach's challenge. The social agenda says, "I'm a person; team relationships are important; I want my coach to care about me other than my skills."

- Girls want to develop a personal relationship through communication with you. This shows that you care about them beyond their athletic abilities. Ask them, "How are you doing?" "What's new?" and "Is everything okay today?" Staying in touch with their emotions, especially when they are injured, is critical. When they answer, you really need to listen to them. Yet for male coaches it is important that caring not turn intimate.
- Girls need to be coached with a positive approach both in words and body language. With boys you can say, "Get out there and take care of business." With girls you need to say, "Let's pull together and work like a team." Frantic facial and hand gestures are displays of body language that can upset players to the point that they're not giving their best.
- Girls need to feel that criticism is not a personal attack.
- Girls process information differently; they want more details, they want to work through each step. Boys will receive information and act on it in a kamikaze fashion.
- Encourage girls to not dumb down. If you see a player whose skills are obviously above those of the other players, chances are she will lower her level of play to fit in with the majority. You've got to try to keep her working at her level and ask her to help the other girls get better.
- When girls talk about having a great team, it's all about how they will work together. Boys usually talk about what a great "forward" or "kicker" they have.
- Girls are generally open-minded enough to listen to what the coach has to say. When you work with boys they will dispute many statements.
- Team makeup, to be successful, must take into consideration that particular girls will play better with some players than other girls they have not bonded with. When a competitive team roster has to be put together, you need to consider which players play the best with each other. That will be your most productive group. Further, the companionship frequently extends to life beyond the game.

In the summer of 1999 a newspaper article was written about the USA Women's Soccer team as they prepared for the World Cup tournament. The writer noted that "fellowship has been a key element in the team's overwhelming success, something the men never have matched—on the field or off." Mia Hamm, a gold medal performer from Atlanta and a goal-scoring leader, stated, "There is never a time you feel you are by yourself or alone. It's a powerful feeling of camaraderie."

A Female Coach's Perspective

Here is an example of one coach's experience training young women:

> *I have some very sensitive girls on my recreation team. It depends on the girl as to how I handle the situation—you have to know how to read girls. I try to use comedy to lighten up the situation. In general, though, I tell them, "Don't get down on yourself if you make a mistake. That's what learning is all about. Nobody's going to get mad at you, and if they do, it's their problem." You have to try to get them to think that way, so that they'll get themselves in a positive frame of mind.*
>
> *I tell them it's just a game, that as long as you play hard, that's what counts. With my more competitive team, I tell them, "Don't be afraid to make a mistake, but don't be afraid and make a mistake. Try not to play scared and hold back. If you play fearlessly and make a mistake in that process, you'll learn something. But you'll never know what you're capable of if you don't go all out." When we are practicing together, I let them know they can't be soft on each other (which girls tend to do). If they don't play aggressively, they won't be ready for a game situation.*
>
> —J.D., parent coach

Male Coach's Perspective

I have chosen to include a variety of perspectives from male coaches, as there are more males coaching girls than females. I didn't have to go very far when I wanted to get some ideas from a male coach about how he views coaching girls as being different from coaching boys. You see, my husband has been coaching girls' gymnastics for twenty-five years. He made the transition from coaching men's collegiate gymnastics to an age-group girls' program. My husband says, "I've learned the hard way that there are things you can't do or say to girls whether they're six or sixteen. For example, you can't tell girls to 'knock it off' when they are fooling around; you have to say, 'Settle down.' I've learned that you can't pop teenage girls on the scale every day [weigh them] and have them feel good about themselves."

The renowned women's soccer coach Aaron Dorrance at North Carolina University has developed an acute awareness of team sport interrelationships. He notes that the toughest part of his job is to get players to feel comfortable competing against each other during team practice. He recognizes that "head-to-head physical confrontation with friends and teammates is not where girls are naturally comfortable." You have to encourage them to let this side of themselves develop on the field of play, that it's okay.

Coach Rick Lyderson, who trains softball players, shared these impressions. "Boys are kind of a kamikaze type. So I encourage them to watch competitive girls for their teamwork, their effort, the way they support each other. Girls will do anything for each other. If one is having a problem, she has eight allies. They pick each other up off and on the field. There is a mutual admiration for what they achieve athletically. Their mutual respect for each other goes well beyond the playing field. One of their motives is to gain respect from other players, which also shows up in their social life."

What Do Girls Want from Their Coaches?

I talked with some female high school athletes to get their perspective regarding what makes a good coach and what makes sports meaningful. I chose this age group because they can articulate what is on their minds, and they've got the experience to back up their observations. Here's what high school girls had to say:

An Ideal Coach

I'm the kind of person who likes to have attention, so I like it when coaches give me personal attention or tell me when I'm doing a good job or when I need work on something. But I hate it when they ignore me. I've experienced being on the bench, and I've experienced being a starter. I noticed that when you're on the bench, the coaches don't work with you so that you can develop the skills to be a starter. Starters are on one level, and the other players are on another level. When you are a starter you get special attention. I'd have to stay after practice and come early to get the help I needed. Lots of coaches only want to work with those players who are winners. Star players get more attention than other people. My ideal coach is someone who listens, someone who demonstrates the activity, who gives me and my teammates a lot of encouragement and pats on the back. I also appreciate a coach who communicates with me along the way about my progress on a regular basis and doesn't wait till there's a big problem to explain the right way to do something.

Having a Responsive Coach

My coach now is very energetic, and I just feel like I can talk to her about anything. She always has her little schedule of what we are going to do, what we need to work on. She tapes our games and makes us watch them even when we don't want to. She shows us what we need to improve. Really talks to us. Communication is really a big thing. If you don't have it, it can break down a whole team. As the head coach, she takes the time for you. You know she's going to be there for you. She's calm and knows the sport. I like the way she helps us mentally and physically.

Having a Nonresponsive Coach

Our varsity coach was a man, and he was used to coaching guys. He stepped in to coach us because we lost our original coach. It seemed like he was thinking, I'll coach the girls because I know how to coach basketball. *He didn't realize there was a big difference between girls' and boys' basketball. He didn't have the time to put into us. I suffered from that personally. When he kicked me out of a game and didn't tell me what I had done wrong, it really hurt. He would not talk to me, he'd just say, "Take a rest." At the beginning of the season I played a lot. Finally at the end of the season I was on the bench all the time. I didn't know what I needed to do to get better. When I asked him for help, he said, "You're fine." He wasn't helping me. A coach needs to take the time to prepare to help each one of the athletes on his team.*

Coaching Your Own Daughter

Some parents go into coaching because they played sports in high school or college and want to provide the same kind of guidance they received. Others coach just because they love a particular sport. Then there are those parents who coach because they think they can make a difference in how their daughter grows up through a sport. The hope of these parents is that they'll be able to give their child lots of attention if they are the head coach of a team. Unfortunately, however, such favoritism can have a negative effect. What if a girl believes deep down that her ability to top her teammates exists only because her parent is there for her? Does that make her ready to compete against other players in a new environment without her parent coach?

Perhaps when you look at your daughter, you see untapped potential. She listens well, she's fast and strong, and above all, she's very coordinated. Yet you've been watching some of her practices and you are somewhat frustrated. You feel that she could do better if someone would push her to meet her aptitude. Perhaps if you were her coach, your firsthand knowledge of her abilities could give her the edge she needs.

If you asked your daughter if she wanted you to coach her, what might she say? What she says and what she feels could be quite different. From her point of view, it would be neat to have Mom or Dad there to provide the TLC during the tough times at practice or in competition. But what about those times when you might be tougher on her than the other girls? In this section we're going to consider these and other issues concerning coaching your own daughter.

Potential Concerns

Here are potential problems that you should consider if you're thinking of becoming your daughter's coach:

• Be careful about giving your daughter more attention than you give the other girls.

- Be careful about not giving your daughter special treatment. You might actually end up neglecting her in order to prove that you're not being biased.
- Be careful about being tougher on her than you are on the other players, especially in the car on the way home or at home.

This is a story about a parent who has dealt with the realities of coaching his daughter.

> *I coach my daughter Chelsea in softball and soccer. I think the toughest thing is to have your daughter take you seriously. Other girls listen to you better than your own daughter. It's often the same as at home; sometimes they listen to you, sometimes they don't. I have to be careful not to show favoritism. On the other side of the coin, I'm tougher on her because you can say things to your daughter that you can't say to other girls. But unlike the other girls, my daughter will just ignore me if she doesn't like what I am saying. And that's not a good thing.*
>
> *The best thing about the experience is that we've developed a closer relationship, and I get to spend time with her. Lots of fathers aren't even involved at all. I think they're missing a lot.*
> —Jim, parent coach

The experience of this parent coach turned out to be positive because the father knew how to control his emotions and had a goal of having a great relationship with his daughter. This is not an easy task, but it can be incredibly rewarding if you are patient.

Reasonable Solutions

If you feel you can coach your daughter's team even-handedly, then review the following recommendations and use them on the field of play:

- Handle your child the same way you would any other girl on the team, in matters both of support and of discipline.
- Make it fun for your daughter to be with you.
- Give your daughter the opportunity to ask questions, just like any other team member.

- When pointing out your daughter's errors in front of others, do so diplomatically—just as you would with any other girl on your team.
- Do not continue to bring up your daughter's mistakes in the car on the way home. Once you hit the car, you're her parent, not her coach.
- Allow her space to make mistakes.
- If you need to critique an assistant coach or referee, do it away from her.
- It's best if you get some feedback from other parents regarding how you are doing as a coach. As tough as it may be, you also need to hear what your daughter has to say about how you're treating her as a team member. It is very easy for a girl to become embarrassed in front of her friends when her parent coach is acting inappropriately.
- Using your daughter as a sounding board, as you drive home from practice or a game, to critique or criticize other team members' play only invites ill will. Take up your concerns with the coach or the assistant coach.

While coaching girls may be a tough job, often the toughest job is to be the child of the coach. Be careful that being your daughter's coach doesn't invade all areas of your family life. Many coaches report a letdown after the season. To prevent this from happening, make sure that during and after season you and your daughter do things that are completely non–sport related. Occasionally parents don't know how to relate to their children if they're not doing sports. They're not quite sure how to interact with their child because there has been such an overemphasis on this part of their relationship. Maintain a healthy sports/nonsports balance in your relationship by keeping the two separate, and you'll both be happier.

The Parent, Athlete, Coach Relationship

To make things run smoothly for all concerned, you've got to keep the lines of communication open. The parents and athlete must know the objectives of the coach, the coach must know what the parents want for their child, and most important of all, the coach must know what the athlete wants for herself.

Advice for Parents

Before you sign up, take these things into consideration:

- Watch the coach in action at a game and practice before you sign up.
- Get together with the coach before the season. After the program expectations have been laid out, talk to your daughter about what is expected from her with respect to attendance at practice and so on. Find out from the coach if your daughter needs special help to get her skills up to speed.
- Listen to and evaluate what current team members and parents have to say about a particular coach.
- Consider what your daughter has to say about the coach and the learning environment.
- Be willing to let the child "own" the sport for herself. Otherwise there will be a time when an overbearing parent will hear the child say, "If you like it so much, you do it."
- Let the coach know you are supportive of his or her efforts. If there are skills to be practiced at home, encourage and help your daughter to do so. The trick is to not make it a chore. Ask her if and when she wants to practice skills, and play with her.
- If you have a disagreement with the coach, go to him or her first instead of being a "locker room lawyer" out in the waiting room or in the bleachers.

Here are some thoughts about the parent-coach relationship from a well-seasoned mother:

> I've been most productive talking to a coach [when a problem arises] by being nonconfrontational and approaching the situation in an intelligent, genuinely concerned way. I tell the coach, "I would like some information regarding . . ." or, "Can you tell me what is going on with such-and-such situation?" If you rush in and the coach feels that you're there just to blame or complain in anger, you won't get very far. You need to sense how the coach is feeling. If you are emotional, cool down and ask questions later.

Advice for Athletes

From the coach's point of view, a player's talent is not the most important factor. Desire and determination are far more significant. If a girl really wants to grab a coach's attention, show her or him the willingness to put in some effort. A coach will go above and beyond the call of duty for a player who's sincere about making progress. When love of a sport is reflected from the inside out, it will show up during the tough times. Even the greatest professional athlete will give the same reason for staying with a sport—"I still enjoy going out there every day."

- Respect the coach's suggestions, because she or he has experience and knows the sport you're trying to learn.
- Let the coach know if you don't understand something or if you're having trouble learning a certain skill. The coach is there to help you.
- Let your parents know if there are problems the coach is not addressing or that you feel uncomfortable bringing up with the coach.

Advice for Coaches

The coach has to be able to communicate on two levels, on one level with the athletes and on another with the parents. In the beginning of the season the coach should set up a meeting that parents and athletes must attend. This should be an informational meeting at which schedules are handed out, policies are reviewed, uniform and tournament costs are announced, and questions are answered. I know one veteran coach who will cancel the parent-athlete meeting if there is not 100 percent attendance. Expectations should be made clear, both for the parents and for the athlete. That way families can decide if they want to go ahead and commit or back out.

One coach told me a lesson that he learned about motivation from one of his athletes. He worked with a young girl who was fairly quiet, and it was difficult to get through to her. To make her feel she was important, one day he went up to her and said, "Are you coming to the tournament this weekend?" She said, "Yes," because that's what she thought he wanted to hear. He said, much to her surprise, "Good, we need you." Megan had never been made to feel so accepted, and she couldn't wait to get home to tell her mom about how the coach *took an interest in her.* From that day on she never missed a practice.

Coaches should try to make the parents feel accepted, also. Give them time to talk with you at the end of practice. Basically, all the parents want to know is how their daughter is doing. Here's what one parent likes about her daughter's coach:

> *I really appreciate when the coach just visits with the parents after practice, whether it's about the needs of the team or my child in particular. It's nice to feel that the coach cares about the whole family. There's good solid rapport, and he tries hard to include the parents in the planning of upcoming events. At meets he always acknowledges that we are there, he's not just looking to see if my child has been dropped off. He tells us what is going on. Because my child's coach has kept us well informed, I feel well versed in the terminology of the sport and knowing what is expected at the competitive level. I feel I know what my child is going through.*

Supportive Coaching Is the Key

If girls are coached in a supportive manner that is sensitive to their needs as young women, at the very least they will enjoy their sports experience. If they continue to be involved with a sport at the competitive level, they will reap the rewards of supportive coaching by being physically skilled and emotionally strong enough to handle the ups and downs of competition.

A coach's job is to oversee the educational process of his or her players. A good coach knows how to observe each player individually, to assess her strengths and weakness and her personality, and then to work with that player to help her improve both her technical and her personal skills. Coaches must also be willing to evaluate themselves and to acknowledge and correct their own deficiencies, whether personal or technical. When a coach creates an environment where every player feels valued, and the players respect their coach, you've got a dynamite combination.

CHAPTER

Role Models Come in All Shapes and Sizes

9

Role models come in all shapes and sizes. Thank goodness. Imagine what it would be like for your five-foot-ten-inch daughter if her only athletic role models were a team of tiny gymnasts on television? Chances are she would never go out for sports and would suffer through her junior high school days as a slump-shouldered girl—unless she had a tall mom who was physically active in sports. Girls need to have role models on a sport by sport basis. When girls see other female athletes who have a similar body shape and size flourishing in the same sport in which they're participating, aspiring young players hold out hope for themselves to be like that athlete—successful and happy with themselves.

One of the best things to come out of the 1996 Summer Olympic Games and the 1998 Winter Olympic Games was the abundance of female role models. There were the ice hockey players validating the aspirations of girls who wanted to wield wooden sticks. And what about the scrappy softball and soccer players, who showed no fear diving face first into the action? Now it's common to wander into any sports-minded girl's bedroom and find a poster or two on the wall of an athlete she holds in high esteem. Behind her idolatry is the simple pleasure of watching her heroine or hero perform with exceptional skill.

We haven't quite reached the day when a shot of Mom in Spandex or Dad in his baseball cap and workout attire is prominently displayed on a child's bedroom dresser. But remember, parents, we need to make sure our girls look beyond television for their role models. We can be role models, too. Believe me, we are being examined by young women, and either admired or rebuked, on a regular basis. So take charge of your image.

In this chapter we'll look at the ways in which parents and coaches—as well as older siblings and sports stars—are role models for both attitudes and actions.

Ideally a parent or coach views physical activity as a way of life and stays fit through recreation and/or sports participation. At the same time, they inspire and encourage children to be physically active. Many parents find it difficult to model the level of activity they would like for their children. But you must try if you are to make the most of your potential as a role model.

What Does Being a Role Model Mean?

Above all, being a role model means you're someone children look up to for support, advice, and inspiration. It also means that you'll do some smart things and other times make mistakes. What do girls have to say about the qualities they look for in a role model, whether it is a parent or a coach? The girls I work with and have interviewed tell me that they want someone who

- can be depended on for inspiration.
- is responsible.
- demonstrates good morals.
- has patience.
- is kind.
- is worthy of respect and who will respect them in return.
- brings out the best in them.
- shows them how to help to be their best and how to help others.

As you go about your daily life, you're not always aware of the times when a child is looking at you as a role model. That means that each day you need to live your life as though someone were watching your every move. That's a tall order. A softball coach I spoke with, a former professional baseball player, had a well-conceived position regarding being a daily role model. I share his thoughts with you because he is both a parent and volunteer community coach.

> *Your actions speak louder than you think. Your actions tell people what you think, so I conduct myself as a role model every day. I want my kids—my children and the kids I coach—to be proud of the way I act. I conduct my life in such a way that I can be proud to be their role model. I can see by the way my daughter introduces me that she is proud of me. I also let parents of my athletes know what I expect of their child when I'm coaching them, and that includes a message about unacceptable behavior. If you think about it, what is the highest compliment someone could give you? That you are a role model. In terms of technical skill, I feel I have a huge responsibility on my part to be knowledgeable. Girls will need the right information to be able to play high school or college sports.*
>
> —Rick, parent, softball coach
> and former professional baseball player

I want to mention that Rick not only does his job well, but he looks like the kind of a coach you would want your daughter to have. He keeps himself in good shape, he maintains a professional appearance with his grooming and clothing, and he always wears a positive attitude on his face. He has seen firsthand how far sports can take a person who chooses to stretch his or her body and mind, meeting challenge after challenge. Helping children, especially girls (and including his daughter), continue their involvement with sports is a very important part of Rick's life.

The reasons that I coach today are far different from the ones I started out with thirty years ago. I have learned along the way to value the traits that girls most want from parents and coaches. That in turn has helped me to value the work I do. Kids want to be able to depend on parents and coaches to take care of them. They want not just to learn sports skills, but to enjoy doing sports, to develop and enjoy relationships and deal with challenges. After thirty years of teaching, I embrace my position as an educator, not just my proficiency as a gymnastics instructor. I'm fairly certain that very few of the students I instruct will be turning somersaults in their sixties, but they will be turning personal skills into careers and thoughts into visions. That's where I can play a supporting role to parents or, in some cases, a leading role for girls who may be in unfortunate family circumstances and don't have a positive role model at home. The people skills and personal values that I can help children to develop are worth more to me in the long run than any other accomplishment in the gym.

Parents and Siblings as Role Models

Are you wondering how to inspire your children athletically since you don't really see yourself as Lindsey Davenport or Michael Jordan? If you're a parent reading this, relax. You don't have to be an athletic trailblazer to be a good role model for your daughter! Whatever image you might have of yourself, know that you have the potential to be a terrific sports role model.

Whether you're raising or coaching children, the first thing to remember is that you're being sized up. How many times has your own child, or one on your team, said, "If you can't do it, how do you expect me to do it?" The success and enjoyment girls find through sports depends on you—you play the number one role. In families where parents are or have been involved with fitness or recreational or competitive sports, the likelihood that children will follow in the same footsteps is great. This is especially true when families dedicate time to play together. By your own behavior, you are teaching them that fitness is part of family togetherness. And if fitness is a focus in your life, you are already a role model for your daughter.

You may be saying to yourself, "I've never even whispered the word *push-up*, let alone done one." It doesn't matter to me if you think you're ready to collect Social Security, collect yourself emotionally and begin just by taking a vigorous walk with your daughter. Perhaps you can walk as she in-line skates. It may be that participating in sports beyond that daily or weekly walk is just not going to happen in your lifetime for a health reason. You can still be a role model by enthusiastically going to her practices and games and giving your daughter the emotional support she needs.

Mom as Role Model

When it comes to sports involvement, moms can model exemplary behavior for their daughters in a number of ways. The following three stories reveal different roles mothers can play. Each of these moms has found a way to be part of their daughter's sporting life.

THE SUPPORTIVE PARENT

When my girls started playing soccer, I wanted to support them. I knew I couldn't coach or run up and down the soccer field, so I asked the head coach, "What can I do to help?" He said I should volunteer to be the team mom. He needed someone to call the participating families to remind them of practices, to coordinate the fund-raising, to organize who was bringing the snacks. I was the first person the head coach would call to get things done. I recall one time I even had to make the team banner, which was pretty challenging for me since I'm not an artsy-craftsy person. Ugh.

It was a great feeling for me that my girls felt that they could rely on me. They would even volunteer me to take other girls home from practice. Because I was the team mom, my girls felt I was actively supporting them. Soccer became something we could share, more than me just "putting them into" a sport.

I think I put extra effort into this because I wanted my children to know the cooperative spirit, that being on a team was an extension of being a family.

—Joyce, team mom, mother of three girls

THE PHYSICALLY ACTIVE AND SUPPORTIVE PARENT

After my second child, I had gained thirty-four pounds. I was really frustrated because prior to that I used the trampoline in my backyard and stayed active all the time. In high school I was a diver, but I knew that it would be nearly impossible to keep that up with a growing family. So last fall I took up bicycling through a local club. I made a commitment to get a baby-sitter so that I would have time just for me two days of the week. My husband joins me on the weekend. It's so good for our girls to see my husband and me ride together. Now that Jacqueline is three and has her own bike, I can't wait until she and her younger sister are older and we all can ride together. We can't wait for the girls to go up that really tough hill that we hate and see them pass us.

The healthy aspect of sports is critical for me. I've learned that your body is very important, so you need to take care of it. When I'm active I eat so much better. I don't want to be a fat mom who can't run on the field with my girls and play soccer. Giving myself the time to get exercise makes me a better mother. I'm in a better frame of mind. I feel so much better about myself, and I have more energy.

—Carrie, mother of two girls

THE COACHING PARENT

When I was growing up, it was frowned upon in my household to be athletic. This was very frustrating because my natural way is to be active. I think of myself as an athletic-jock-grown-up tomboy. I knew when I had my daughter that I would do everything I could to get her into sports since I didn't have a role model when I was a girl.

I first started coaching soccer with my boys when they were young. It was kind of funny and sad at the same time, because the first time I ever kicked a ball was when my son was seven. After helping coach the boys, I wanted to do more. I went to coaching classes and did all kinds of things so that I could do the best I could for the kids. The next thing that happened was that I became an assistant coach for a man training a girls' program. His lack of believing in the girls really put me off. I realized then that I wanted to be a coach for girls, since there weren't any female role models.

I eventually became the head soccer coach. I have learned so much from the girls on my team. One day a very brave little girl came up to me and said, "You haven't played me, and I don't care if we win or lose because I have nothing to do with this game." I thought about this for a long time, asking myself, Why are we out here, anyway? I knew my role had to change from focusing on winning to focusing on each girl. As I *worked with that young girl, she turned into the kind of player you just couldn't keep off the field.*

My philosophy was, Just do your best. You win by playing the best you can, whether we win or lose. I also wanted the members of my team to know that it's okay for girls to be aggressive in sports. I taught them that they should never back down. There's nothing wrong with playing hard. Finally, I wanted them to realize that a team has to work together. Of special importance to me was not allowing anybody to be ridiculed. I would not tolerate unkindness. Through coaching I felt that I could have a positive influence on girls' lives and be the role model I never had.

—Judy, mom turned coach, one daughter and one son.

My Mom

How did my mom serve as a role model? She was a supporter, the one who took us on long walks down to Hammond Pond, where we searched for pollywogs; to the Charles River in Boston for tree climbing and running; to tap and swim classes at the local recreation center. No matter the season of the year, she insisted that we play outdoors by riding our bikes or building ice forts out of outrageous amounts of New England snow. She encouraged us to be active rather than moping around the house—television was not an option. My mother was the cheering squad at the playground, probably driven crazy by countless entreaties of "Watch me!" She was someone who helped me fully enjoy my childhood by just having fun, by being active, by sharing the moments that will never return except in my fondest memories.

Dad as Role Model

"Some things only a dad can do," says columnist Kathleen Parker. There's no question that a dad who plays an active role in his daughter's athletic education can help to create benefits for her that will last a lifetime. Let's look at the ways in which fathers can be positive role models when it comes to sports.

The Supportive Parent

When Jennifer and Haley made a commitment to play sports, I made a commitment to get them to softball practice and games. But I'm also big on homework. My girls know that they must get their studies in before they go to practice. So it gets done. When they commit, they have to commit 100 percent.

When they first started playing, it was easy to give them support just for being on the team. I knew I would support them whether they were successful individually or as a team. I wanted them to enjoy the game, to learn as much as they could about the game.

With sports it is easy to get wrapped up in the competitive part of it. So I tried to make it important to give positive support for all the girls on the team. That comes by going to games and, when the girls are at practice, noticing that they're making progress. My daughters know that if they want me to help pitching or catching balls, I'll be there. I want to see them go as far as they want to go.

—Curt, father of two girls

THE PHYSICALLY ACTIVE AND SUPPORTIVE PARENT

I think for health reasons I've always stayed active after high school and college sports. I feel it keeps me more alert mentally. I still play softball, pickup basketball games, and work out year-round so that I can enjoy life to the fullest. As I look at the older population, I see that the people who stay active have much more going on in their lives.

From the very beginning when my wife and I started our family, we always did recreational activities together—biking, swimming, and camping. Even when my daughter Shannon was a preschooler, I took her to see sporting events. When I was coaching girls' basketball she'd see that, and eventually she asked me to play with her. My wife and I also played in a recreational coed softball league. It provided a nice balance because the main focus was participating and having fun.

It was in junior high school that Shannon finally settled on soccer as her favorite sport. She was fast and understood strategy. As she improved in high school, she told me she wanted to play college sports. We had talked a lot about my career in college sports, and it appealed to her. During her senior year we went to many college campuses to review pro-

grams I did everything I possibly could to help her make her dream come true of being a Division I athlete. I'm so proud of her.

—Dave, father of one daughter and one son

THE COACHING PARENT
I always felt that by staying in shape, I could get out on the basketball court and play, to do some of the things that I was asking my high school girls to do. I notice that they listen with more respect when they see me playing. Once they saw some of their own progress, I began to tell them why year-round conditioning was important. I really tried to educate them about the fitness aspect of life, not just sports. It was kind of interesting. Some of the top athletes would spend time hanging around the weight room, talking about what they were doing with sports and their life outside the gym. This was a terrific way for me to have an even greater impact on their lives. You never could have hung out in the weight room fifteen years ago and gotten to know girls in a more casual environment.

—David, father of one daughter and one son

MY DAD
Where did my own dad fit into the role model picture? He was somebody who taught our family of five to play softball and tennis, to swim, to fly kites on the beach at low tide, to ice- and roller-skate, and to balance on a pair of homemade stilts—and did all these things joyously with us as an active participant. Dad always reminded me that I would never know what I was capable of accomplishing unless I tried. He supported me ceaselessly as he saw my passion for a sport unfold through gymnastics lessons, lessons that were sometimes painful but always precious. He believed that I should be raised as a competent person, not merely as a girl. He always let me know that striving was valued, that maybe I wouldn't be the best at whatever I did, but I could try my best. He's someone who to this day can still turn a cartwheel. My dad is my hero.

Siblings as Role Models
In my family I was the firstborn. I do have a twin sister, but I was still first. I was also the first in our family to be captivated by the

sport of gymnastics during high school. It wasn't long before my sister and three younger brothers gave it a whirl. They all joined the high school team, and our family name became synonymous with gymnastics over a twelve-year span at Newton High School in Massachusetts. One brother followed in my footsteps beyond high school and became a competitor at the same university I attended, the University of Massachusetts. I'll always remember those days when we all got together and did handstands and handsprings out on the front lawn of our home. My mother didn't think it was so great when multiple pairs of feet suddenly appeared about eye level in the kitchen while she was cooking dinner, but we didn't want her to miss our spectacular performances.

What's great about sibling support is that if your brother or sister is also in sports, it provides a more intimate way to share your joys of learning something new, your frustrations of trying to perform skills, and your concerns about teammates and your coach. You can learn from siblings in a less formal way than from coaches or parents. Unlike parents who are former athletes, they're not relying on memories of how things were when they were competing. Sisters and brothers who play sports understand the demands on energy, teammate relations, what it feels like to master a particular skill. Siblings can empathize with your feelings about winning and losing. I quite enjoyed having my sister at gymnastics practice. When my brothers picked up the sport, we could go to workshops together and teach at the same summer camps. Plus, it was fun to have a shared topic of conversation, a shared passion.

CAN'T MISS WITH SIS

In the eyes of nine-year-old Haley, her twelve-year-old sister, Jennifer, is pretty neat. Jennifer has made herself into a top-notch pitcher for her local softball team. Haley has always looked up to her for guidance and support. Fortunately Jennifer takes her role model position seriously, but with a loving approach. She wants her younger sister to be all that she can be. Haley admits that what she likes about her sister is that she says, "You can do it, and don't stop until you can." In Haley's words:

> She is always encouraging me with all my sports. When I watch her play softball, I see that she's serious because she's

trying to concentrate. And she goes to watch me at my soccer games. If she didn't, I would miss her. When I first learned to swim she would encourage me so I could be on the big-girl team. Now when she goes to watch my swim meets, that makes me want to do well to show her. I like to have her help me with all my sports because she teaches me. It feels great to have my sister be there for me.

A Brother Like No Other

Many girls who are excellent basketball players developed their skills because of the opportunity to play pickup games with older brothers. In a local newspaper's account of a young girl basketball player, her brother stated, "Playing with a guy helped her. I was more physical and more skilled than girls her age." His sister agrees. "Playing with the guys really helped me improve my skills. It pushed me. Guys are stronger, bigger, and more physical. If I can beat them, I can beat any guard. . . ."

A high school soccer player happily recounts her relationship with her brother: "I have my own cheering section. My brother and I are really close because we are so close in age. He's always there for me. If I have a bad game, he'll always be the first one to say, 'You did this good,' 'You did that good.' I do the same for him. He always makes sure he comes to every one of my games. He could do plenty of other things on a Friday night, but he's there rooting for me. We always go to each other's games. It's a family thing. I think the sports have brought us closer together."

Peers as Role Models

The more I coach and work with girls, the more I realize that parents and coaches can provide a valuable lesson by teaching girls to be helpful to one another. Once you plant the seed of supportiveness by recommending that girls help one another, helpfulness and compassion will eventually become second nature. Instill this idea of girls helping girls by taking advantage of situations as they pop up or by designing circumstances. When I'm in the gym training young girls, I always try to find a situation where each child can demonstrate an activity to another child who needs help. If you make this a big part of practice, eventually they'll say, "Oh, I know how to do that. Can I help her?" Here are some thoughts from girls who have benefited by receiving help from one of their peers and come to view them as role models.

> *Tanya gave me her attention and her time to learn when I was a nobody. She would teach me what the coach was saying. It made me feel good because Tanya could come down to my level even though she was better athletically. I like her strong attitude because she doesn't allow herself to become overwhelmed. I notice that she shrugs it off when she makes a mistake and just goes on to the next thing.*
>
> —Cari, high school soccer player

> *My friend would always do her best, and if she messed up, her attitude was, "That was then, this is now." She would always tell me to not get too upset. I liked the way she was easygoing and had fun. I want to be like that. She wasn't one of the girls who wanted to grow up too fast.*
>
> —Kelsey, junior high field hockey player

> *My teammate gives me little tips on how I can be a better swimmer. She encourages me. When I was new on the team, she made me feel welcome.*
>
> —Tina, swimmer

> *The person I look up to has gone through injury and overcome lots of problems. Her sportsmanship shows all the time by having a good attitude toward everyone on the team. Sometimes it can get petty, but my friend says we are all one team, and we shouldn't talk about each other behind the scenes.*
>
> —Jennifer, softball player

Besides specifically helping another athlete on their immediate team, girls can help other girls within the sport community by volunteering their time to teach younger children. Parents can go a long way toward helping their daughters understand the concept of "giving back" early on in their lives if they suggest this. Check with the YMCAs and the Boys and Girls Clubs to find out if your daughter could be an assistant to a head coach. Perhaps there is even an elementary school with an after-school program that could benefit by your daughter's help. This will require some support from you in terms of transportation. It will be well worth it.

Coaches as Role Models

Most people are used to the customary descriptions of a great coach—someone who helps girls build their skills and develops a winning team. But there's so much more. Young female athletes have some descriptions of their own that they would like to express based on their experiences with coaches they respect and enjoy.

> *I like my coach because he is very flexible. He tries hard to get along with the players by being friendly and talkative. A good thing is that he makes time to talk to everyone, to try to find a way to help us be successful in all areas of our lives. He's very encouraging. I'd like to be as positive as he is. He's a funny person, fun to be around.*
>
> —Tina, high school swimmer

> *Coaches shouldn't expect girls to know everything the first day. They need to help you practice the basics, or you won't succeed as much as you could. If they don't help you learn the basics, you feel like giving up. My coach doesn't think winning is everything. I used to have a coach who was just the opposite, he thought he was awesome, everything had to go his way. Nobody liked that.*
>
> —Kelsey, elementary school softball player

> *I appreciate a coach who is strict and won't let you goof off. They're organized so that when you come to practice, you know what you're doing. You get a lot more out of practice. Yet they'll say things like "Nice try" and encourage you. They don't put you down. And they don't need to make you run laps for punishment.*
>
> —Jennifer, elementary school softball player

> *When I grow up, I want to be a fun person like my coach, someone I could have a relationship with, someone who cared about me.*
>
> —Kari, high school field hockey player

As you can see, girls want more than just to be on a winning team. A thought that was expressed over and over was that a good coach goes beyond the teaching of the sport. That person is able to help the athlete take away something special in her character development, something that stays with her after she leaves the sport. Coaches who truly desire to develop their players in body, mind, and spirit can one day look forward to receiving a letter like the following. It was written by a graduating senior, Alaina, who received extraordinary support from a man who was not only a classroom teacher, but her coach in after-school sports. She wrote this letter to him because she wanted him to know how much he influenced her life, especially during troubled times, and how his support helped prepare her for a career as a paramedic.

> *Dear Coach: On Monday I was reminded of how you influenced me during my three years at Escondido High. In your presence I have always felt important, never inferior or childlike. I hold you in very high regard. Your ability and choice of seeing each student as an individual are very important to me. I know that I was never an ideal student, and your patience toward me was above and beyond what most teachers would ever give. High school was a very chaotic time for me, and your patience, especially early in the morning, made a big difference. Thank you for not getting mad at me. I always felt that you saw potential in me that even I was blind to. Still today that encourages me and gives me hope in the future. My work in athletics training was never anything that someone else could not do. But it was often overlooked. You and Coach Rossetta always made me feel like an invaluable and irreplaceable asset to the athletic program. Thank you for making me feel so special. I know of no way to repay you for all of this. I can only hope that this letter encourages you to continue being a wonderful teacher, coach, and person. Most important, please know that you are appreciated.*
>
> *—Alaina, upon graduating senior high school*

After Alaina read the letter to me, she stated that there was no way she could repay her coach. I told her that when he read this letter, it would be with teary eyes—and it would be payment enough.

Athletic Superstars as Role Models

At some point in your daughter's life, it's likely that a particular high-profile athlete will capture her imagination. Maybe it's the celebrity athlete's phenomenal accomplishments or their fierce determination, style, or personality. It's likely that those reasons for admiration will change over time. Having superstar competitors be role models works best when young athletes know a lot about their hero's background. Sometimes they come from very financially restricted childhoods. Instead of having the best gyms or playing fields to do their training, they trained wherever possible. And while it certainly helps to be very talented, many great athletes, by their own admission, have average abilities. Yet their inner strength combined with a crystal-clear vision helps carry them through the daily struggles of practice. Cynthia Cooper, for instance, a Women's National Basketball Association player, states that her training situation is governed by discipline. She notes that even in the off-season, she still gets up at six-thirty A.M. so that she maintains consistent habits.

Certainly some superstars have habits that no parents would want their child to have—yelling at referees, throwing tennis rackets, grabbing an opponent by the throat. Without naming names, the professional athletes who display this unnecessary behavior are phenomenally competitive, but also incredibly unashamed of showing it.

To make sure that your daughter is not edging toward the kind of role model who is out of control, attend her tournaments so that you can observe and understand her behavior. For your daughter to have a healthy attitude, you must be very clear about what you will and will not accept. I used to know an athlete whose behavior was so self-centered and out of control that she alienated every last one of her teammates. The problem was that neither the coach nor the parents stepped in to change the behavior because they wanted the young lady to make it to the top. On more occasions than not, it was not fun to be around her no matter how talented she was.

MY ROLE MODEL

When I was a competitive gymnast, I followed the career of a Russian gymnast, Ludmilla Tourescheva. She was dignified under pressure (no pouting, no tears), she was physically very strong, yet all her moves had a graceful, balletic quality. Strangely enough, thirty years later I had the opportunity to accord Ludmilla the fame she so richly deserved. As a member of the board of directors for the International Gymnastics Hall of Fame, I was on the selection committee that chose to induct her. I never would have guessed in a million years that I could be part of my sports hero's life. When I met her at the induction ceremony in 1998, she was every bit as gracious as I had imagined her to be. Through a translator I was able to tell her of my great admiration for her ability. Also through the translator she told me that I looked as though I were still in good shape. What a button buster that was!

REALITY CHECK

There will always be some girls who admire superstars because of the fame that goes with the job. The travel, the cars, the money, the notoriety, can be pretty inviting. But often children don't realize the hard work that goes into winning an athletic scholarship, which may then lead to fame and fortune for only a very few. This came to my attention when I was a guest speaker on Role Model Day at one of the local junior high schools. There were children who wanted to play professional sports until the subject of education was brought up. When I mentioned that recruiters found athletes through high school and college educational programs, it took a little of the glow off the flame of fame. In my experience it is just a fantasy for children to expect to be a superstar until they understand the amount of time and education that must be dedicated to such a goal.

MALE AND FEMALE ROLE MODELS

It only makes sense to encourage your daughter to respect both female and male sports celebrities—as long as those "superstars" are worthy of a child's admiration. One dad, whose teenage daughter is a soccer player, mentioned that she admires Olympic female soccer player Mia Hamm because of the publicity and honor she has brought to the sport. When his daughter grows up, she wants to be everything that Mia is. She also respects professional male soccer player Slobo Ilijevski for his community involvement and dedication to fund-raising for local groups. The teenager appreciates her role model's generous nature and the fact that he acts like a regular person.

LOOKING THROUGH A CHILD'S EYES

Unless a special event is set up for children to meet and work with superstars, they'll probably never have direct contact with them. However, the indirect contact can be just as important. *Sports Illustrated for Kids,* a magazine that covers the lives of superstars on and off the field of play, includes a letters section that is most revealing of what children think. The young athletes who write are observant and know their sport. Here's a sampling of some of the mail from the magazine's readers:

> *Dear Editor: Last season in the WNBA, I kept hearing about how the centers and forwards made great shots right under the basket. Well, who do you think got the ball to those players? The point guards! That's the position I play. And that's why I admire guard Teresa Weatherspoon of the New York Liberty!*
> —Becky, age 13

> *Dear Editor: Thanks for writing about ABL free-throw ace Carolyn Jones of the New England Blizzard. Her tips on shooting free throws helped me win a game for my team.*
> —Michael, age 10

This last letter caught my eye because it was written by a young *boy* who had read a story about a female basketball player in the magazine.

It's All About Giving Back to the Community

I have always admired great athletes who "give back" to the sport that made them develop a passion, reach for goals in life, and become famous. Your daughter should know about famous athletes who have done just this. One such person is five time Olympic track star Willye White, who created the Robert Taylor Girls Athletic Program in Chicago's South Side. If anybody has worked her way up in the world and educated others to pursue their own personal development, it's Willye White. Raised by her grandparents, White was taught that she could work in the cotton fields or make another future for herself. It didn't take long for her to realize that she wanted more for herself than backbreaking work. By the age of twelve she had already discovered her love of running on a track and soon became the Mississippi high school state champion. So talented and dedicated was she that White qualified for her first Olympics by the age of sixteen. The extraordinary career of Willye White lasted a remarkable twenty-seven years.

After an injury forced her to retire from competition, White turned to teaching. Her goal was to create a program where girls could focus on developing self-esteem through after-school activities that included sports. In an interview with *Parade* magazine, she is quoted as saying, "It took me fifty-seven years to find the job of my life. This is my ministry. I am creating productive citizens for the year 2000 and beyond." Although Willye White never had children herself, she has undoubtedly influenced the lives of the hundreds she has worked with.

If you're a parent, I encourage you to talk with your daughter and explore her thoughts about teachers or coaches who have meant something to her. Should she have someone in mind, suggest to her that she write a note to that special person. It certainly makes the recipient feel good and reminds him or her of what's important. This is also another way you can be a role model, demonstrating that communicating appreciation is an admirable trait.

Every once in a while someone will write to me and let me know that my involvement has touched them in a remarkable way. This letter came to me from an employee:

Dear Susan: Thank you for inviting me to the premiere screening of the HBO sports documentary Dare to Compete. *That was quite an event. I was really impressed by the women I met at the reception. They were successful, professional, and dedicated to promoting sports. In other words, they were a lot like you. Someday I hope I can be in that same category.*

In the meantime, I want to get involved with promoting

sports any way I can. You helped me realize the importance of sports. It's not about gymnastics or baseball, it's about making life a better experience. So, whether it ends up being my cause or my career, it's something I want to support. Thank you for inspiring me.

I cried.

Protecting a Girl's Right to Play Sports Her Way

10

Messages about who we are and what we can do are passed along from generation to generation. As I have said, for me, the first message about sports was instilled by my dad. He always encouraged me to try whatever I wanted to do, though I doubt he had ever heard of the phrase *gender equity* back in the early sixties. If he had, it would have only added fuel to the fire of his personal philosophy. He believed that my activities should never be limited by the fact that I was a girl. He did everything possible within his power to give loads of opportunities to me and my twin sister. That included standing up to his mother regularly, who thought her granddaughters did very weird things when they did gymnastics. Little did my dad or my grandmother know that my attachment to sports would lead to skydiving and other equally dangerous activities—but that was after he finished paying for college!

Playing high school sports, though, was the first time I noticed that athletics for girls and boys might be different. The girls' gymnastics team had to practice in back of the bleachers when the boys were playing a basketball game. Funny, when I tell this to girls I coach today, they say, "I never would have stood for that!" Little do they know on whose shoulders they stand.

When I went on to college sports, the training conditions had improved greatly from my high school days. Women shared fabulous training facilities with men and had well-designed locker rooms. I was so busy training and enjoying gymnastics that I had no idea about budgets, prime-time scheduling, tutors, and special dining arrangements. I did notice that our transportation to away games was by station wagon, not the university bus. (This arrangement did not include my senior year, when I lived off campus and had to thumb a ride to the gym before I could even ride in the station wagon.) But for the most part, and as far as my teammates and I were concerned, things were relatively comfortable. What did we know? If there were back room issues, such as budgeting, our coach protected us from them.

In the years since my own college days, the pursuit of gender equity (equal opportunities regardless of sex) has led to impressive accomplishments in the world of girls' and women's sports. This is especially true at colleges and universities and on the international scene at the Olympics and world championships. But it took more than coaches to make sure that girls and women got the sports opportunities they deserve; it took federal legislation.

Title IX: The Turning Point That Gave Girls a Chance

After the close of the 1996 and 1998 Olympiads, many people asked how the women got to be so good so fast. During the 1996 Summer Olympic Games, the "Year of the Women," American women won far more gold in the overall medal count for the United States than the men. Of the 101 medals awarded to the United States, 69 were won by women. The driving force behind all this achievement was Title IX, an education amendment passed in 1972 that guaranteed gender equity in federally funded programs. When Title IX was enacted, only one in twenty-seven girls played high school sports. Now it's one in three. In colleges and universities in 1972, there were 31,000 women athletes, compared with 110,000 in 1998. Participation is not all that has changed. Athletic scholarships for young women rose dramatically from a national average of less than $100,000 to $179 million because of schools being forced to follow Title IX guidelines.

Title IX states:

*. . . No person in the United States shall, on the basis of sex,
be excluded from participation in, be denied the benefits of, or
be subject to discrimination under any education program or
activity receiving federal financial assistance. . . .*

Try not to let the wording throw you off track. Title IX means
that any educational system that receives federal money must not
practice sex discrimination in the programs they offer. When the
law was written, it was designed to target only sex discrimination
and apply to *any* education program that receives federal funding. If
the requirements aren't followed, federal money can be cut off. However, the focus has shifted to include athletic programs at schools
and universities, parks and recreation facilities, and within intramural athletic organizations. This does not necessarily mean that
the same amount of money must be spent on the athletic programs
at a given institution for both sexes. The main thrust is to make the
programs comparable. This is done by following specific written
guidelines.

How Educational Programs Meet Legal Requirements
To meet the requirements of Title IX, schools need to show that
they can pass a three-prong test. Yes, that's right. *Schools* have to
pass a test. Ask and answer for yourself the following questions regarding your daughter's school:

- Do the programs match the abilities and interests of girls and
  young women?
- Are female athletic opportunities proportionate to the ratio of females in the student body?
- Does the school have a history of expanding programs for females?

If you spend a little time finding out the answers to these questions regarding your daughter's school, you will have begun the
process of educating yourself about gender equity. Most public
schools are taking the necessary steps to comply with Title IX.
However, if you believe some inequities still exist at your school,
this chapter will provide you with specific ways to deal with them.

Parents, please know that *you* are your daughter's best advocate for a value-driven, balanced education—that includes athletics.

How the Legal System Works for You

Finding out that bias exists is one thing, having an approach to deal with tough issues is quite another. When you need to take action to make sure your daughter gets a sporting chance, there are legal policies and related measures that can back your position. You may be tempted to call your attorney, but don't choose that as your first course of action. Fortunately there are others methods to effect change. It would be much less costly and less inflammatory to talk to other parent groups and find out what is being done successfully by individuals as well as athletic organizations across the country to make sports a part of every girl's life.

You can then remedy an unjust situation by using the three elements of legislation that make up Title IX—the law itself, the regulations, and the policy interpretations. Following is a brief explanation of each part of the legal package.

THE LAW

The passage of Title IX by Congress meant that the education rights of females were recognized and guaranteed. The elements of the law cover sexual discrimination within education programs. The federal funding element is placed in the law as an enforcement tool. If violations of the law are discovered, funding can be taken away.

THE REGULATIONS

Technically, after Congress passes a law, regulations must be created to implement the law. The executive branch of our government is responsible for developing and adopting regulations. Once that is done, regulations carry the full force of the law. Regulations state that the laws and policies must be followed.

POLICY INTERPRETATIONS

Colleges and universities that receive federal funding have been given guidelines to know if they are in compliance with Title IX. Policy interpretations do not have the full force of the law, but when a lawsuit or complaint is being investigated, all of the areas in the following list will come under review. All higher educational institutions that receive federal funding are required to have a written procedure for you to follow to make a complaint if you allege discrimination. The requirements as outlined by the policy interpretations for athletics cover thirteen specific components:

- Athletic financial assistance
- Accommodation of abilities and interests
- Coaches
- Dining and housing facilities and services
- Medical and training facilities and services
- Practice, competition, and locker room facilities
- Publicity
- Recruitment of student athletes
- Scheduling of games
- Supplies and equipment
- Support services
- Travel and per diem allowances
- Tutors

High schools must meet some but not all of these guidelines. For instance, they do not provide financial assistance (scholarships), dining and housing, recruitment of student athletes, travel allowances, and tutors.

Financial aid is really the critical area for evaluating compliance, meaning that the dollars spent must be proportionate to the percentage of females in the athletic program. Compliance may be measured by benefits received—clothing, travel, and tutors, for example.

THE OFFICE OF CIVIL RIGHTS INVESTIGATOR'S MANUAL

This manual offers guidance for the Office of Civil Rights (OCR) to evaluate complaints submitted by high school or college athletes. The OCR is an arm of the U.S. Department of Education. There are approximately ten regions throughout the country that have designated offices to handle legal affairs.

THE EQUITY IN ATHLETICS DISCLOSURE ACT

Parents of young women who want to play college sports should be familiar with the Equity in Athletics Disclosure Act. In 1995

Congress passed this act in order to require colleges to provide yearly reports itemizing expenses for women's and men's athletic programs. This information is made available only if parents, students, or others ask for it specifically. Parents today are smart shoppers, and they want to know that the college they are sending payments to will be committed to providing their daughter with the sports opportunities she desires. Unfortunately this same disclosure of information does not apply to high schools or community programs.

This disclosure act was an important measure, but it did not go far enough. Knowing that there was room for improvement in how colleges reported details of expenditures in athletics, two congresswomen, Carol Mosley-Braun and Nita M. Lowey, wrote a bill named the Fair Play Act. Its purpose is to include the information previously mentioned as well as coaches' salaries and the amount of scholarship money being awarded. These statistics would be made available to the Department of Education, which in turn would be required to publish the data on the Internet, set up a toll-free number, and inform all high schools throughout the nation that the information is available to them.

Due to the use of legal measures by some families whose goal it was to make sports programs equitable on college campuses, there have been great changes in those institutions forced to take the difficult steps necessary to come into compliance. Athletic directors who have been watching this drama unfold are getting the message loud and clear: Do it yourself or the government will do it for you. Full compliance across the nation, though, still has a long way to go, generally owing to weak leadership and staff resistance. Yet it won't be long before high schools will face the same abundance of challenges. Public awareness has been raised, and athletes will push to make substantial improvements with the support of knowledgeable and proactive parents.

Gender Equity in Sports = Educational Opportunity

Your daughter cannot afford to miss out on the golden opportunities for personal development that sports provides. Sometimes that means an opportunity to get bashed and bruised, but talk about lessons learned per bump! Seriously, one of her key opportunities may be to step up to a leadership position on her team or work through a series of qualifying tournaments that teaches her the power of persistence. Through countless sports-related learning experiences, athletics offer a unique opportunity for a girl or young woman to enhance her sense of self-worth and develop valuable interpersonal skills. For this reason alone, gender equity should be important to you and worth fighting for.

It's not just parents who need to appreciate the value of a sports education, it's school administrators as well. They need to look at athletics as part of a school's core curriculum, not merely a mandated fringe activity. In many cases if programs are not provided in public schools, many lower-income girls do not participate in sports at all, and this is truly a shame.

The Foundation Concepts of Gender Equity

There's a great Title IX workshop kit distributed by the National Association for Girls and Women in Sport that outlines three critical reasons why educators should value equity in sports—they are identified as the legal, educational, and moral imperatives.

LEGAL

The Title IX law is the guideline for deciding whether or not schools will continue to get federal funding. Either a school can comply with the law or risk loss of funding and pay for compensatory damages to the parties who have been discriminated against. Schools live and die by their budgets, so this is a major concern.

EDUCATIONAL

The learning of such life skills as risk evaluation, teamwork, decision making, leadership, and assertiveness through sports is simply part of the educational process. Studies show that the girls who participate in sports are more likely to graduate from high school, show an increased desire to continue higher education, and in general get higher grades and are less likely to skip classes.

MORAL

Equity is the most basic educational principle and is taught by example. Without this, girls will be led to believe that discrimination is acceptable.

These imperatives typically apply to public education. But what if you choose a private school? What if you choose a private military school? Fortunately the battle for equity on that turf has been fought and won. Military schools such as Virginia Military Institute (VMI) used to provide their own brand of discrimination. Not anymore. In an attempt to maintain single-sex education, a "separate but equal" program was established for women at the nearby Mary Baldwin College in Virginia. Realizing that separate but equal was unconstitutional, the issue was brought before the Supreme Court. In a ruling supporting Title IX, Justice Ruth Bader Ginsberg wrote, "Generalizations about the way women are" cannot justify excluding women from programs. If the goal of the institution is to produce "citizen soldiers, surely that goal is great enough to accommodate women." Since 1996 women are now attending VMI, fully participating in the fitness training expected of each and every student through required classes (boxing, wrestling, swimming, principles of physical education, and drug and alcohol abuse training) and elective classes (golf, tennis, gymnastics, racquetball, weight training, lifeguarding).

Multiplying Opportunities and Facing Challenges

In order for you to multiply opportunities for your daughter and other girls, you'll need to know what challenges you may face and how to overcome them. What are the conditions that might hold girls back from receiving what they are legally entitled to? When you begin to look at sport programs offered at your daughter's school, you may be pleasantly surprised or have a rude awakening.

Start with the big picture. Does the school offer the same access to athletics for girls as for boys? As you review and evaluate policies, please make sure that you hear what all sides have to say—talk to athletes, coaches, administrators, and other parents before you come in with your guns blazing. As you go through this evaluation process, you will find that from state to state, and community to community, there are many common issues in both public education and local community programs.

Challenges in Public Education

Opportunities for girls in public schools can easily be evaluated by going over the concerns in the following list. Remember, your goal is to create equal opportunities. Find out if these policies are in action at your daughter's school:

- Playing on a boys' team is possible when no girls' team is provided. Generally a girl should be eligible to play if she passes the tests for sound conditioning and appropriate skill level. Ask what the athletic tests are before tryouts so that your daughter has time to prepare her skills and level of fitness.
- The abilities and interests of female athletes are being met in the athletic program. Not having the same number of teams for females as for males may not necessarily be the concern. What girls do need to have are opportunities to participate in the sport they want. If girls can demonstrate there is enough interest to warrant a field hockey team and it is not offered, technically the school should do something to meet the need.
- Competition is equally scheduled during prime spectator time for females and males. Prime-time scheduling of practice and competitive events needs to be evenly distributed. Everyone needs to benefit from prime-time booking so that spectators will come and watch the action. In some schools, instead of the girls playing their big games during the week, they play on Friday night before the boys play.
- Support received by Booster Clubs is balanced. All programs must benefit equally from funding regardless of the source. If a specific male team receives money, and there is not an equivalent offering for a female team, this constitutes a violation.
- The degree of coaching available to teams is allocated fairly. Look at how hiring is handled for coaching positions. Sometimes teachers at a school have special sport experience as coaches, sometimes it is the physical education staff, and sometimes it is professionals from outside the school system. If a coach hired for a female's team cannot deliver full-time training, yet a coach for a male's program can, the school's program is not in compliance.
- Spending is proportionate. Collegiate institutions that receive federal money and offer financial assistance or scholarships must award money proportionate to the male/female population. If 52 percent of the population is female, women should get 52 percent of the scholarship money.

- Cheerleading or pep squads are equally scheduled for girls' and women's events. Having visible support by the school is just as important for girls as it is for boys. Girl athletes and their coaches do not want to feel like second-class citizens.
- Quality equipment and facilities are provided for physical education classes. Girls should be assured of having quality physical education classes that meet their interests and teach the importance of physical activity. Just because a girl does not want to be part of a team doesn't mean she's not interested in taking challenging courses in physical education, nor should it mean that her physical education should be cut back.
- Travel and provision of uniforms must be equal in terms of benefits. Take a basketball program, for example. Both men and women need clothing and travel money. But it is possible that outfitting the men's team is more expensive than outfitting the women's team. So while it may cost more for the men to be in uniform, as long as every woman on the basketball team is in uniform, the benefit is equal. The same applies to travel. Say that both the men's and women's teams are scheduled for eight tournaments. It may be that the women have to travel farther than the men to get to their opponent's school, and therefore the cost of travel would be higher. As long as travel budgets allow for each of the men's and women's programs to travel to eight tournaments, the benefits are equal.

If you are concerned about a possible violation, you might be wondering, "Is there anything that can be accomplished simply by talking to my daughter's PE teacher?" The answer is yes. This is the place you must start. The PE teacher may then have to go to the athletic director, who in turn may have to contact the county department of education. Ultimately, on the secondary education level, the principal is responsible for compliance with Title IX.

A good rule of thumb is to look at a program through the eyes of girls who feel that they are left out of the picture. If this reflects your daughter's position, encourage her to speak with her PE teacher or athletic director. Go with her to talk to school personnel if she feels uncomfortable bringing up the subject. Or suggest that she get together with a group of girls and set up a meeting. Perhaps the athletic director doesn't realize that there are girls who would play golf, for example, if only they were encouraged.

When you're seeking changes within the school, be aware that change is tough. Begin by working on the items that can be changed at little or no cost. Try to make those changes immediately. Making those changes will increase the likelihood of cooperation from administrators. Then you'll have to plan for more costly changes on a timetable that both the school and the students can live with.

Challenges in Community Programs

In most communities, low-cost or free sport programs for girls are scheduled through nonprofit organizations and city recreation programs. These programs usually schedule more offerings to families than the local public school system. Review the seasonal brochures that are mailed to your home to understand what percentage of programs represents girls' needs. Talk with program directors to find out why you're provided with these particular choices if you sense inequality. If you want to get a grip on the total picture, ask these six questions:

- What sports teams are offered for girls as compared with those for boys? Check to see if there are enough offerings to support the interests of girls.
- Are any of the offerings coed? If a program is not offered for girls, will girls be allowed to join the boys' program?
- What noncompetitive activities are offered for girls? Ask about physical education activity where motor and sport skills are developed through a variety of daily offerings. The goal is to promote a less threatening environment. Once girls become more confident with their bodies and skills, they often opt to try the recreation leagues for specific sports that provide competition for even the lowest level of player.
- Are the locker facilities secure? A girl should not have to worry that a boy or a man could easily walk into the locker or shower area.
- If there is only a boys' volleyball team, how do you start one for the girls? Does a petition sheet need to be passed around for girls to sign? Can an interest list be kept?
- Are there any women coaches? Many times girls will sign up for a recreation class if there's a woman teacher. This is especially true if a girl has not had any sport experience with a male coach.

A Step-by-Step Plan to Insure Equal Sports Opportunities

It takes both insight and action to secure for your daughter what is rightfully hers. Making your voice heard can be scary. Put as much effort as you can into solving your problem within the educational system first. Take legal action only as a last resort. As you act on what you believe to be right, armed with the full strength of Title IX, you will begin to feel that you have power over your life—and your daughter's. You are not alone. After reading over these suggestions, you may even come up with your own creative ways to remove the existing restrictions that hold your daughter back from participating in and enjoying sports.

Solutions Within the Educational System

The best advice I have to give is to try to work with coaches and administrators at the outset. Remember, nobody's perfect, and you need to go into meetings with an open mind and goodwill. Give credit where it is due, begin a discussion of the issues that need to be addressed, and effect compliance with the law without going through costly and emotionally painful legal action. Here are some recommendations to follow as you work to build improved programs at your daughter's school or community program.

- Start with the administrator in charge of the program. It's best not to go over his or her head immediately to find a resolution to your problem.
- Whether you are a parent, a coach, or a student at the college level, find out the name of the Title IX officer representing your school or community program. This is the person with whom you would register an in-house complaint if necessary. This person will investigate the complaint in-house as opposed to going outside the institution in question. Middle schools and high schools do not have Title IX officers. Go to the principal or the athletic director for help.
- Surround yourself with people who seek fairness in analyzing an athletic program. It's up to you whether you form a loose-knit or-

ganization or something more formal. Contact representatives involving all specialty areas—parents, students, coaches, physical education teachers, and administrators.

- Be open to finding a solution and show potential adversaries that you are seeking to be fair and objective in finding solutions. In many cases you are working for a minority that depends on the cooperation of the administration. Keep decision makers open to your side of the story.
- Demonstrate to administrators that there is a clear interest in getting a new program off the ground. Round up the support of girls (and their parents) who would participate on a specific team if it were offered.
- Advocate immediate changes that require little or no cost. This might involve such issues as scheduling, publicity, and assignment of pep squads, which reflect that the girls' programs are as worthy as the boys' programs.
- Outline suggested changes and the dollar amount necessary to put the changes into effect. This will likely include uniforms, travel money, and hiring more coaches. Put a budget together for all interested parties to review.
- Work with the media to publicize your plans once you have reached agreement with all those affected by a given policy.

It is sometimes necessary to go to a board of education meeting to make a presentation. Find out when the board meets and if you need to have your issue placed on the agenda before you testify.

Athletics has become a setting for judicial test cases. One of the most historic cases to test Title IX was a six-year legal battle that reached the Supreme Court involving Brown University. The institution was sued on behalf of present and future women athletes by a law firm in Washington, Trial Lawyers for Public Justice. The case was brought to trial in 1991 because Brown had tried to eliminate the girls' gymnastics and volleyball teams as well as two men's teams in a budget-cutting effort. The women cried foul and went after the rights they believed were violated under Title IX. According to columnist Richard Carelli, "The Supreme Court refused to free Brown University of rulings that the Ivy League school discriminated against female athletes." The federal lawsuit was settled with Brown agreeing to keep approximately the same percentage of women in sports as in its student population. This ruling did much to constitute a warning to the entire collegiate population of the nation, that foot-dragging by administrations would not be tolerated.

Solutions Within the Community Setting

The way to solve sports inequity disputes that involve community programs cannot be found in a simple blueprint because Title IX is usually not applicable. According to the Women's Sports Foundation, ". . . there is no government agency that is a 'watchdog' for recreational sports leagues. Therefore it is necessary to consider other laws that may apply:

- Public accommodation laws: Almost all states have public accommodations laws that prohibit certain types of discrimination in public facilities. . . . Some states even have gender equity laws that specifically apply to public facilities, and many municipalities have broad nondiscrimination laws.
- The U.S. Constitution: the Equal Protection clause of the 14th Amendment states that 'no state shall . . . deny to any person within its jurisdiction the equal protection of the laws.'

"In determining which of these laws may apply to a recreational program, some of the relevant factors to analyze include (1) how the league is funded (whether it receives public or private funds); (2) whether the league has any connection to the state that shows state involvement in the discrimination; and (3) how a recreational league is organized."

You do not have to file a lawsuit to protect your daughter's rights. Going to court should be your last option. Use political pressure instead. Make sure you have your facts straight, get together with the person who has immediate responsibility for the situation, meet with the board of supervisors or the board of recreation, start a letter-writing campaign, contact the media, and call the Women's Sports Foundation for help.

Here is a story about resolving inequity in sports participation when concerned parents went to bat for their daughters: The West Valley Girls Softball League in Los Angeles charged that their teams

were being denied access to the same parks boys used to play baseball. The parks where boys played had lighting for night games and
better fields. The softball players and their parents decided to play
hardball with one of the city's park departments by filing a suit with
the American Civil Liberties Union to get equal access to the local
parks. To date, the city has done a complete turnabout and has provided better sites for the girls to play their games. It is further making an effort to increase communication so that parents know what
programs are available for their daughters.

Who Else Can You Turn to for Help?

Do you ever feel you're fighting the equal sports opportunities
battle by yourself even though the law is on your side? Where else
might you go for information, assistance, or just somebody to talk to
who's been there?

National Nonprofit Organizations

The following groups are national nonprofit organizations that
have a history of working for the rights of women and girls. Write or
call their national offices or local branches to get the help you need.

- American Association of University Women (AAUW). This organization "promotes equity for all women and girls, lifelong education, and positive societal change." It has contributed to the
  funding of many projects that provide educational information
  about gender equity. They have produced a very complete semi-
  nar packet with transparencies and materials that can be copied
  for handouts at workshops. They can be contacted at 800-326-
  AAUW, ext. 160.
- National Organization for Women (NOW). A nationwide nonprofit organization that in 1993 sued the California State University system and won, citing a decline in women's participation in
  sports from 36 to 30 percent over a thirteen-year period. Participation and scholarships rates must be raised to within 5 percent
  of the proportion of the female student body by 1998–99. NOW
  has a Legal Defense and Education Fund, which can be reached
  at 212-925-6635.
- National Women's Law Center. In 1997 the center, using information from the Equity in Athletics Disclosure Act, went after

colleges and universities believed to be in violation of Title IX. Dealing with the issue of sports scholarships, it filed complaints with the U.S. Education Department's Office of Civil Rights, stating that there was a significant gap between the average amount men and women received. Reach their office at 202-588-5180.

- Women's Sports Foundation. "A nonprofit educational, membership-based organization that promotes and enhances the sports and fitness experience for all girls and women." The foundation works to influence sports policy on the national level and monitors legislation, Title IX enforcement, and policies at organizations that govern sports. Call them at 800-227-3988 for advice and information.

Contacting Your Political Representatives

Almost all of us at some time or another have held a strong enough opinion that we've said, "I'm going to write to my representative." If you feel you must go this route, try to be brief and to the point. If there is a problem, spell it out and ask your representative to help you solve the problem by telling her or him what you want done.

Whether you start a call-in or a write-in campaign, be sure you state how a particular issue will affect your family or a family member. If other families are involved, ask each family to write their own letter, then bundle them and mail them all together. Personal letters are great because each family has its own story to tell.

You might even request that one of your representatives support girls in sports by being present at an awards banquet or a key community meeting. Stick with a positive message. Inform elected officials of the benefits of athletic participation for young women.

Using the Media to Raise Sports Equity Awareness

When you think about contacting someone in the media, do you feel about as qualified as a 5K runner trying to compete in a marathon? The truth is you don't have to be a public relations expert to get the word out. Think about how truly proud you are of your daughter and her team. Don't you tell all your friends and anyone who'll listen to you? That's called word-of-mouth advertising. Never underestimate its power. The resources you can use to get the word out about girls in sports are divided into three areas: print media (newspaper and magazine stories), radio, and television. Here's what you'll need to do before you approach the media.

- Identify the contact person and phone number of the individual who is responsible for a competition or special event. That way a newspaper reporter has a specific person to speak with regarding an upcoming or completed event.
- When writing your competition or special event information, keep it to one page, double-spaced—the who, what, why, where, and when details. State the name of the club hosting the event, give the name of the competition, and note where will it be held and when (during the day or the evening).
- Include a separate fact sheet if necessary, specifying the ages of the girls, previous history of the team, and name of the communities in which they reside.
- Send in a photo with a biographical sketch of an individual or team you think is newsworthy. Indicate why you think your daughter or team is special.
- Put together a "frequently asked questions" sheet with questions and answers.

Strategy 1: Using Print Media

CONTACT YOUR LOCAL NEWSPAPER

Newspapers can't survive without dozens of human-interest stories. Yours is one of them. Let me give you some ideas of what you can write about besides just a win-loss record. You could focus on how long a team has been in training for a special competition. There are always fund-raisers to advertise. What about notifying the public about the team banquet at the end of the season? Have the girls been to a special camp where a "superstar" was part of the teaching staff? Are you planning a clinic? Do you know a girl who has overcome a physical challenge? Have any girls received scholarship money? Any of this information is "news."

If you're just starting to communicate with a newspaper staff, send a season schedule and all results of competition to the sports department. Instead of mailing, you should fax results to the sports editor. When you give the newspaper enough notice, a photographer may come to your event. If not, find a parent who can take publicity photos and send them along with your results. When a special story is written about your team, keep up good relations by following up with a phone call to thank the writer. Most important of all, respect deadlines!

Once you have established a relationship with the sportswriters for a newspaper, they will be more open to dealing with the tougher issues you may want to pursue, such as the paper's ratio of reporting girls' and boys' events. If your local sports department is not open to your presentation, there are other ways to spread the word. Try contacting someone in the lifestyle section or local news.

At the same time, support your daughter by helping her gather photos of individual athletes or teams accompanied by stories to be put in her school's newspaper. This will raise the awareness level of students and teachers on campus.

SUBMIT LETTERS TO SPORTS, HEALTH, AND WOMEN'S MAGAZINES

Publishers of periodicals such as *Sports Illustrated for Kids* have made an effort to highlight up-and-coming female athletes. This is especially true if they are involved in traditionally male-dominated sports such as wrestling and ice hockey. Letters to the editor from young athletes are welcomed and printed. I enjoy the "Kids Who Care" column because it highlights athletic kids who are doing good deeds off the field of play. Send in a photo and your daughter's special story, or write a brief story about your daughter's sports accomplishment and send it along with a photo.

Some magazines that consider material for publication are *Child, Family Circle, Family Life, Good Housekeeping, Ladies' Home Journal, McCall's, Parenting, Parents, Working Mother, Girls' Life, Jump, Fitness, Living Fit,* and *Self.*

Strategy 2: Getting on the Radio

Local radio stations are always shopping for "knowledgeable" guests. Look for someone in your group who is an informed and credible person to interview. What can you talk about? How about the development of life skills as a benefit of girls' sports? This could be done at the end of a season when a conference title has been won. You could talk about how girls learned to keep the pressure on when things looked grim. How about finding some experienced parents who can talk about fighting the system to help their daughters get into college sports? These people can be terrific sources of information for parents who will face similar issues down the road. Timing is also important. Stay in touch with what is happening with your sport on the national scene. You might tie into the frenzy of some national event like the basketball playoffs, for example, with a story about your daughter's high school basketball team's winning season.

In order to get on a radio show, you'll have to identify which stations support community efforts. Call them on the phone and find out who is the director of programming. Send a letter to that person stating your concerns, and follow it up with a phone call.

Strategy 3: Attracting Television to Your Event

We can truly thank television for igniting the message that female athletes come in all shapes and sizes—and that they can excel at a variety of sports! You may be saying to yourself, "Yes, but only the hot shots get broadcast coverage. How do we get airtime for our hometown programs?" Keep in mind that local news shows and cable companies are always willing to consider community stories. Bring something positive to the table. Highlight a special accomplishment by a girl who has average talent but an above-average level of persistence. Emphasize a unique training approach used by a dedicated coach. Try to get a cable company to send a camera team to a girls' competition to produce a highlight film. Remember, if you want exposure, make it easy for media representatives to reach your spokespersons.

If you are feeling particularly strong about an issue, go ahead and write to major sports networks like NBC Sports or ESPN. Let the folks at the top know of your desires, your concerns, your support. Lydia Stephens, vice president of programming at ABC, says, "Every letter we receive represents one hundred more viewers who are thinking about writing."

I have had my own successful experience with the media: one of my business ventures included operating a sports center with a family concept. I felt that what we had to offer was pretty unique, so I steeled my nerves and called one of the local major networks to see if I could rouse some interest. Was I ever delighted and shocked when I was told that my idea was newsworthy and that a TV crew would be sent to my fitness center. It took a lot of guts to make that phone call, but it taught me a valuable lesson. Pick up the phone.

Reaping the Reward of Equal Sports Opportunities

Title IX has been around for over a quarter of a century. A whole generation of women has been brought up under its powerful guidelines. Every time a female athlete is in a commercial or on the news, or is simply enjoying a school sports program that wasn't available twenty-five years ago, she bears witness to this life-changing drama. The families who have raised their daughters to participate in sports know firsthand the gains in self-confidence and personal skills this provides. Lucy Danziger, editor of *Women's Sports and Fitness* magazine, says it best:

> *[Sports] has given us a new paradigm, outside the gym and beyond the fashion magazines, where our self-image is shaped in terms of skills, achievements, and commitment, not muscle tone or dress size. . . . I look forward to the next Olympics, when American women winning event after event will no longer be considered a story about gender breakthroughs, but individuals, each one a great athlete.*

I couldn't agree with her more. I was in Atlanta when our women struck gold, not only as one of the countless sweaty spectators, but as one of the thousands of architects who had helped lay the foundation for our women competitors—as an athlete, as a coach, as a role model. What a glorious feeling.

Helping Your Daughter Stay with Sports

11

I often ask myself why sports has been a mainstay in my life. Is it because I had a carefree childhood where sports and play outdoors, not just on my street but in my whole community, was a safe way of life? Is it due to my terrific experience as a college competitor? Is it due to my parents encouraging me and participating with me in sports? Or is it because I simply can't sit still and sports is fundamentally about being active? There's got to be a bit of each element etched into my spirit. It's odd, though, while sports and recreation are a given in my life, the reasons that I stay involved change with time. In college, being in the weight room was a way for me to build my strength so that I could master demanding gymnastics skills. Now, bustling through my fifth decade, I visit the gym regularly so that I can enjoy chocolate-chip cookies and brownies fearlessly. There's more. I love having the physical strength (and because of it, the courage) that allows me to do whatever captures my imagination. I'm definitely not waiting for retirement to play golf, so every Sunday I walk the course, enjoying being outdoors and improving my skills at the same time.

The main reason girls *stay* in sports, like anything else in life, has to do with how much they enjoy what they're doing and how good they feel about themselves. Some issues are more important than others. There are also reasons that girls drop out of sports, mostly having to do with their relationship with themselves, the coach, or their parents. This chapter will help you understand what drives girls to stick with sports and what drives them crazy.

Seven Reasons Why Girls Stay with Sports

Whether you are reading this as a parent or a parent coach, this list of the top seven reasons why girls stick with sports should serve as a wake-up call. If you want girls to stay involved with sports, you must understand what's important to them. The Youth Sports Institute at Michigan State University completed a study in 1988 regarding the participation and attrition rates of American boys and girls in sports from ages ten to eighteen. The reasons girls gave for participating and staying in sports were ranked in the order of the following summaries.

#1—To Have Fun

The popular song "Girls Just Want to Have Fun" says it all. The main goal of parenting and coaching in youth sports should be to create an environment where girls can have fun while learning athletic skills. In our adult lives, too often we overlook the need to have fun by staying active. As a grown-up, admitting to having fun means you're taking time away from your adult or parental responsibilities. But girls go into sports because it's fun for them to be physically active and to be with some friends. Sports is a total shift away from academics, where kids may feel confined to a chair in a classroom where it is required to succeed.

Frequently enjoyment comes from mastering a new skill. When your daughter wants to return to practice because she can look forward to succeeding, it's a sure sign you and she are on the right track. Our role is to make sure that girls are in a situation where they can joyfully achieve sport skills. If only we could allow this one concept to be our guiding light, I guarantee we would see the sunny side of our girls more often.

Enjoying sports can show up in unexpected ways. I used to have a group of young girls in my gymnastics school who were more impressed with the midafternoon snack than anything else. They'll probably never forget the peanut butter–filled celery sticks with raisins, which we called "ants on a log."

#2—To Stay in Shape and Get Exercise

Many girls I've spoken with validated the Michigan State University study. They told me they thought sports was a fun way to stay in shape and get exercise, in particular during the teen years. Several mentioned that they were "hyper" personalities. Sports allowed them to let out a lot of their energy. Once they got in shape, they liked the feeling.

I was notably struck by a seventeen-year-old's comments about how being in shape enhanced her self-confidence. Heidi said, "I know I can do things. The other day a guy followed me. He was in a car and I was walking. Because I'm in good shape I knew I could run fast and get away. What would I do if I was overweight? I couldn't do anything. If someone is harassing me now, I know I can handle myself because I'm used to handling my body." This single event demonstrated to her the depth of her self-confidence. It made a deep impression on Heidi—and on me.

#3—To Learn and Improve Skills

I can't say I remember my youthful thoughts about wanting to improve my skills, although it became my focus in college. For me, the benefits of participating in sports were intrinsic. I clung to the idea that if I kept at something, I could improve to the point that it became rewarding.

Most girls want to get better at sports and are motivated when they see skillful players living it up and enjoying themselves. They want to copy them, to experience the fun they seem to be having. This starts as a small kernel of curiosity. If an activity looks appealing, your daughter will want to try it. If she believes she can learn a skill or two, she will want to improve because it makes playing the sport easier and more enjoyable. Once girls get a taste of the idea that they can improve, it feeds on itself. I think thirteen-year-old Jennifer says it best: "I worked on my skills all season, and at the last softball game I hit a double. It felt so good when I made it, I almost started dancing on second base."

#4—To Do Something They're Good At

We all feel best about ourselves when we're doing something we're good at. It's just part of parenting that you help your daughter explore her athletic potential so that she can not only find something she enjoys, but find something that really makes her tick. In my case, because I was open to trying almost any sport, I was bound to find a sport that was exactly right for me. My parents didn't suggest gymnastics, but the school district offered it, which makes me believe that the schools can have a significant impact on a girl's attitude toward sports if they choose to do so. School sports, for some high school girls, is the one place where they can shine.

#5—To Enjoy the Excitement and Challenge of Competition

Every morning when I teach my preschool class, I am reminded that the competitive spirit starts very early and without much provocation. In addition to bouncing on the trampoline and tumbling, we have a practice of running the length of the gym, about eighty feet, several times. "Ready, set, go" are the three most exciting words these little girls can hear. There is never an occasion when one child isn't trying to beat another. Everybody gets a rush when they try to make their little legs sprint faster than those of the person next to them. It seems that the excitement of "me against the world" or "I won" is already part of their motivation.

The first time I really understood that competition could be exciting was when I had enough skills to be a challenger. There is definitely no thrill to entering competition when you have don't have enough preparation under your belt, but as my skill base grew, the excitement grew as well. Every time I competed against higher-level athletes, I understood the possibilities and it made me step up mentally. And I did. It was a fairly reliable reaction. Twenty-five years later I had that same feeling of being pumped up by competition out on the golf course as I competed in local tournaments.

#6—To Be Part of a Team

For many girls, being on a team creates a feeling of camaraderie that is exceptionally fulfilling. Belonging to the group is the greatest sensation there is. Sharing the struggle, the glory, and the pain with peers is equally important. Girls delight in the kind of shared experiences sports teams provide, where making new friends and relationships are valued. Working together for a common goal means you're pulling for your teammates and your teammates are pulling for you. Rather than being singled out for mistakes or successes, the unspoken message is, "We're in this together, I'm needed, my role is important, and other girls depend on me."

Here are some thoughts from a high school athlete who was a three-sport team member. She sums up the team experience in a nutshell. Denise said, "Playing as part of a team, I have a lot of close friends. The people I can relate to are on my team, they have similar interests. Otherwise I wouldn't stay after school for two hours. You have someone to laugh with when your muscles are aching and you can't run anymore. Playing sports can get old really quick unless you have someone there to cheer you on or just help you get back up emotionally."

#7—To Make New Friends

Girls who are outgoing look upon sports as a stimulating way to make new friends. Even though changing grade levels in school year to year can provide new friendships, girls don't have the same interaction with their classmates that they do with their teammates. They look forward to meeting other girls who have similar interests and energy, to interact with and get to know them. Sports can give girls a chance to meet people they wouldn't otherwise come into contact with. It can be a particularly good thing for girls who attend small private schools or are home schooled, providing them with a wider range of friends.

Here are one seventeen-year-old athlete's thoughts on the social value of sports: "At school you can only meet so many people. Being in sports is more like a real world than school. You're out playing on the field and you really have to deal with people. You're not forced to be quiet, and you can find out more about their personalities, what other people value. It's good to be in organized city sports because you meet a variety of different kids, especially when you are younger."

Other Reasons That Spur Participation

The Michigan State University study revealed that other issues also had an important effect on girls' participation in sports. In essence, most of these issues contribute greatly to their self-esteem. Some of the other reasons cited for continuing participation are listed here.

Wanting to Win

With some athletes, no matter what the age group, the need to "win" is a very dominating feeling. This trait springs from one's core personality and is rarely a quality that can be taught. For some girls, every time they enter an athletic contest it is strictly with the intent of winning, though this is not necessarily winning at all costs.

The need to win may be apparent not just during an athletic contest, but during training as well. The competitor may show up to practice early or stay later or train an extra day a week. One of my friends' daughters, Jennifer, was a "need to win" kind of athlete. An excellent softball player, she couldn't get enough training information. She was constantly working on her skills. Having played third base on a losing team for a couple of seasons, she finally realized that if she knew how to be a pitcher, she could be a major factor in winning a game. Jennifer went to her coach and asked to be trained in this new position. When the coach was busy and couldn't help her, she asked her dad or her mom to catch balls for her. She even switched teams to gain further advantage. It wasn't long before Jennifer mastered pitching and did what she wanted to do—be in a controlling position to win. That's the intense side of Jennifer. The fun side of her says, "The best thing about winning is to splash the coach."

To Be Like Someone They Admire

Several years after I left my gymnastics program in New Jersey, one of my former students caught up with me in California. Helena and I had quite a bit of news to share, but it was the end of our phone visit that made a huge impression on me and left me somewhat stunned. Helena revealed that she had always wanted to grow up and be the kind of person I represented to her. To that end, she trained long and hard to be a great gymnast, served an apprenticeship to become a gymnastics coach, and tested to become a rated gymnastics official. In her heart she wanted to make a difference in the lives of the girls who came under her guidance the same way I had unknowingly touched her young life. When the conversation was over, I could barely recount it to my husband through my tears and shaken voice.

You just never, never, never know how you influence those impressionable lives around you. If you are a parent doubling as a parent coach, carry this story with you. Ponytails may be flying by you seemingly uninterested, but don't let that fool you. Open up your heart every day to the possibility that you are someone girls can admire.

To Participate on a Team That Travels

Once a team hops on the bus, the "social" factor comes into full play. Such trips are often the only times that girls get to visit with each other in a casual way outside of practice. Just like at a sleepover, girls will create their own world in which one tries to outlaugh the other.

I've been on both ends of the travel adventure—as an athlete and as a coach. One of my most unforgettable trips as a competitive gymnast was the first time I flew in an airplane to the national championships. I was eighteen years of age: you're with your team, you've got a mission to accomplish, and you're energized to the max. Things got better—this was also my first experience of staying in a hotel. Did anybody mention we were supposed to get some sleep? The next morning came all too soon. If we weren't fully alert after breakfast, we certainly were when we walked into the sports arena and felt the full impact of TV lights. The competition was a struggle, but in my mind that was only one part of the experience. That trip to Southern Illinois University was one of many out-of-town adventures with my team, and I just loved exploring new places, seeing new things. A whole new world opened up for me. My family came from modest means, and if I hadn't been on a university team, it might have been years before I even left my home state. I'll always cherish my college trips with my teammates.

On the other side of the coin, I have spent many an hour in the car driving girls to and from competition. The trips that were the most fun were the out-of-state road trips. It might be possible, but I don't think I've seen more candy available on Halloween than I saw come out of these girls' gym bags. The gymnasts' stories about school, friends, and parents were endless and always pitched at a volume louder than the radio's. When we stopped for meals, it was a per-

formance in and of itself, finding the best booth to sit in and order-
ing the right amount of French fries and Coke. Memories are made
of this. A couple of summers ago I heard that a few of the girls who
were longtime competitors and buddies located each other and had
a great reunion. Sharing the stories of our many travels was a highlight of their conversation. Your daughter will also enjoy such experiences if they are available to her.

To Feel Important

If you've ever had the chance to have your picture in the newspaper or have an article written about just you and your special accomplishments, you know what an incredible pump it is to your
self-esteem. You pass your friends in the grocery store and they bring
up your recent accomplishments; relatives cut out and mail to you
the newspaper article that recounts your personal story; others
phone you with excitement and respect for your success. You feel
like a million dollars, and your parents feel like billionaires.

One of the greatest sensations in life is to feel like an important
contributor to your team. Maybe you've scored the winning goal or
earned enough points to help qualify your team for nationals. When
the team is counting on you to come through and you can, it's a major feather in your cap. Your teammates know it, your parents know
it, the parents of your teammates know it, and the coach counts on
it. This is a wonderful gift to give to young women.

To Have Something to Do

It can get pretty boring going home to an empty house or just an
average home where you're not connecting with anyone because
everyone has their own schedules. Girls who are outgoing and have
a high energy level are the ones who get bored or lonely easily.
Sports are good for them. Julie, an animated fourteen-year-old, said,
"I cannot sit at home on a couch like a lot of people can. I don't like
to just sit and do the same thing over and over. I'd rather be on a losing team; it's frustrating, but still fun. Even if you're not very good,
you have something to do instead of sitting at home."

To Receive Awards

The first time you hold a medal or a trophy in your hand for winning an athletic contest, it feels better than getting an A on a test.

Winning an athletic award is uniquely special because you've gone beyond competing against yourself; you've triumphed over a tough obstacle—your opponent. The award is a public acknowledgment of your worth, and at the same time it becomes part of a private hall of fame in your bedroom. This is a priceless confidence booster for any young girl.

The younger the age of the child, the more important it is to have what I call a "frequent tryer" award. This is essentially a participation award given to each child who takes part in an athletic competition. Everybody goes home feeling good when you have low-key competition and a fun-first attitude. As one parents notes, "[When] everybody gets ribbons, [and] nobody cries, everybody is pretty much happy."

Reasons Why Girls Don't Stay with Sports

Unfortunately, statistics show that between the ages of ten and seventeen there is a decrease in girls participating in sports and related activities. The following are reasons that girls typically give for why they drop out. As you ferry your daughter from one sports venue to another, think of what you can do to help prevent these issues from becoming a barrier between your daughter and the athletic activities she enjoys.

Too Much Emphasis on Winning

A shocked and frustrated freshman cheerleader, Vicki was astounded by the attitude of her teammates. What she had observed as enthusiasm during tryouts was in reality a total emphasis on competition. The only goal of the squad was to win the national title. Sadly, the seasoned cheerleaders didn't care about Vicki as an individual. After practice, all she came away with was a negative feeling; she felt that she couldn't do anything right, that she was unworthy.

Even if girls aren't putting pressure on themselves, there's always the possibility that parents are overemphasizing the importance of winning. Are you the kind of parent who keeps statistics on your daughter starting at age five? Have you gone up to her after a soccer game and said, "That was great, you had three assists," when possibly she didn't know what an assist was? She was in her glory just making contact with the ball. Over and over, the girls I talk with in youth sports wish that they could tell their parents and coaches, "Relax, it's just a game."

Always on a Losing Team

It doesn't matter how enthusiastic a coach is, players who are new to competition will rarely have a chance to come out on top. Add a long hot afternoon to the picture, and nobody will listen to a coach's pep talk when they feel like losers. After every punishing game, girls will try to cheer each other up, but watching the high fives of the opposing team week after week eventually gets to be just too much. Thinking about the next practice and how to improve just doesn't happen until the girls have to show up. On top of this, if the best player on the team decides to leave and be part of a winning team in another town, you're likely to have mutiny. Should your daughter have a competitive spirit, she too will soon be asking for a transfer. If this is a likely scenario for your daughter's team, suggest not keeping a win-loss record or play in a league that is more balanced in terms of ability.

Character is really built on losing teams, and girls have to learn how to deal with losing by increasing self-discipline and developing persistence. Every bit of psychological research finds that people will cease doing the thing for which there is no reward. Somewhere along the way, girls will need to enjoy the good feeling of winning. But it's up to the coach to mentally prepare girls for competition, which inevitably includes losing.

Too Much Physical Stress

One of the newest problems in youth sports is overuse injuries. Girls are being asked to practice skills over and over to master them, but this can have a negative effect on their developing bodies. Pain and loss of range of motion in the arm and leg joints are common overuse injuries. A sound conditioning program and a coach who's not in a hurry to produce star athletes will go a long way toward reducing injuries.

Does your child have the strength and flexibility to be doing the skills she is asked to do? Recently a harried parent called to schedule her daughter for a private gymnastics lesson so that she could learn special skills for cheerleading tryouts—the girl had only two days left to get ready. The mother insisted that her daughter could be available for two or three hours of training at a time. The next day the girl came in for her first training session. She was very weak and struggled at best. She lasted a half hour. After the lesson the mother signed her up for another session the next day. The appointment was never kept because the girl was in pain, couldn't move easily, and had no desire to punish her body again. In such instances both parents and children underestimate how physically demanding a sport can be.

How do you know what is too much activity for your daughter to handle? As the aspiring cheerleader above found out, if you are not active on a daily basis, even a half hour of physical exertion can be too much. Likewise, the stronger a girl is, the more likely she will be able to handle rigorous activity. So look at her general activity level, her physical strength, and her basic motor skills. We have talked extensively in chapter 3 about those core skills. In the end, your biggest indicator that there is too much physical stress will be pain. If your daughter is in such pain that it is difficult for her to get out of bed the next day, she's not physically ready for what she wants to do athletically. The key is to keep active regularly and develop the large muscles of the legs and arms so they're ready for action.

One of the greatest producers of stress is a dramatic increase in hip and or breast size, which makes girls become very self-conscious. All the activities that seemed natural are no longer natural. Physical actions seem to slow down, and balance is greatly affected. Skills that were difficult to perform before are incredibly more difficult now. Teens feel that if they work harder to keep their weight under control, something will change. But there are some things over which they have little control. It's not just skills that are affected. Large breasts can result in upper back soreness and dents in the shoulders due to the pressure from bra straps. But teens want parents and coaches not to act as if their increased size is impossible to overcome. They still are and want to be motivated just like any other athlete. This becomes highly critical as peer pressure is a mounting factor.

Players Are Too Rough

Elaine, a soccer player for one of the local high schools, told me that she has noticed a general trend over the past few years toward players becoming more competitive, being more physical and, in turn, more dangerous. This made her feel extremely uncomfortable. When she learned more ball handling skills, she was less fearful, but that did not change her feelings about the roughness of the game. Her mother felt that this very physical play was adopting the male standard of competition, which she thought was unnecessary. Her observation was that most of the girls "wanted to play a less physical game, not bang into each other like bumper cars. The heavier, muscular girls could use their weight to gain position. Finesse was missing. The more physical girls made assaults behind the referee's back, and it became an accepted standard." Elaine managed to stick out the season, but she never returned to soccer after high school.

When playing sports, children should not be put in danger by being asked to perform at a level for which they're not physically or mentally ready. In order to know if game play is indeed too rough for your daughter, sit in the bleachers and evaluate the situation for yourself. If your daughter is not able to learn a strategy to protect herself or does not want to play under these conditions, by all means move her to a less jolting level or program.

Inconvenient Game and Practice Times

Lucky is the girl who has a parent to drive her around after school. Yet for the many girls whose parents both work, elaborate carpool schedules must be worked out whenever they need a ride to or from practice. It can be an embarrassment to always depend on someone else for transportation. Many times when I've driven by our neighborhood high school, I've seen the team bus unload with various end results. Some girls have parents waiting for them, some go over to the fast-food restaurant and feed their starving appetites, and some just sit on the curb—and wait.

For some families, competing interests take priority—music lessons, religious commitments, Girl Scouts, tutors. Some older girls must set aside a portion of their precious after-school time to baby-sit younger siblings. With so many demands on children's and parents' schedules, carving out the necessary time for practice and games is a constant challenge.

From my perspective, I want to encourage parents to do whatever it takes to keep their daughters in after-school sports. It is such a small capsule of time that can be enjoyed and profited from. Look at your own life. When you look back, do you see too many missed opportunities? What are your daughter's chances of learning and playing in organized sports after she graduates from high school or college and must be gainfully employed? Do what you can to ride-share—have another parent drive to practice and you pick up. If you can't drive at all, offer to pay for gas. Maybe you could trade services, where another family drives and you cook dinner.

They Want or Need to Get a Job

Around the junior year of high school, girls are overwhelmingly impacted by our consumer society. They want clothes, CDs, money for movies and meals out—and they don't want to continually ask their parents for money. Many girls are faced with the fact that their parents don't have a lot of extra money. Their solution is to get a job. Amy, a senior in high school, said, "I was never forced to get a job. It was my choice to gain employment and my choice to quit the team because of it. My coach didn't think I needed a job because it took me away from soccer. I didn't like being yelled at because of it. I can't handle that. I also needed to start saving for college."

Girls whose financial needs outweigh their desire to play sports are in a tough spot when it comes to "sticking to it." Unless a girl's passion for her sport and stamina are great enough to enable her to juggle a job and team practice, she'll likely drop out of sports. Still, as a parent you can encourage your daughter to stay involved in some kind of physical activity—even if she no longer has the time for team participation. Do something as simple as power walking in a mall or in your neighborhood. If it's financially possible, have her join a fitness center. You may need to offer your companionship and go for a walk with her, work out with a fitness video at home, or go for a bike ride. Perhaps you could encourage her to find a friend who will go jogging with her.

Parents Don't Want Them to Play

It's easy to voice your opinion and play down the role of sports when you're the breadwinner parent and the carpool driver. You may feel that being on a roller-hockey team is a waste of time since your daughter can in-line skate in the street. As far as you're concerned, it won't lead anywhere, and it won't result in a scholarship to college.

Perhaps one of your concerns is that a particular sport is too dangerous. If your daughter does not have the physical and emotional strength to deal with the demands, you are right to back off. On the other hand, you may be able to help her build her strength to be able to play that sport. Strengthening the large muscle groups like the biceps in the upper arms, the large muscles of the upper leg, and the stomach and back muscles will contribute significantly to learning skills and being safe. Building muscle strength can be done with timeless exercises like pull-ups, sit-ups, jumping up stair steps, and leg raises while lying on the stomach.

A potential concern is that your daughter may waste her time in a sport for which she has limited potential. There are times when you might be inclined to make an assessment of your daughter's ability and say something harsh, perhaps, "You'll never be tall enough to play basketball, so don't even bother." If your daughter loves basketball or her best friend is on the team and she really wants to play with her, your offhand remark can become a major zinger. One of my friends who admitted to this faux pas said it took a year before her daughter could come to her and express how hurt she felt.

Be careful not to discourage your daughter. Whether or not she shows it, she takes what you say about her skill and her efforts very seriously. And remember that although it may not result in a marketable skill or a college scholarship, involvement in sports helps your daughter develop social awareness and self-esteem as well as physical competence. Are you sure you want her to give up such a valuable opportunity for personal growth?

Need More Time to Study

It's understandable that girls need to keep up with their studies if they want to play sports. In high school this becomes a critical issue for girls who choose to apply to college. Much to my frustration, however, the preferred method of discipline is to keep girls out of sports when they need to improve their grades. Parents believe that if they take away something kids love, they'll work hard to earn the privilege back. And for the most part, they do. But I believe that girls backslide when they leave the field or the gym for weeks at a time. Rhythm and coordination must be reestablished. It takes a great amount of time and effort to build skills in the first place, and when the pattern is interrupted, some skills have to be relearned. I urge you to consider taking away television time, CDs, the computer, going out with friends, anything but the sports environment, which contributes mightily to a girl's growth and personal balance. As one young teen commented, "Some parents are stuck in their little world of 'My kid can't get bad grades.' They think that we should only get straight A's and that sports will interfere."

A Final Message to Coaches

Throughout this book we've been talking about ways to insure that girls take an active interest in sports—and maintain their involvement during their school years and beyond. Coaches can have such a positive influence on a girl's sports experience. Hopefully you will be the kind of coach who helps transform some girls' interest into a real passion. What better reward could you ask?

One of the most important things to remember is to keep the child focused on skill development rather than the outcome of the competition. Not every kid is motivated by pressure. Give them a skill to pay attention to, rather than winning in the beginning. After skills develop, there is a time and place for winning. Remember, too, that the lower the skill level of the player, the more patient you must be. And the younger the child, the more they seek to please the coach. Always give them an easy way to please you. The following are key points to keep in mind as you train and guide the girls on your team.

- Relax, it's just a game.
- Put the emphasis on participation.
- Understand the needs of the players.
- Always strive to be a better teacher.
- Work to constantly acquire a better knowledge of the sport.

A Final Message to Parents

If you suspect that you're getting too intense about your daughter and sports, write this question on a slip of paper and tape it on the bathroom mirror: *What can I do to make sure my child gets the best experience out of this sport and still has a really good time?*

Do whatever you can to encourage your daughter—whether it's letting her know she's ready to attempt the next level or a particular sport or noticing something specific that she did well and telling her. If she enjoys a challenge, support that—but let her experience success, whatever that takes. Encourage her instead of pressuring her. One thing that girls know for sure is that they don't want the same kind of pressure on their sports performance that they have on academics.

Think about whether you're weighing the value of your daughter's experience appropriately. Are you coming at it from an economic point of view: "I'm spending a lot of money, so I hope it's worth it"? Are you coming at it from a time commitment perspective, saying: "If I'm going to spend all this time driving you around and waiting for you, you better be sure that this is what you want to do"?

It takes some family discussion to find a comfortable balance between the value of sports in your daughter's life and the degree of commitment you and the rest of your family want to make. I hope that the stories and information in this book have convinced you that being active in sports is one of the most enriching experiences a girl can have. Here are some important guidelines to follow as you encourage your daughter to "stick with it."

- Stop yelling in the car on the way home.
- Never put her in the middle between you and the coach.
- Stay away from comparisons.
- Show up, be supportive, no shouting at the ref or coach.

In the final analysis, parents can make sports a memorable family affair if they follow the advice of twelve-year-old Nicole: "Sit down, watch the game, do us a favor and be proud of us."

Use These Ideas to Support Your Daughter

The next time you wonder what to do with your daughter on the weekend or what to get her for her birthday, think sports and give these ideas some thought. You can do a little seed planting while you're being innovative and generous. Even if you think some of these suggestions are a little wacky, try them anyway. In the future, the way she thinks, the way she acts, maybe the way she'll raise her own daughter, could easily be influenced the way you try new things.

- Purchase a gift of sports equipment. Or get your daughter a gift certificate to a sporting goods store and let her make the choice.

- Go see a high school or college sports event. Instead of a going to a movie on Friday night, try visiting your local high school or college. Generally there are competitions going on from September through May. If there is a junior college in your area, you can count on them having games on Saturday afternoons. If you are fortunate enough to live near a Division I university or college, you will have an opportunity to see terrific athletes in action, as Olympians often come out of college sports programs. You can obtain a schedule with a simple phone call to the school's physical education or athletic department.
- Buy a sports video. You might already have an idea of what sports your daughter enjoys. If you don't, try paying attention to what she points out on television. In any event, competition or highlight videos are good with Friday nights and popcorn.
- Try a mother-daughter or father-daughter fitness class. Shop around for a sports or fitness program that welcomes young people. This works best with preteens and teenagers. It is a great way to have time "just for her" when coming and going in the car. If the fitness idea doesn't pan out, what about a martial arts class—they're gender free. Be open to suggestions and listen to your daughter. Consider what *she* wants.
- Set up a party or sleep-over to watch a special sporting event on television. If adults can have a major bash for the Super Bowl or the World Series, girls can also use a favorite sports event as an excuse for a party.
- Have a birthday party at a gymnastics school or a batting cage. Several years ago I started offering gymnastics birthday parties to families, and this has been a great success. Ask if your local gym or rec center offers such programs.

Some Final Thoughts

Many young athletes I spoke with were eager to have their feelings known about why they stayed in sports. One of the best interviews was done with an adult, Wanda, who was the mother of a female softball player.

> *My daughter is a pitcher in high school, and though I currently don't have any children in this community league, I continue to help organize and coach, because over the past ten*

years my husband and I have seen the benefits of playing sports from six years of age to high school for our daughter.

Sports may be the savior when self-esteem is needed at fourteen or fifteen years of age, when they need to say no to drugs. As the girls have become better, more seasoned players, they become stronger individuals. They are part of a group that hasn't had any drug problems or lost control over their personal lives. That starts here on the softball field. My daughter likes herself. She is number one with herself. She has the personal strength to dress the way she wants to dress. If she doesn't want to go to a party and get drunk, she doesn't have to.

I've also seen the carryover to other areas of her life. She has gained the ability to play other sports because she's learned how to learn. It's been a terrific life experience to see how she has learned to work with other people. She's a leader on her high school team. As she has gotten better and better, she's able to be the top person. Now as a teenager, she is a leader for the youth players on the team that she once belonged to. Another thing that I've seen my daughter learn is to speak her mind. I like that, as a parent.

Some of these kids may never come back and play softball, but at least they've learned they can do something. They always had a good time. Our last year in bobby sox, when we went to the regional tournament, we treated them as though this were the best event in their lives. It's so great to watch the girls as they get older. They are doing well in high school, and many go on to college. They're good kids. You can see that something has changed them.

I couldn't have said it better myself. That is truly the gift of allowing girls to play "sports her way." You never know where sports may take you. If anyone had ever told me when I was fifteen, cartwheeling around the gym, that one day I would be the director of the 1984 Olympic Gymnastics Competition, I would have said, "Ridiculous!" But it happened. Not overnight. But it happened, one day at a time, one dream at a time. Dream on.

Appendix

Sport Organizations

Amateur Athletic Union
c/o Walt Disney World Resort
P.O. Box 10,000
Lake Buena Vista, FL 32830
www.aausports.org
407-934-7200

American Volkssport Association
1001 Pat Booker road, Suite 101
Universal City, TX 78148
www.ava.org
210-659-2112

Boys and Girls Clubs of America
1230 W. Peachtree Street, NW
Atlanta, GA 30309
www.bgca.org
404-815-5700

Girls Incorporated National Headquarters
120 Wall Street, 3rd Floor
New York, NY 10005
www.girlsinc.org
212-509-2000

YMCA of the USA
101 N. Wacker Drive
Chicago, IL 60606
www.ymca.org
888-333-YMCA

YWCA of the USA
Empire State Building
350 Fifth Avenue, Suite 301
New York, NY 10118
www.ywca.org
212-273-7800

Support Organizations

Amateur Athletic Foundation
2141 West Adams Boulevard
Los Angeles, CA 90018
www.aafla.org
323-730-9400

American Alliance for Health, Physical Education, Recreation, and Dance
1900 Association Drive
Reston, VA 20191
www.aahperd.org
703-476-3400

American Association of University Women
American Association of University Women Foundation
1111 16th Street, NW
Washington, D.C. 20036
www.aauw.org
800-326-AAUW

American Sport Education Program
P.O. Box 5076
Champaign, IL 61825
www.ASEP.com
800-747-5698 (x2930)

Girls Count
225 East 16th Avenue, Suite 475
Denver, CO 80203
www.girlscount.org
303-832-6600

National Alliance for Youth Sports
2050 Vista Parkway
West Palm Beach, FL 33411
www.nays.org
561-684-1141

National Council of Youth Sports
116 First Terrace, Suite 709
Palm Beach Gardens, FL 33418
www.ncys.org
561-625-1197

National Association for Girls and Women in Sport
1900 Association Drive
Reston, VA 22091
www.aahperd.org/nagws
703-476-3450

National Association for Sport and Physical Education
1900 Association Drive
Reston, VA 22091
www.aahperd.org/naspe
800-213-7193 (x410)

National Institute for Child Centered Coaching
(Family Development Resources)
3160 Pinebrook Road
Park City, UT 84098
www.familydev.com
800-688-5882

National Youth Sports Coaches Association
2050 Vista Parkway
West Palm Beach, FL 33411
www.nays.org
800-729-2057

President's Council on Physical Fitness and Sports
200 Independence Avenue, SW Room 738H
Washington, D.C. 20201
202-690-9000

Program for Athletic Coaches' Education
Youth Sports Institute
Michigan State University
East Lansing, MI 48824
517-353-6689

(The) Women's Sports Foundation
Eisenhower Park
East Meadow, NY 11554
www.WomensSportsFoundation.org
516-542-4700

Office for Civil Rights
U.S. Department of Education
400 Maryland Avenue, SW
Washington, D.C. 20202
202-205-5413

Publications

Jump (For Girls Who Dare to Be Real)
Weider Publications Inc.
21100 Erwin Street
Woodland Hills, CA 91367
www.fitnessonline.com
818-884-6800

Sports Illustrated for Women
Time & Life Building
Rockefeller Center
New York, NY 10020
www.sportsillustrated.com

Sports Illustrated for Kids
P.O. Box 60001
Tampa, FL 33660
www.siforkids.com

Women's Sports + Fitness
P.O. Box 50033
Boulder, CO 80322
www.womenssportsandfitness.com
800-274-0084

High School Associations

(The) National Federation of State High School Associations
P.O. Box 20626
Kansas City, MO 64195
www.nfhs.org
816-464-5400

National High School Athletic Coaches Association
P.O. Box 5020
Winter Park, FL 32793
407-679-1414

Colleges and University Associations

(The) National Collegiate Athletic Association
700 Washington Avenue
Indianapolis, IN 462061
www.ncaa.org
317-917-6222

National Association of Intercollegiate Athletics
6120 South Yale Avenue, Suite 1450
Tulsa, OK 74136
www.naia.org
918-494-8828

National Junior College Athletic Association
P.O. Box 7305
Colorado Springs, CO 80933
www.njcaa.org
719-590-9788

National Governing Boards (By Sport)

Archery	719-578-4576
Badminton	719-578-4808
Basketball	719-590-4800
Bowling	414-421-9008
Boxing	719-578-4506
Canoe/Kayak	518-523-1855
Cross Country	317-261-0500
Cycling	719-578-4581
Diving	317-237-5252
Equestrian	212-972-2472
Fencing	719-578-4511
Figure Skating	719-635-5200
Golf—American Junior Golf	770-998-4653
Gymnastics—U.S.A. Gymnastics	317-327-5050
Ice Hockey	719-576-8724
Judo	719-578-4730
Lacrosse	410-235-6882

Luge	518-523-2071
Racquetball	719-635-5396
Rowing	317-237-5656
Sailing	401-849-5200
Shooting	719-578-4670
Ski and Snowboard Association	435-649-9090
Softball	405-424-5266
Soccer	312-808-1300
Speedskating	440-899-0128
Synchronized Swimming	317-237-5700
Swimming—U.S. Swimming, Inc.	719-578-4578
Table Tennis	719-578-4583
Taekwondo	719-578-4632
Team Handball	770-956-7660
Tennis	212-244-7171
Track and Field (Athletics)	317-261-0500
Volleyball—U.S.A. Volleyball	719-228-6800
Waterpolo	719-634-0699
Weightlifting	719-578-4508
Wrestling	719-598-8181

International Organizations

United States Olympic Committee
One Olympic Plaza
Colorado Springs, CO 80909
www.usoc.org
719-632-5551

Arco Olympic Training Center
1750 Wueste Road
Chula Vista, CA 91915
www.usoc.org
619-656-1500

INDEX